# Bek's Introduction to SQL Programming

"That Pelican Database Book"

First Edition

## *Jon Bek*

*Santa Barbara City College*

Bek's Introduction to SQL Programming

"That Pelican Database Book", First Edition

Jon L. Bek

Textbook Resources may be found at: https://bekplanet.com/books

Library of Congress Control Number: 2024912269

ISBN: 979-8-89379-807-4

ABOUT THE COVER:

THE CALIFORNIA BROWN PELICAN, A COASTAL ICON, SHOWCASES DISTINCTIVE FEATURES SUCH AS A CHOCOLATE-BROWN AND WHITE PLUMAGE, WITH A WINGSPAN THAT REFLECTS BOTH GRACE AND RESILIENCE. KNOWN FOR THEIR SYNCHRONIZED FLIGHT PATTERNS ALONG THE PACIFIC COASTLINE, THESE BIRDS HAVE MADE A REMARKABLE RECOVERY FROM NEAR-EXTINCTION DUE TO PESTICIDE THREATS. THEIR CLIFFSIDE COLONIES, PERCHED ON ROCKY OUTCROPPINGS, OFFER A GLIMPSE INTO THEIR COMMUNAL AND NURTURING BEHAVIORS. THE PELICAN'S VOCALIZATIONS CONTRIBUTE TO THE COASTAL AMBIANCE, CREATING A MELODIC SYMPHONY. THE SPECIES WAS SUCCESSFULLY REMOVED FROM THE ENDANGERED LIST IN 2009, MARKING A CONSERVATION TRIUMPH AND EMPHASIZING THE SIGNIFICANCE OF PRESERVING NATURAL HABITATS.

NOTICE OF LIABILITY

Trademarks

COVER PHOTO: PELICAN OVER VENTURA HARBOR
PHOTO BY SUSAN BEK

# Contents

# Contents

# Contents

# Preface

The intent of this book is to provide a free eBook and affordably priced print textbook resource for students, offering an introduction to SQL programming appropriate to a short course in the subject. The focus is on a practical, primarily hands-on approach to the subject. The text is not intended as a substitute for a comprehensive study of database design. Consequently, this text does not delve into selected and important fundamentals, such as database design, normalization, construction of Entity Relationship Diagrams, and so forth. These are left as a matter for either a comprehensive, semester-length course, or additional short courses focusing on those elements. Similarly, it also omits coverage of many worthy advanced SQL programming concepts and constructs, such as correlated sub-queries, performance tuning, dynamic SQL, Common Table Expressions (CTEs), JSON objects, etc. These are deferred to follow-up courses dedicated to advanced SQL programming techniques. The book is purposed for the support of a course of about one-half of a semester, organized into approximately seven units of study, plus a final unit devoted to summative assessment. The text is appropriate for an audience possessing limited, introductory computer skills, and no prior experience with databases, programming, or the SQL language is required.

# Chapter 1- Introduction to SQL Programming and Relational Databases

## What is a Relational Database?

At the heart of the digital age's vast web of information lies a remarkable innovation that has reshaped the way data is stored, managed, and accessed: the relational database. What makes a database truly "relational" is its ingenious design centered around the principles of relationships, tables, and the mathematical framework of relational algebra.

Imagine a virtual world of interconnected tables, each one representing a specific aspect of reality—a snapshot of information that captures everything from customers and orders to products and suppliers. These tables, also known as relations, form the bedrock of a relational database. Each relation is akin to a digital filing cabinet, meticulously organized with rows and columns.

The essence of the relational model lies in the ability to forge relationships between these tables, emulating the complex interactions that define the real world. For instance, consider an e-commerce scenario wherein customers place orders for various products. A relational database would effortlessly intertwine the **Customers** and **Orders** tables through a shared attribute like the customer's unique ID.

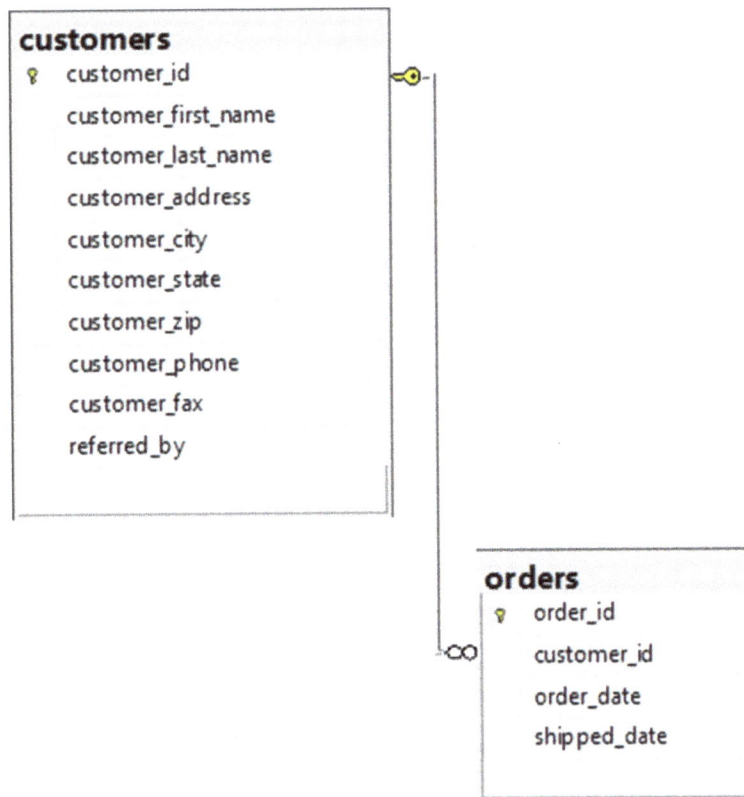

**customers**
- ⚷ customer_id
- customer_first_name
- customer_last_name
- customer_address
- customer_city
- customer_state
- customer_zip
- customer_phone
- customer_fax
- referred_by

**orders**
- ⚷ order_id
- customer_id
- order_date
- shipped_date

*Figure 1 - Customer:Orders Relation*

Enter relational algebra—a mathematical language that serves as the engine propelling these connections. Just as mathematical symbols and formulas allow us to solve complex equations, relational algebra provides a systematic way to query, manipulate, and extract meaning from the labyrinthine network of data relationships. It acts as the intermediary, translating our human inquiries into a language the database understands.

Relational algebra's foundational concepts—selection, projection, joins, and set operations—mirror our intuitive way of thinking. Selection acts as a filter, extracting specific rows that meet certain criteria. Projection narrows down the scope, isolating specific columns of interest. Joins merge different tables, revealing how they intertwine, while set operations allow us to combine and compare datasets.

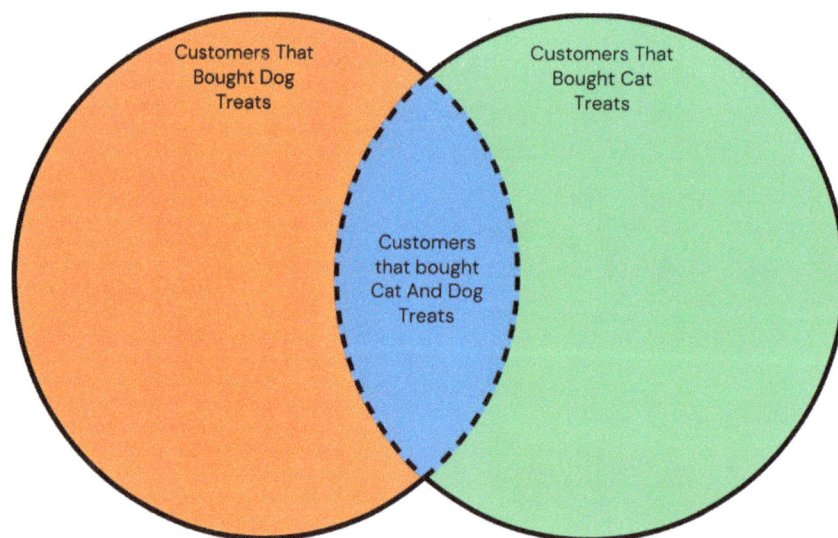

*Figure 2 - SQL and Set Operations*

Consider querying a database to uncover the products a particular customer has ordered. Relational algebra makes this possible: selecting the customer's ID from the **Customers** table, joining it with the **Orders** table, and then further joining to the **Order Details** table, and ultimately to the **Items** table to unveil the coveted information.

*Figure 3 - Relations in a database schema*

With relational databases, this mathematical language doesn't just remain an abstract concept; it's the underpinning logic that drives the scenes. Every query executed, every report generated, every insight derived—all are realized through systems of relations and algebra.

So, what makes a relational database truly relational? It's the connectedness of tables through relationships between linking (key) fields, a relational algebraic structure. The ability to traverse this structure transforms raw data into actionable knowledge, allowing us to explore the depths of interconnected information and harness the power of relationships to uncover truths hidden within the digital tapestry of the modern world.

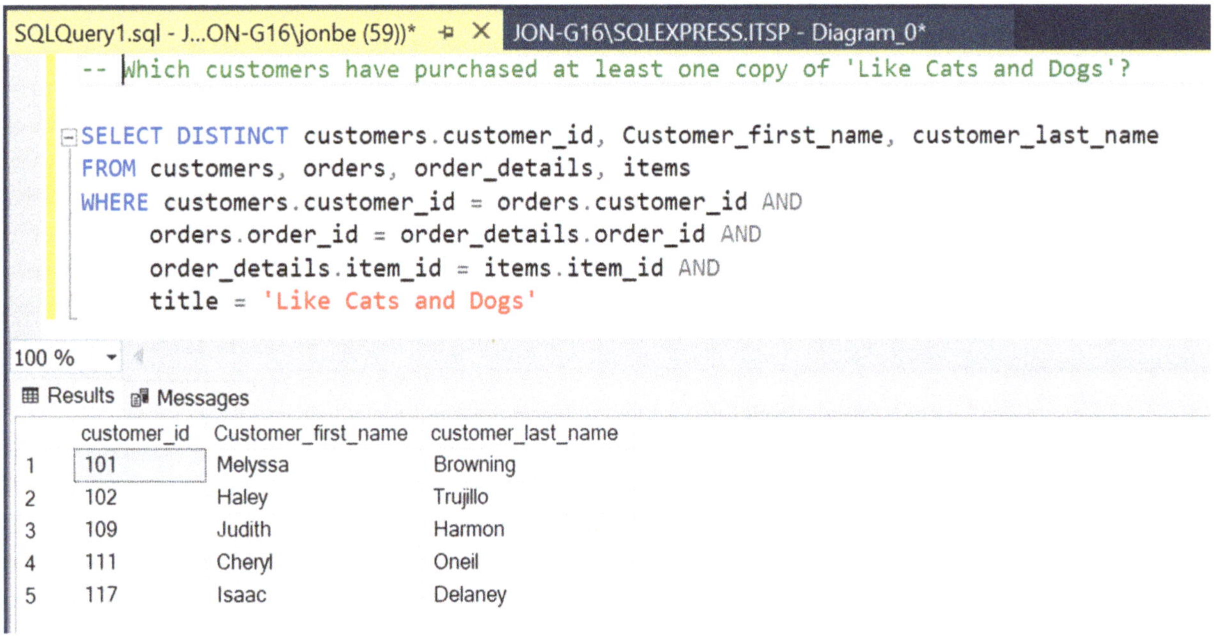

*Figure 4 - Exploring connectedness through SQL relations*

Relational databases have become the foundation of countless applications across various industries, from business and finance to healthcare and e-commerce. They provide a powerful and structured way to manage and retrieve data, allowing for efficient data storage, retrieval, and manipulation while maintaining data accuracy and integrity.

# Chapter 1

Relational Databases and Relational Algebra: What is an "Algebra"?

In mathematics, where abstract concepts are expressed through symbols and operations, the term "algebra" takes on a role of profound significance. It is a gateway to unlocking the hidden patterns and relationships that govern the world of numbers, variables, and structures. To grasp the essence of what an algebra truly is, we must explore mathematical thought.

Imagine a vast landscape of mathematical expressions, equations, and transformations, each a piece of a puzzle waiting to be solved. This puzzle-solving endeavor is at the heart of algebra. At its core, algebra is a system—a structured framework—through which we manipulate and explore mathematical objects, ranging from numbers to variables, using a set of defined rules and operations.

The term "algebra" derives from the Arabic word "al-jabr," which roughly translates to "reunion of broken parts." This encapsulates the essence of algebra elegantly—a tool for reuniting disparate elements, unraveling complexities, and revealing hidden symmetries. In the same way that an artist assembles a mosaic from countless tiny fragments, algebra allows us to piece together mathematical relationships, providing a deeper understanding of the world around us.

## Al-Khwarismi: Algorithms and Algebras

The two terms—algorithm and algebra—take us on a journey through time, culture, and intellect. These words are intricately connected, carrying the weight of centuries of human thought and innovation.

The word "algorithm," memorializes a remarkable Persian scholar of the 9th century, Al-Khwarizmi. Within his pioneering work, "Al-Kitab al-Mukhtasar fi Hisab al-Jabr wal-Muqabala," lies the first trace of the term "algorismus," a Latinization of Al-Khwarizmi's name. This treatise, a beacon of mathematical enlightenment, introduced the Western world to the concept of manipulating numerical symbols to solve equations—a practice that would later evolve into modern algebra.

Fast forward to the 21st century, and the term "algorithm" has evolved to encompass key concepts of computing and logic. An algorithm is a blueprint of instructions—a meticulously crafted recipe—that guides a machine or a computational process toward solving a problem or completing a task.

*Figure 5 Pencil sketch imagining 9th century scholar Al-Khwarismi*

Now, let's pivot to "algebra". Etymologically, "algebra" draws inspiration from Al-Khwarizmi's treatise. His "al-jabr" referred to the process of transposing, rearranging, and manipulating equations—a revolutionary approach for balancing equations. Over the centuries, algebra transformed from a pathbreaking treatise into a discipline of its own, evolving to encompass not just numerical manipulation, but also the abstraction of mathematical concepts into symbols and formulas.

# Introduction to SQL Programming and Relational Databases

Algebra provides a universal language for describing patterns, making predictions, and solving problems across various domains. It's not just a static set of rules; rather, it's a dynamic framework that adapts to the challenges at hand. This adaptability is a testament to algebra's versatility—a feature that has made it an indispensable tool not only in mathematics but also in physics, engineering, computer science, economics, and countless other fields.

At its simplest, algebra may involve basic arithmetic operations—addition, subtraction, multiplication, and division—performed on numerical values. But its true power lies in its capacity to handle variables, allowing us to represent unknown quantities and work with symbolic expressions. Algebra provides a bridge between the concrete and the abstract, enabling us to formulate and solve equations that capture complex relationships.

Through algebra, we are able to manipulate symbols to reveal hidden truths, solve intricate puzzles, and traverse the landscape of mathematical thought. It's a journey that has enriched our understanding of the universe, empowered technological innovations, and illuminated the path to new frontiers of knowledge.

In essence, an algebra is more than a mere mathematical tool; it's a dynamic and ever-evolving language that allows us to explore abstraction, connect seemingly unrelated concepts, and bring order to the complexity of numerical and symbolic relationships.

## SQL Databases-- Nearly Magical?

In the complex field of relational databases, where vast troves of data lie waiting to be unearthed, a silent but ingenious player takes center stage: the *query optimizer*. This unassuming yet formidable entity is the unsung hero behind the scenes, wielding a profound impact on the efficiency and performance of SQL databases. To truly appreciate the role of a query optimizer, we must study how and what it does, and understand why SQL is often hailed as a "fourth generation language."

Imagine a bustling library of information, where queries are the eager readers seeking knowledge from the volumes of data stored within. Each query, a question to be answered, requires careful consideration in how it's executed. Enter the query optimizer—a master of efficiency and execution, poised to turn these questions into orchestrated symphonies of data retrieval.

The primary responsibility of a query optimizer is to transform the abstract queries written by users into efficient execution plans that the database engine can follow. These execution plans outline the sequence of operations, the order in which tables are accessed, and the methods employed to retrieve and join data. In essence, the query optimizer acts as a conductor, harmonizing the intricate interplay of data manipulation.

Here's where the magic happens. The query optimizer leverages its knowledge of the database's structure, the statistics of the data, and a deep understanding of query processing techniques to make crucial decisions. It's a chess player navigating a vast board, contemplating each move with the goal of minimizing resource usage and query execution time.

*Figure 6 – The Query Optimizer creates the SQL execution plan*

Through a series of intricate optimizations, the query optimizer can transform a seemingly straightforward query into a finely tuned masterpiece. It decides when to use indexes for efficient data retrieval, how to perform joins to minimize processing overhead, and when to employ caching strategies for rapid data access. Every choice is meticulously evaluated, factoring in the complexities of the database's physical storage, system resources, and the nature of the query itself.

Now, let's circle back to SQL's status as a "fourth generation language." The concept of generation in programming languages refers to the level of abstraction they offer. First-generation languages were low-level assembly languages, while second-generation languages were closer to machine code. Third-generation languages, like C and Pascal, introduced higher-level abstractions for ease of programming.

SQL, however, transcends even these advancements. It's often referred to as a "fourth generation language" due to its unique ability to empower users to define what they want (***declarative***) rather than how to achieve it (***procedural***). This declarative nature aligns perfectly with the aspirations of a query optimizer. This is likely the reason that your computer science professor or database administrator (DBA) seems to think that SQL (relational) databases are nearly magical: As a SQL programmer, you use the SQL language to create SQL program code that concisely describes the solution set for a data query problem – yet you do *not* have to provide the programming code details to instruct the computer as to the detailed step-by-step process (algorithm) needed in order to generate that solution.

The query optimizer embodies this fourth-generation spirit by taking user-defined queries and crafting efficient execution plans without requiring explicit, procedural instructions. It operates at a level of abstraction that embodies the very essence of SQL: the ability to focus on the desired outcome, leaving the intricate details of implementation to the database system itself.

In this dance of abstraction, the query optimizer reveals its true significance. It's the invisible hand that transforms user intent into efficient data retrieval, optimizing performance and resource utilization. It exemplifies the profound impact of fourth-generation languages—languages that empower users to express complex concepts effortlessly, unlocking the full potential of data-driven endeavors.

# Introduction to SQL Programming and Relational Databases

## Relational Databases and SQL

Relational databases and SQL are inherently intertwined. SQL is the standardized language used to interact with and manipulate relational databases. It provides a means for users to define, manipulate, query, and manage data stored in a relational database management system (RDBMS).

## "Standard" SQL? Why So Many Dialects?

Standard SQL language is known as ANSI SQL (American National Standards Institute Structured Query Language). ANSI SQL serves as the foundation for defining the syntax, semantics, and core features of the SQL language. It provides a common set of standards that relational database management system (RDBMS) vendors and developers can adhere to, ensuring a level of consistency and compatibility across different database systems.

However, despite the standardization efforts, various database vendors have implemented their own versions of SQL, often referred to as SQL dialects. These dialects introduce vendor-specific extensions, optimizations, and variations on the standard SQL syntax. Some of the well-known SQL dialects include:

Transact-SQL (T-SQL)
Developed by Microsoft and used primarily with Microsoft SQL Server, T-SQL extends ANSI SQL with additional features, functions, and procedural programming capabilities. It supports features like stored procedures, triggers, and user-defined functions.

PL/SQL
Developed by Oracle, PL/SQL (Procedural Language/Structured Query Language) is an extension of SQL that includes procedural programming constructs. It's used for writing stored procedures, triggers, and other programmatic logic within the Oracle Database system.

PL/pgSQL
This is the procedural language for PostgreSQL, an open-source RDBMS. Similar to PL/SQL, it allows users to write stored procedures and functions with PostgreSQL.

MySQL/MariaDB SQL
MySQL and its fork MariaDB share a common SQL foundation, but each has introduced its own extensions and optimizations, especially in areas like storage engines and system functions.

SQLite
SQLite is a lightweight, embedded database engine. While it adheres closely to the SQL standard, it lacks some advanced features and optimizations found in larger RDBMSs.

NoSQL Databases' Query Languages

Some NoSQL databases have their own query languages inspired by SQL. For example, MongoDB uses a query language called MongoDB Query Language (MQL), which shares similarities with SQL but is tailored to the document-oriented nature of MongoDB.

These dialects of SQL are needed for several reasons. These include provision of vendor-specific features, optimizations, advanced capabilities, additional data types, and historical reasons (such as innovations introduced by a vendor, which were subsequently standardized in a later ANSI Standard update).

Despite these dialects, many database operations and queries can still be written in a standards-compliant manner. However, when developing applications or working with specific database systems, it's important to be aware of the dialect-specific features and syntax to ensure optimal compatibility and performance. And do not be naïve; commercial database companies are quite intentional in their attempt to obtain influence and market share through the provisioning of proprietary SQL language extensions.

## Different Types of SQL

Different types of SQL statements serve distinct purposes, each contributing to the management, manipulation, and querying of data. Let's delve into the narrative explanation of these various types of SQL.

## Data Definition Language (DDL)

Imagine you're an architect designing a magnificent skyscraper. Before construction begins, you need to create a blueprint that outlines the structure's foundation, floors, walls, and rooms. Similarly, in the realm of databases, the Data Definition Language (DDL) is like the blueprint for your database.

DDL statements are used to define and manage the structure of your database. They enable you to create, modify, and delete database objects such as tables, indexes, and constraints. Just as an architect specifies the dimensions and materials for each building component, DDL statements define the data types, columns, keys, and relationships that make up your database's foundation.

For instance, when you use a **CREATE TABLE** statement, you're essentially crafting the structure of a new room in your data skyscraper. **ALTER TABLE** statements allow you to modify existing rooms, adding or removing columns like rearranging walls. When you drop a table, it's like tearing down a room to repurpose the space for something else. DDL statements are the architects' tools for shaping the physical layout and organization of your database.

# Introduction to SQL Programming and Relational Databases

## Data Manipulation Language (DML)

Now that you have your database's structure in place, it's time to furnish those rooms and bring them to life with data. Think of the Data Manipulation Language (DML) as your interior designer's toolkit. Just as the designer arranges furniture, decor, and artwork to create a functional and appealing space, DML statements allow you to populate, modify, and manage the data within your database's tables.

***INSERT*** statements are like placing furniture in the rooms; they add new rows of data to your tables. ***UPDATE*** statements allow you to change the color of the walls or replace furniture with newer items. ***DELETE*** statements, on the other hand, are like removing items that no longer fit the design concept.

With DML, you can ensure that the data in your database evolves over time while maintaining its integrity and coherence. It's the dynamic aspect that transforms empty spaces into vibrant living areas.

## Data Query Language (DQL)

Now that your database is both architecturally sound and stylishly furnished, it's time to explore its contents and extract valuable insights. Enter the Data Query Language (DQL), your investigative reporter within the database world.

DQL statements, primarily the ***SELECT*** statement, allow you to retrieve specific data from your database. Just as a reporter interviews people to gather information, DQL queries tables and retrieves rows of data based on specified criteria. You can filter, sort, aggregate, and even join data from different tables to unveil patterns, trends, and answers to your questions.

DQL is like having a magnifying glass to examine the intricate details within your data skyscraper. Whether you're a business analyst seeking sales trends or a researcher uncovering patterns in scientific data, DQL equips you to discover meaningful insights buried within the vast database landscape.

In this narrative journey, DDL constructs the structure, DML decorates it with data, and DQL shines a light on its secrets. Together, these types of SQL statements orchestrate the creation, transformation, and exploration of databases, turning raw data into a dynamic, informative, and functional environment.

# Chapter 1

A Timeline of Database Technologies

The history and evolution of databases is a tale of innovation, addressing the ever-growing need to efficiently store, manage, and retrieve vast amounts of information. Prior to the emergence of relational databases, several key developments laid the groundwork for this technology.

## Hierarchical and Network Databases (1960s)

In the early days of computing, hierarchical and network databases were prevalent. Hierarchical databases organized data in a tree-like structure, with parent-child relationships. Network databases, on the other hand, employed a more flexible graph-like structure, allowing for multiple relationships. These systems were efficient for certain applications but lacked the ability to handle complex relationships between data elements. Moreover, once constructed, making fundamental changes to the underlying data model was complex and labor intensive (which is to say, expensive!).

## Codasyl and IBM's IMS (1960s)

The Conference on Data Systems Languages (CODASYL) developed the CODASYL Data Base Task Group in the 1960s, which led to the creation of the CODASYL Data Model. IBM's Information Management System (IMS) was one of the first implementations of this model. These systems were widely used for mainframe computing and enabled organizations to manage large volumes of data more effectively.

## Relational Model and SQL (1970s)

The breakthrough moment came with the introduction of the relational model by Edgar F. Codd in 1970. This model proposed organizing data into tables (relations) with rows (tuples) and columns (attributes), facilitating efficient querying and manipulation. Structured Query Language (SQL) emerged as the standardized language to interact with relational databases, providing a powerful tool for data manipulation and retrieval.

# Introduction to SQL Programming and Relational Databases

## IBM's System R and Oracle (1970s-1980s)

IBM's System R project and the subsequent commercialization efforts by companies like Oracle and Ingres played a crucial role in popularizing the relational model. Oracle's introduction of the first commercially available relational database management system (RDBMS) in 1979 marked a significant milestone, making relational databases accessible to a wider range of users.

---

**Larry Ellison, Founder, Oracle Corporation**

Larry Ellison, the visionary founder of Oracle Corporation, embarked on a remarkable journey that would revolutionize the world of technology and business. Born Lawrence Joseph Ellison on August 17, 1944, in New York City, he would eventually become a driving force behind the rise of relational databases and enterprise software solutions.

*Figure 7 - Larry Ellison*

---

## Normalization and ACID Properties (1970s-1980s)

The concept of normalization, aimed at minimizing redundancy and improving data integrity, gained prominence during this period. Additionally, the ACID (Atomicity, Consistency, Isolation, Durability) properties became foundational for ensuring the reliability and integrity of database transactions.

## Microsoft SQL Server and MySQL (1980s-1990s)

The 1980s and 1990s saw the rise of Microsoft SQL Server and MySQL, bringing relational database technology to Windows and open-source platforms, respectively. This expanded the reach of databases and made them more accessible to smaller businesses and developers.

## Object-Relational Databases (1990s-2000s)

The limitations of purely relational databases led to the development of object-relational databases, which aimed to bridge the gap between relational and object-oriented programming paradigms. These databases could store and manage complex data types, such as images and multimedia content, more efficiently.

## NoSQL Databases (2000s-2010s)

As internet-driven applications and massive data volumes gained prominence, NoSQL (which stands for Not Only SQL rather than "No SQL") databases emerged as an alternative to traditional relational databases. These systems offered greater scalability and flexibility for handling unstructured and semi-structured data.

## NewSQL and Cloud Databases (2010s)

NewSQL databases aimed to combine the benefits of traditional relational databases with the scalability of NoSQL solutions. Additionally, cloud-based databases provided easy scalability, accessibility, and cost-efficiency, revolutionizing how organizations manage and deploy their data.

The evolution of databases, culminating in the rise of relational databases, transformed the landscape of data management. These technologies laid the foundation for modern data-driven applications, enabling businesses and individuals to harness the power of data for insights, decision-making, and innovation.

## Rise of Relational Databases

In the mid-20th century, as the world began to grapple with the growing complexity of data management, a brilliant and visionary computer scientist named Edgar F. Codd emerged as a pioneer. Born in England and armed with a deep understanding of mathematics and logic, Codd's journey would lead him to a revolutionary breakthrough that would forever change the landscape of database science.

# Introduction to SQL Programming and Relational Databases

---

**Edgar F. Codd: Pioneer of the Relational Model**

*Figure 8 - E.F. Codd*

Edgar Frank "Ted" Codd (August 19, 1923 – April 18, 2003) was a British-American computer scientist widely recognized as the visionary behind the development of the relational model for database management. Born in Portland, Dorset, England, Codd displayed exceptional mathematical talent from a young age. He earned a degree in mathematics and chemistry from the University of Exeter and later pursued a Ph.D. in mathematical logic from the University of Michigan.

Codd's revolutionary work in the field of databases began during his tenure at IBM's San Jose Research Laboratory in the 1960s. His pioneering research led to the creation of the relational model, which laid the groundwork for a more flexible and efficient approach to organizing and retrieving data. Codd's contributions revolutionized the way data was stored, manipulated, and queried, and his legacy continues to influence the world of database systems and information management.

---

During his tenure at IBM's San Jose Research Laboratory in the 1960s, Codd was confronted with the challenge of managing data in an increasingly intricate digital world. Traditional methods of organizing information were proving to be inadequate, leading Codd to question the fundamental principles underlying data management. Drawing inspiration from mathematical set theory and his background in logic, Codd embarked on a quest to reimagine the way data was stored, manipulated, and queried.

Codd's vision crystallized into what would become known as the relational model—a radical departure from conventional wisdom. He proposed a bold idea: why not represent data as interrelated tables, each comprised of rows and columns? This simple yet revolutionary concept marked the birth of a new era in database science. No longer confined by rigid hierarchical structures or file-based systems, data could now be organized into elegant, flexible tables that preserved the inherent relationships between pieces of information.

Central to the relational model was the concept of the primary key—a unique identifier for each row within a table. This ensured that every entity could be unequivocally identified and linked across tables, fostering data integrity, and eliminating redundancy. Codd's model also introduced the concept of constraints—rules that governed the validity of data relationships, paving the way for standardized practices in maintaining data quality.

But Codd's innovation didn't stop there. He understood that a new approach to querying this data was necessary. Thus, he introduced a powerful and versatile query language—Structured Query Language (SQL). With SQL, users could interact with databases in a standardized way, unleashing the potential to extract, manipulate, and transform data with ease.

As Codd's relational model gained momentum, the implications reverberated across the computing world. Businesses, institutions, and researchers began to grasp the transformative potential of this paradigm shift. The relational model offered a higher level of abstraction, shielding users from the complexities of data storage and enabling them to focus on insights and analysis. This newfound flexibility paved the way for greater innovation in applications ranging from finance to healthcare to scientific research.

Codd's work didn't just advance data management; it ignited a revolution. His ideas catalyzed a fertile field of research, inspiring the development of relational database management systems (RDBMS) that would become the bedrock of modern computing. The relational model's impact was not only immediate but also lasting, as its principles of data integrity, normalization, and standardized querying became cornerstones of database design.

In essence, Edgar F. Codd's genius lay not just in his mathematical prowess but in his ability to envision a world where data was liberated from its constraints and structured in a way that mirrored the complexity of reality. His relational model, born from a blend of mathematics, logic, and sheer imagination, shattered the old paradigms and laid the foundations for the data-driven world we inhabit today—a world where information flows freely, relationships are seamlessly traced, and insights are waiting to be discovered. Edgar F. Codd's legacy continues to shine as a guiding star in the ever-evolving constellation of database science.

## Principles of the Relational Model

Codd's seminal papers outlined the following principles of the relational model:

1. Information Representation: Data is represented in the form of tables, consisting of rows (tuples) and columns (attributes). Each row represents a distinct entity, and each column represents a characteristic or property of the entity.

2. Primary Keys: Each table must have a primary key, which uniquely identifies each row in the table. This ensures that each entity in the table is uniquely identifiable.

3. Data Integrity: The relational model enforces data integrity through a set of constraints, including entity integrity (each primary key value must be unique and not null) and referential integrity (relationships between tables are maintained).

4. Structured Query Language (SQL): Codd introduced a query language, SQL, for interacting with relational databases. SQL provides a standardized way to retrieve, manipulate, and manage data stored in relational databases.

5. Data Independence: The relational model promotes data independence by separating the logical representation of data from its physical storage. This allows changes to the physical storage without affecting the logical structure of the data.

# Chapter 2 – Creating Tables and Databases

## Introduction to SQL Scripts and Query Clients

Imagine you are a skilled chef in a bustling kitchen, crafting exquisite dishes to perfection. To streamline your culinary creations, you rely on well-crafted recipes that detail every ingredient, step, and technique. Similarly, in the world of databases, creating SQL scripts is like developing your own set of recipes—a practice that offers significant advantages over composing new SQL queries every time they're needed.

## Purpose of Creating SQL Scripts

SQL scripts are pre-written sets of SQL queries, commands, and statements that are saved for reuse. Their purpose extends far beyond mere convenience. They provide a structured and organized way to manage, maintain, and manipulate data within a relational database. Here's why creating SQL scripts is essential:

- Consistency and Accuracy: Just as a recipe ensures consistent flavors, SQL scripts ensure consistent query execution. By using standardized scripts, you minimize the chance of errors that might arise from manually composing queries each time.
- Efficiency: Think of SQL scripts as your sous chef, ready to assist at a moment's notice. Instead of reinventing the wheel with every query, scripts allow you to quickly access tried-and-true solutions, saving time and effort.
- Reusability: Like having a collection of go-to recipes, SQL scripts can be reused across projects, tasks, and even databases. This reusability enhances productivity and promotes best practices by leveraging tested code.
- Documentation: Just as a recipe details ingredients and cooking steps, SQL scripts provide documentation of your data manipulation processes. This documentation aids in understanding the purpose and logic behind each script, making collaboration and troubleshooting easier.
- Version Control: Like keeping track of recipe iterations, you can maintain versions of SQL scripts. This is particularly helpful when changes are required or when collaborating with a team.
- Automation and Scheduling: Just as a slow cooker prepares meals over time, SQL scripts can be scheduled to automate tasks. For example, you can schedule scripts to run backups, updates, or data imports at specific intervals.

# Chapter 2

## Benefits of Using SQL Scripts

Creating SQL scripts offers a range of benefits that extend beyond immediate convenience:

- Faster Development: Just as using a recipe speeds up cooking, SQL scripts accelerate development. Reusing existing scripts eliminates the need to start from scratch, allowing you to focus on the unique aspects of each project.
- Consistency in Database Changes: Like maintaining consistency in cooking techniques, SQL scripts ensure that database changes are applied uniformly across different environments.
- Error Reduction: Just as following a recipe reduces kitchen mishaps, using scripts reduces the risk of introducing errors or inconsistencies in your queries.
- Scalability: Similar to scaling recipes for larger gatherings, SQL scripts can be easily adapted to handle larger datasets or more complex operations.
- Collaboration: Like sharing recipes with other chefs, SQL scripts can be shared among team members, promoting collaboration and knowledge exchange.
- Efficient Troubleshooting: Just as a chef can adjust a recipe to fix a dish, SQL scripts can be modified and fine-tuned to address issues or changing requirements.

In the grand culinary symphony of database management, SQL scripts are your secret ingredients for efficiency, consistency, and success. By crafting these "recipes" for data manipulation, you empower yourself and your team to navigate the complex world of databases with precision, agility, and confidence.

## Query Clients

Query clients play a pivotal role in enabling developers, database administrators, and data analysts to interact with and manage the underlying database systems effectively. These query clients serve as powerful tools that facilitate tasks such as querying, designing, modifying, and maintaining databases. Two prominent examples of query clients are MySQL Workbench and SQL Server Management Studio (SSMS).

## MySQL Workbench

Imagine you're a skilled artisan crafting intricate pieces of furniture. To bring your creations to life, you need the right tools, workspace, and precision. In the world of databases, MySQL Workbench serves as your well-equipped workshop. Developed specifically for MySQL databases, this graphical user interface (GUI) tool offers an array of features to streamline database development, querying, and administration.

*Database Design and Modeling*

Much like sketching out blueprints for your furniture, MySQL Workbench allows you to visually design and model your database schema. You can create tables, define relationships, and set data types using an intuitive visual interface.

*SQL Querying*

Just as a carpenter meticulously shapes each piece of wood, MySQL Workbench empowers you to craft SQL queries with ease. Its integrated SQL editor lets you write, test, and optimize queries, ensuring that you retrieve the precise data you need.

*Performance Optimization*

Just as the artisan fine-tunes furniture for optimal function and aesthetics, MySQL Workbench provides tools to analyze and optimize query performance. You can identify bottlenecks, analyze execution plans, and enhance query efficiency.

*Data Migration*

Similar to moving your furniture to a new location, MySQL Workbench facilitates smooth data migration between different database systems. You can import, export, and synchronize data with minimal effort.

*User Management*

Managing who has access to your furniture pieces is crucial (imagine that your pet dog or cat is not allowed on the couch). Similarly, MySQL Workbench enables you to administer user privileges, ensuring secure access to your database.

# Chapter 2

SQL Server Management Studio (SSMS)

Picture yourself as a conductor leading a symphony orchestra. To create harmonious music, you need to coordinate the efforts of various musicians and sections. In the context of SQL Server databases, SQL Server Management Studio (SSMS) serves as your conductor's baton, orchestrating the management of your database environment.

## *Database Development*

Just as the conductor guides musicians in rehearsals, SSMS provides a platform for developing, testing, and debugging database applications. Its integrated development environment supports coding, scripting, and debugging SQL objects.

## *Database Administration*

Similar to overseeing the orchestra's performance, SSMS enables you to manage and maintain your SQL Server databases. You can create, modify, and optimize database objects, including tables, stored procedures, and indexes.

## *Querying and Scripting*

Just as the conductor coordinates the timing of musical pieces, SSMS allows you to execute and analyze SQL queries. Its robust query editor supports syntax highlighting, IntelliSense, and execution plans for efficient querying.

## *Performance Monitoring*

Like monitoring the orchestra's tempo and dynamics, SSMS provides tools to monitor and diagnose database performance. You can identify resource bottlenecks, analyze execution statistics, and fine-tune query performance.

# Creating Tables and Databases

Just as the conductor ensures order and security during performances, SSMS enables you to manage user access, permissions, and security settings within your SQL Server environment.

In the world of relational databases, MySQL Workbench and SQL Server Management Studio are like masterful tools that empower professionals to interact with databases creatively, efficiently, and effectively. Whether you're designing schema blueprints or conducting a symphony of data, these query clients play a critical role in making the process seamless and productive.

*SQL Code Examples Provided in This Text*

This textbook is intended as a vendor-agnostic approach to introductory SQL programming. And though the American National Standards Institute (ANSI) publish standards for the SQL Language, it is impossible to ignore the important dialectic and syntactical variations implemented by leading DBMS vendors. This forces a hard choice on the author, and necessarily the readers of such a text: to provide example code for only one SQL dialect; to neglect important and necessary proprietary extensions and variances from the ANSI standards; or to provide examples in at least two popular SQL dialects so as to illustrate both dialectic commonality and divergence to the reader. The author has selected this last option, understanding that this unfairly imposes on the reader the special burden of having not only to learn SQL, but to simultaneously learn about two divergent dialects of the SQL language. The author's thought is that although this is burdensome to the reader, it also most realistically reflects the SQL marketplace, which requires database administrators to either have fluency in the SQL variants of multiple products, or to be blindly bound to the brand-specific choices and limitations of a single vendor. The author recommends that at times when reading multiple versions of SQL code unduly encumbers the learning process, that the reader temporarily ignore the dialect in which they are not presently working and focus on the code examples relevant to the learning environment and laboratory they have chosen to use for their hands-on exploration of the subject.

The two SQL dialects for which code examples are provided throughout this text are SQL Server (formally this dialect is known as TRANSACT SQL), and MySQL. Happily, many code examples are, in fact, common to both dialects. To help clarify this for the reader, all code provided in the text begins with one of three SQL comments (denoted using the double-dash comment operator), as follows:

```
-- COMMON SQL
```

- This code operates without modification on both the SQL Server and MySQL platforms.

```
-- SQL SERVER
```
- This code operates correctly in the SQL Server database environment.

```
-- MySQL
```
- This code operates correctly in the MySQL database environment.

Databases and Table Creation Scenario

Let's explore the creation of databases and tables using a scenario:

In the bustling city of Techville, a passionate entrepreneur named Alex decided to bring her dream of opening a modern and efficient bookstore to life. Alex understood the importance of managing data effectively to run the business smoothly. To achieve this, Alex turned to the widely used relational database system, SQL Server, to create and manage her bookstore's data.

Alex knew that databases were organized collections of data, and SQL Server was a reliable choice for her venture. To begin, Alex had to write SQL statements using Data Definition Language (DDL), which is specifically designed for creating and modifying database structures.

With a clear vision, Alex opened SQL Server Management Studio, a powerful tool for working with SQL Server. In the query window, Alex started writing the script to create the database, which she named "create_bookstore.sql." The SQL script for this important step looked like this:

```
-- COMMON SQL
CREATE DATABASE alexbooks;
```

This script was the foundation on which the entire bookstore's data management would be built. Alex executed the script, and SQL Server responded with a success message, indicating that the database had been created.

Next, Alex needed to define the structure of the database by creating tables to hold different types of data, such as books, authors, customers, and orders. Each table would have columns (also known as fields) representing various attributes of the data.

For example, to create a table to hold book information, Alex wrote the following SQL code:

```
-- COMMON SQL
USE alexbooks;
```

```
CREATE TABLE books (
    book_id INT PRIMARY KEY,
    title VARCHAR(255),
    author_id INT,
    publication_year INT,
    price DECIMAL(10, 2)
);
```

In this code, Alex created a table named **books** with columns for the book's ID, title, author ID, publication year, and price. The **book_id** column was designated as the primary key, ensuring uniqueness for each book in the table.

Primary Key

Take a moment to review the **CREATE TABLE** statement in the previous code. Notice that **book_id**, in addition to being defined as an **INTEGER** data type, is also defined as a "PRIMARY KEY" or PK. In SQL database programming, a primary key is a unique identifier for each record in a table. It ensures the uniqueness of each row by preventing duplicate values in the specified column or set of columns. Additionally, a primary key column cannot have **NULL** values, as it must contain a valid and unique identifier for every record in the table. The primary key is used to establish relationships between tables and is a fundamental concept for maintaining data integrity within a relational database. In this example, records can be uniquely identified using the value of just one field (**book_id**). In some situations, we will use a combination of the values of two or more fields to ensure uniqueness. A PK that is composed of more than one field is known as compound or composite primary key. In general, every table should possess a primary key.

Similarly, Alex created a table named **authors** with columns for the **authorID**, author's last name, and author's first name:

```
-- COMMON SQL
USE alexbooks;

CREATE TABLE authors(

    author_id INT PRIMARY KEY,

    Lname NVARCHAR(35),

    Fname NVARCHAR(35)
```

```
);
```

Table Relationships

Alex understood that relationships between tables were crucial for meaningful data connections. To establish these relationships, Alex used foreign keys. For example, to relate the **books** table to the **authors** table, she wrote:

```
-- COMMON SQL
ALTER TABLE books
ADD FOREIGN KEY (author_id) REFERENCES authors(author_id);
```

This code linked the **author_id** column in the **books** table to the corresponding column in the **authors** table, creating a strong connection between the two.

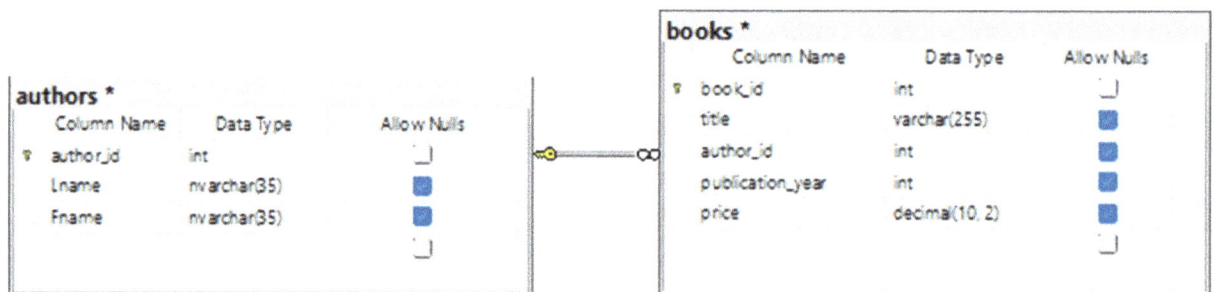

*Figure 9 - Primary key:Foreign key relation*

With the database structure in place, Alex was well on her way to creating a successful bookstore. The carefully crafted SQL scripts using Data Definition Language had laid the groundwork for efficient data management, allowing the bookstore to keep track of books, authors, customers, and orders seamlessly.

# Creating Tables and Databases

> **Foreign Key**
>
> Now, take a moment to review the ***ALTER TABLE*** statement in the code above. Notice that ***author_id*** field from the ***books*** table is being linked to the primary key field of the ***authors*** table (also named ***author_id*** in this table). In SQL database programming, a foreign key (FK) is a field or a set of fields in one table that refers to the primary key in another table. It establishes a link between the two tables, enforcing referential integrity. The foreign key in one table points to the primary key in another table, creating a relationship between them. This relationship ensures that values in the foreign key column(s) correspond to existing values in the primary key column of the referenced table. Foreign keys are crucial for maintaining data consistency and integrity in a relational database.

In the heart of Techville, the bookstore's database, powered by SQL Server, became the backbone of Alex's entrepreneurial journey, showcasing how a well-designed relational database system could transform a dream into a thriving reality.

## Data Types for Columns: Selection and Optimization

The selection of appropriate data types for table columns is a critical decision. Data types determine the kind of data that a column can store, the space it occupies, and how it is processed. Each data type is designed to accommodate specific types of data, and making the right choice is essential for efficient data storage, retrieval, and manipulation. In this section, we will discuss various common SQL data types, their characteristics, and the considerations that guide their selection. For your convenience, a reference for common MySQL data types may be found in Appendix F, and a similar reference for SQL Server data types in Appendix G.

### Numeric Data Types

#### INTEGER

The ***INTEGER*** data type is fundamental in SQL for storing whole numbers. It occupies a fixed amount of space, typically 4 bytes, and is used when you expect to store numbers without fractional components. It's ideal for columns representing counts, quantities, or identifiers. Choosing ***INTEGER*** over larger numeric types, such as ***BIGINT***, can optimize storage when precision is not a concern.

*DECIMAL/NUMERIC*

For scenarios requiring precise decimal or floating-point numbers, the **DECIMAL** (or **NUMERIC**) data type is suitable. This data type allows for specifying the exact number of digits before and after the decimal point. It is essential for financial data, where precision matters. However, it consumes more storage compared to **INTEGER** due to its flexibility.

Character Data Types

*VARCHAR*

The **VARCHAR** data type is used for variable-length character strings. It's versatile and efficient in terms of storage as it only occupies space proportional to the length of the stored data. For columns containing textual information, such as names, addresses, or descriptions, **VARCHAR** is often the preferred choice. The maximum length is specified when defining the column.

*CHAR*

In contrast to **VARCHAR**, the **CHAR** data type stores fixed-length character strings. It is suitable when you have consistent data sizes for a particular column, like fixed-length codes or abbreviations. However, it may waste storage space if the actual data is shorter than the defined length.

Date and Time Data Types

*DATE*

The **DATE** data type is used to store calendar dates, including year, month, and day. It is ideal for columns representing birthdays, booking dates, or any other information involving dates. **DATE** data types are efficient in terms of storage and allow for various date-related operations.

# Creating Tables and Databases

*TIMESTAMP*

When you need to store both date and time information with higher precision, the ***TIMESTAMP*** data type is preferred. It includes date and time down to fractions of a second. This data type is commonly used for tracking events, such as database record modifications, where timing is crucial.

Boolean Data Type

*BOOLEAN*

The ***BOOLEAN*** data type stores true or false values. It is used for binary decisions, representing conditions like "yes" or "no," "true" or "false." For columns requiring logical flags or binary indicators, ***BOOLEAN*** is the natural choice. It consumes minimal storage, typically just one bit.

Data Type Selection Considerations

Choosing the right data type depends on several factors:

1. Data Integrity: Select a data type that enforces the necessary constraints and ensures data integrity. For instance, using ***DATE*** for date columns helps prevent invalid date entries.

2. Storage Optimization: Consider the volume of data and storage constraints. Using smaller data types like ***INTEGER*** instead of ***BIGINT*** when a larger range of values or greater precision is not critical can optimize storage.

3. Query Performance: The data type affects query performance. Well-chosen data types can speed up data retrieval and processing, reducing the need for data type conversions.

Data Type Conversions

When data is moved or manipulated within SQL, data type conversions may be necessary. Implicit conversions are automatically performed by the database system when a compatible data type is expected. However, explicit conversions may be required when dealing with incompatible data types. It's crucial to be aware of potential data loss or unexpected results when performing conversions, especially from a larger to a smaller data type. Consequently, understanding SQL data types and their appropriate usage is fundamental to effective database design and optimization. By selecting data types based on the nature of the data, considering storage efficiency, and handling data type conversions with care, SQL programmers can build efficient and robust database systems that meet their application's needs.

## NULL Values in SQL

Understanding and managing NULL values is a fundamental aspect of ensuring data integrity and query accuracy. In this section, we will explore the concept of NULL values, their implications, and strategies for handling them effectively within your SQL databases.

### Understanding NULL

NULL is a placeholder in SQL that represents missing or unknown data. It is not the same as an empty string or zero; rather, it signifies the absence of a value. NULL values can appear in any column, whether it's numeric, character-based, or date-related. Consider a scenario where you have a database of customers, and some customers have not provided their email addresses; in this case, the email column would contain NULL values for those customers.

### Implications of NULL

Understanding NULL values is crucial because they can have far-reaching implications:

- **Unknown Information**: NULL indicates that the actual data is unknown or not applicable. This can be useful in scenarios where you cannot provide a meaningful default value.
- **Query Complexity**: Dealing with NULL values can add complexity to SQL queries. You need to consider how to handle NULL values in your SQL statements to get accurate results.
- **Data Integrity**: NULL values can affect data integrity. In some cases, they might be entirely valid (e.g., optional fields), while in others, they could signify missing or incomplete data.

## Managing NULL Values

### *Default Values*

One strategy to manage NULL values is to set default values for columns. When a new row is inserted and no value is provided for a particular column, the default value is used instead. This approach can be handy for ensuring consistency in your data and simplifying queries.

For example, you might set a default value of "N/A" for the email column in your customer database. This way, if a customer doesn't provide an email address, it defaults to "N/A" rather than NULL.

### *Permitting or Prohibiting NULL*

When designing your database schema, you face a pivotal decision: whether to permit or prohibit NULL values in a column. This choice depends on the specific requirements of your application and the meaning of the data.

- ***Permitting NULL Values***: Allowing NULL values is suitable when you genuinely expect certain data to be missing or unknown at times. For example, in an e-commerce database, the ***shipdate*** column for a customer order might allow NULL values because a product may have been ordered, but the order has not yet been shipped.
- ***Prohibiting NULL Values***: Prohibiting NULL values is preferable when you require complete and consistent data. For instance, in a product catalog, the ***Price*** column should likely prohibit NULL values to ensure every product has a defined price.

### *Impact on Data Integrity*

The decision to permit or prohibit NULL values has a profound impact on data integrity:

- ***Permitting NULL:*** While it provides flexibility and allows for more realistic data representation, it demands extra caution in handling NULL values during queries. You must anticipate and account for NULL values in your SQL statements.
- ***Prohibiting NULL:*** This approach enforces data integrity by mandating that every column has a defined value. It simplifies queries and ensures data consistency. However, it may not be suitable for all scenarios, as it might not accurately represent real-world data conditions.

*Final Thoughts on Null*

Understanding the concept of NULL, its implications, and the strategies for handling it effectively are essential skills for every SQL practitioner. By setting default values, making informed choices about permitting or prohibiting NULL values, and carefully considering the impact on data integrity, you can create databases that not only store data but also do so with precision and accuracy, meeting the needs of your application and users. In subsequent material, we will discuss advanced SQL techniques for querying and manipulating data, building on the foundation established here.

---

## Defining Constraints and Keys

Ensuring data accuracy, integrity, and relationships between tables is of paramount importance. This section explores the crucial task of defining constraints and keys in SQL databases, covering unique keys, foreign keys, enforcing referential integrity, and the use of CHECK constraints for data validation.

*The Importance of Constraints*

Imagine a library where books are organized without any order or system. Chaos would reign. Similarly, in SQL databases, constraints serve as the organizational rules that maintain data order and relationships. They ensure that data adheres to predefined standards, preserving the integrity of your database.

*Unique Key Constraints*

The Unique Identifier

A ***unique key constraint*** is a rule that enforces the uniqueness of values in a column or a set of columns within a table. It ensures that each value in the specified column(s) is distinct, preventing duplication of data.

For example, in a ***Student*** table, you might define a unique key constraint on the ***StudentID*** column. This ensures that every student has a unique identifier (*note that by definition, a primary key field is constrained to be both non-NULL and unique*).

## Ensuring Uniqueness

Unique keys are vital for maintaining data integrity and facilitating data retrieval. They ensure that critical information, such as primary keys or email addresses, remains distinct. Attempting to insert a duplicate value into a column with a unique key constraint will result in an error, preventing data duplication.

### *Foreign Key Constraints*

Now let is consider the defining role foreign key constraints play in the relationship between database entities (tables).

## Building Relationships

Relational database tables often share relationships. A **foreign key constraint** establishes a link between tables by specifying that the values in a column (the foreign key) must correspond to values in another table's primary key column (the referenced key).

For instance, consider an ***Orders*** table and a ***Customers*** table. The ***CustomerID*** column in the ***Orders*** table can be a foreign key that references the ***CustomerID*** primary key in the ***Customers*** table. This enforces a relationship where each order must be associated with an existing customer.

## Enforcing Referential Integrity

Foreign key constraints play a pivotal role in **referential integrity**, ensuring that relationships between tables are maintained. They prevent actions that would compromise these relationships, such as inserting records with non-existent foreign key values or deleting records that are referenced by others.

By enforcing referential integrity, foreign key constraints guarantee that your data remains accurate and meaningful. Attempting to violate these constraints will result in errors, preserving the integrity of your database.

*CHECK Constraints for Data Validation*

While unique and foreign keys primarily deal with data uniqueness and relationships, **CHECK constraints** expand the scope of constraint rules to validate data based on specific conditions. They allow you to specify conditions that must be true for data to be valid.

For example, in a ***Products*** table, you might define a CHECK constraint that ensures the ***Price*** column contains values greater than zero. This constraint prevents invalid data, such as negative prices, from being inserted.

Enhancing Data Quality

CHECK constraints are invaluable for enhancing data quality and enforcing business rules. They help maintain consistent data by rejecting entries that violate specified conditions. By applying CHECK constraints, you can ensure that your database contains only accurate and meaningful data.

*Final Thoughts on Constraints*

Defining constraints and keys is akin to laying the foundation of a sturdy building. Unique key constraints guarantee data uniqueness, foreign key constraints establish relationships and enforce referential integrity, and CHECK constraints validate data based on specific conditions. These tools collectively ensure the integrity, accuracy, and meaningfulness of your database. With a solid understanding of these constraints, you can craft SQL databases that not only store data but do so with precision and reliability, supporting your application's needs and providing confidence in data integrity. In the following material, we will explore techniques for optimizing queries and performance.

---

Modifying Existing Tables

The ability to adapt your database structure to changing requirements is essential. In this section, we will explore the art of modifying existing database tables, covering the use of ***ALTER TABLE*** statements for altering table structures, adding, modifying, and dropping columns, and renaming tables and columns to keep your database in sync with evolving needs.

# Creating Tables and Databases

*The Need for Modification*

Imagine a library where the shelves remain fixed, unable to accommodate new books or adapt to changing genres. Such rigidity is impractical in the world of databases. The ability to modify tables is a fundamental aspect of database maintenance and evolution.

*ALTER TABLE Statements*

The **ALTER TABLE** statement is your key to modifying table structures in SQL. It allows you to make changes to an existing table, ranging from adding new columns to altering existing ones, and even dropping or renaming columns.

Adding Columns

One common task is adding columns to a table. Consider an **employees** table that initially had basic information like names and salaries. As the organization grows, you may need to add columns for additional information, such as job titles or departments. The **ALTER TABLE** statement enables you to do this seamlessly:

```
-- SQL SERVER
ALTER TABLE employees
ADD COLUMN JobTitle VARCHAR(50), DepartmentID INT;
```

```
-- MySQL
ALTER TABLE employees
ADD COLUMN JobTitle VARCHAR(50),
ADD COLUMN DepartmentID INT;
```

This statement adds two new columns, **JobTitle** and **DepartmentID** to the **Employees** table.

Modifying Columns

As requirements evolve, you may need to modify the data type or constraints of existing columns. Suppose the **Salary** column in the **employees** table needs to accommodate decimal values to represent salaries more precisely. You can use the ALTER TABLE statement to achieve this:

```
-- SQL SERVER
ALTER TABLE employees
ALTER COLUMN Salary DECIMAL(10, 2);
```

```
-- MySQL
ALTER TABLE employees
MODIFY COLUMN Salary DECIMAL(10, 2);
```

This statement changes the data type of the *Salary* column to DECIMAL with 10 digits and 2 decimal places.

Dropping Columns

Sometimes, you may need to remove columns that are no longer relevant or necessary. For instance, if you decide to track employee salaries in a separate *Salaries* table and no longer need the *Salary* column in the *employees* table, you can use the ALTER TABLE statement to drop it:

```
-- COMMON SQL
ALTER TABLE employees
DROP COLUMN Salary;
```

This statement removes the *Salary* column from the *Employees* table.

*Renaming Tables and Columns*

Changing the name of a table or column is another common task in database maintenance. Perhaps your *employeeInfo* table would be more appropriately named *employees*, or you want to rename the *FirstName* column to *GivenName.* The **ALTER TABLE** (MySQL) and system stored procedure **SP_RENAME** statements facilitate these changes:

```
-- SQL SERVER
-- Renaming a table
EXEC sp_rename 'employeeInfo', 'employees';

-- Renaming a column
EXEC sp_rename 'employees.FirstName', 'GivenName', 'COLUMN';
```

# Creating Tables and Databases

```sql
-- MySQL
-- Renaming a table
ALTER TABLE employeeInfo
RENAME TO employees;

-- Renaming a column
ALTER TABLE employees
RENAME COLUMN FirstName TO GivenName;
```

These statements demonstrate how to rename a table and a column, respectively.


## Final Thoughts on Modifying Tables


The **ALTER TABLE** statement is your versatile tool for making these changes, whether you need to add, modify, drop columns, or rename tables and columns. By mastering these techniques, you can ensure that your database remains flexible and aligned with the evolving needs of your applications, maintaining its relevance and efficiency. In the following section, we will explore advanced SQL techniques for optimizing and fine-tuning database performance to ensure that your database operates at its best.

---

## Best Practices for SQL Script Execution


In SQL programming, efficiency, organization, and precision are paramount. This section explores best practices for executing SQL scripts, emphasizing organization, version control, error handling, debugging techniques, transaction management, and the critical concepts of rollbacks and commits.


## Organizing SQL Scripts


Imagine a library where books are scattered without any order. Finding the right book would be a daunting task. Similarly, in SQL programming, organizing your SQL scripts is essential for clarity and efficiency.

**Best Practice**: Group related SQL statements in separate scripts or files. For instance, have one script for table creation, another for data insertion, and yet another for querying.

*Version Control*

Version control is the backbone of software development and database management. It allows you to track changes, collaborate seamlessly, and, most importantly, roll back to previous states if needed.

**Best Practice**: Use a version control system like Git to manage SQL scripts. Commit changes regularly, provide clear commit messages, and consider branching for different development phases.

*Error Handling and Debugging*

Errors are part of the programming journey, but dealing with them effectively is essential. SQL provides tools for error handling and debugging.

**Best Practice**: Surround SQL code with error handlers (e.g., BEGIN...EXCEPTION...END blocks) to catch and handle errors gracefully. Implement proper logging to record errors for later analysis.

*Transaction Management*

Transactions are essential for maintaining data consistency and integrity. A transaction groups one or more SQL statements into a single unit of work. It either succeeds entirely or fails completely.

**Best Practice**: Wrap related SQL statements in transactions, using ***BEGIN TRANSACTION*** and ***COMMIT*** to mark the start and end. If an error occurs, use ***ROLLBACK*** to undo changes and maintain data integrity.

*Rollbacks and Commits*

Rollbacks and commits are the gatekeepers of data changes within a transaction. Understanding when to use them is vital.

**Best Practice**: Commit your transaction only when you are sure all the related SQL statements are error-free and should be permanently applied to the database. Use ***ROLLBACK*** when an error occurs or when you want to discard the transaction entirely.

# Creating Tables and Databases

*Final Thoughts on Script Execution Best Practices*

By organizing your SQL scripts, implementing version control, mastering error handling and debugging, and understanding the nuances of transaction management, rollbacks, and commits, you equip yourself with the skills and knowledge needed to navigate the SQL landscape with confidence and precision. These practices are the pillars of efficient and reliable SQL development, ensuring that your database remains a resilient and efficient repository for your data. In the material which follows, we will discuss advanced SQL techniques and emerging trends to prepare you for the ever-evolving world of SQL programming.

## Advanced Topics and Considerations

As you delve deeper into SQL programming, it's essential to explore advanced topics and considerations that go beyond the basics. In this section, we will journey into the realm of generating and executing SQL scripts programmatically, dynamic SQL and parameterized queries, and delve into security best practices and permissions management.

*Generating and Executing SQL Scripts Programmatically*

Manually crafting SQL scripts for every task can be time-consuming and error-prone. To overcome these challenges, developers often turn to programmatic script generation and execution.

***Advanced Consideration***: Leverage programming languages like Python, Java, or C# to generate SQL scripts based on dynamic criteria. Automate routine database tasks, such as data imports, migrations, or report generation, by programmatically generating and executing SQL scripts.

*Dynamic SQL and Parameterized Queries*

Static SQL queries have their place, but dynamic SQL offers adaptability and flexibility. Dynamic SQL allows you to construct SQL statements at runtime based on user inputs or changing requirements.

***Advanced Consideration***: Use parameterized queries to mitigate SQL injection risks in dynamic SQL. Parameterization separates SQL code from user inputs, enhancing security and improving query performance.

```
-- SQL SERVER
-- Dynamic SQL with Parameters
DECLARE @sql NVARCHAR(MAX);
SET @sql = 'SELECT * FROM Employees WHERE Department = @dept';
EXEC sp_executesql @sql, N'@dept NVARCHAR(50)', @dept = 'Sales';
```

```
-- MySQL
-- Dynamic SQL with Parameters
SET @sql = 'SELECT * FROM employees WHERE DepartmentID = ?';
PREPARE stmt FROM @sql;
SET @dept = '1';
EXECUTE stmt USING @dept;
DEALLOCATE PREPARE stmt;
```

*Security Best Practices and Permissions Management*

Securing your database is not a luxury; it's a necessity. Implementing robust security practices and managing permissions are paramount in safeguarding sensitive data and preventing unauthorized access.

***Advanced Consideration***: Adhere to the principle of least privilege, granting users only the permissions they need for their specific tasks. Implement strong authentication mechanisms, such as multi-factor authentication, and regularly review and update access controls to mitigate security risks.

```
-- COMMON SQL
-- Granting Minimum Permissions
GRANT SELECT ON Employees TO ReportingUser;
```

```
-- SQL SERVER
-- Implementing Strong Authentication
ALTER LOGIN ReportingUser WITH PASSWORD = 'NewStrongPassword';
```

```
-- MySQL
-- Implementing Strong Authentication
ALTER USER 'ReportingUser'@'%'
IDENTIFIED BY 'NewStrongPassword';
```

# Creating Tables and Databases

*Final Thoughts on Advanced SQL Topics*

As you ascend to the advanced levels of SQL programming, you'll encounter challenges and opportunities that demand a deeper understanding and more sophisticated approaches. The ability to generate and execute SQL scripts programmatically empowers you to automate and streamline database operations. Embracing dynamic SQL and parameterized queries allows for adaptability and security in your database interactions. Finally, adhering to security best practices and mastering permissions management is vital in ensuring the confidentiality and integrity of your data.

These advanced topics and considerations are the culmination of your SQL programming journey, equipping you with the knowledge and skills to tackle complex database tasks and navigate the evolving landscape of data management and security. Your journey in SQL programming continues, as you explore emerging trends and cutting-edge techniques to stay at the forefront of this dynamic field.

---

## Cross-Database Compatibility

Working with different database systems is a common challenge. Databases like MySQL, PostgreSQL, and SQL Server may have subtle but significant differences in syntax, data types, and constraints. The passages which follow explore the intricacies of cross-database compatibility, offering insights into considerations when creating scripts for various database systems.

*The Landscape of Compatibility*

Imagine a world where people speak different languages, use different currencies, and have unique customs. Similarly, various database systems have their own dialects of SQL, making it essential to navigate the landscape of compatibility.

**Consideration**: Recognize that different database systems have their own SQL variants. MySQL, PostgreSQL, SQL Server, and others adhere to the SQL standard to varying degrees, but they also introduce their own extensions and quirks.

*Syntax Variations*

The syntax differences among database systems can be likened to dialects of the same language. Simple SQL statements might be portable across systems, but more complex queries may require translation.

***Consideration***: Be aware of variations in SQL syntax when creating scripts. Familiarize yourself with the specific syntax rules and keywords for the database system you are using.

```
-- Example: LIMIT/OFFSET vs. TOP
-- SQL Server
SELECT TOP 10 * FROM Employees OFFSET 20 ROWS;


-- MySQL
SELECT * FROM Employees LIMIT 10 OFFSET 20;
```

*Data Type Variations*

Differences in data types can be a stumbling block when porting scripts between database systems. While some data types are common, others are specific to certain systems.

***Consideration***: Choose data types that are compatible across database systems whenever possible. For example, use *VARCHAR* instead of *TEXT*, as *VARCHAR* is more widely supported.

```
-- Example: Different Text Types
-- SQL Server
CREATE TABLE Products (Description NVARCHAR(MAX));

-- MySQL
CREATE TABLE Products (Description TEXT);
```

*Constraint Challenges*

Constraints, such as primary keys, unique constraints, and foreign keys, play a crucial role in maintaining data integrity. However, their implementation can vary across database systems.

***Consideration***: Be mindful of constraint syntax differences when designing your database schema. Test your scripts on the target database system to ensure constraints are applied correctly.

# Creating Tables and Databases

```
-- Example: Creating a Primary Key

-- SQL Server
CREATE TABLE Employees (EmployeeID INT CONSTRAINT PK_Employees
PRIMARY KEY);

-- MySQL
CREATE TABLE Employees (EmployeeID INT PRIMARY KEY);
```

*Final Thoughts on Cross-database Compatibility*

Cross-database compatibility in SQL programming is akin to being a multilingual traveler in a diverse world. While the core principles of SQL are universal, each database system introduces its own nuances and dialects. To navigate this terrain effectively, it's crucial to understand the syntax, data types, and constraints specific to the database systems you work with.

By recognizing the variations in SQL syntax, choosing compatible data types, and being mindful of constraint implementation, you can bridge the gaps and create SQL scripts that work seamlessly across different database systems. This skill is invaluable for database professionals who must daily deal with a variety of different SQL database engines, ensuring that their scripts and applications are useful with minimal modifications across diverse environments.

# Chapter 3 – Single Table Queries

Introduction to Single Table Queries

As we learned in the previous chapters, SQL (Structured Query Language) serves as the cornerstone of interaction with relational databases. SQL enables us to retrieve, manipulate, and analyze data stored within these databases. One fundamental aspect of SQL is constructing queries, which are requests for specific data from a database. These queries can be quite simple or incredibly complex, depending on the nature of the information we seek. Let's delve into the process and significance of constructing single-table queries.

Single-Table Query Scenarios

Here are three example scenarios where a single-table query is useful. Studying different examples should help to cement your understanding of the utility of this kind of query.

### Scenario 1: Employee Information Management

Consider a company that needs to store and manage information about its employees. In this scenario, a single table could be used to store details such as employee ID, name, job title, department, hire date, and salary. A single-table query could be constructed to retrieve a list of all employees within a specific department, making it easy for HR managers to review and manage staff distribution. The single table here helps centralize employee data and allows for efficient querying based on various attributes.

### Scenario 2: Online Retail Product Catalog

In an e-commerce context, an online retail store may need to maintain a product catalog. This catalog could include product ID, name, description, price, category, and availability status. With a single table, the store can organize all product information in one place. A single-table query could then be used to fetch a list of products within a particular price range or category, aiding customers in their shopping experience. The simplicity of a single table in this scenario streamlines product management and querying.

### Scenario 3: Student Enrollment Tracking

For an educational institution, tracking student enrollments is crucial. A single table could be utilized to store student details such as student ID, name, date of birth, program, enrollment date, and contact information. Constructing a single-table query allows administrators to generate a list of students enrolled in a specific program, helping them manage class sizes and resources more effectively. The single table approach simplifies student data management and reporting.

In all these scenarios, the single table serves as a repository for specific types of data, allowing for organized storage and efficient querying without the need for complex relationships between multiple tables. This simplicity can be advantageous in scenarios where the data doesn't require intricate interconnections and relationships, making single table queries a practical solution.

Imagine you're managing a book store's database, and you need to retrieve information about the books available. This is where single-table queries come into play. A single-table query involves working with just one table in the database. Recall that database tables commonly reflect specific real-world (or business-world) entities, so we would expect that the collection of books would reside in one table, in contrast to, say, librarians or library employees, which would reside in a different table. This is perfect when you're interested in data contained within a single entity, like books in our case. The image below provides useful information about the *books* table for our example, which will be used when querying this entity:

# Single Table Queries

**books (bookstore)**

| Column Name | Condensed Type | Nullable |
|---|---|---|
| BOOKID | bigint | No |
| ISBN | nvarchar(13) | Yes |
| Title | nvarchar(30) | Yes |
| PubDate | datetime2(0) | Yes |
| PubID | bigint | Yes |
| Cost | decimal(5, 2) | Yes |
| Retail | decimal(5, 2) | Yes |
| Category | nvarchar(25) | Yes |

*Figure 10 - Constituency of the Books Table*

## Basic SELECT Statement

A SQL query consists of several key elements: the ***SELECT*** clause, the ***FROM*** clause, the ***WHERE*** clause, and the ***ORDER BY*** clause. The ***SELECT*** clause determines which columns you want to retrieve from the table. The ***FROM*** clause specifies the table you're querying. The ***WHERE*** clause allows you to filter the data based on conditions. Lastly, the ***ORDER BY*** clause arranges the results in a specified order.

### Constructing Your Query

Imagine you're tasked with retrieving the titles and ISBN numbers of all the computer books in stock which were published after the year January 1, 2001. You start by writing your query:

```
-- COMMON SQL
SELECT Title, ISBN
FROM books
WHERE Category = 'COMPUTER' AND PubDate > '2001-01-01'
ORDER BY PubDate;
```

*Explanation*

| | |
|---|---|
| *SELECT Title, ISBN* | You're specifying that you want to retrieve the 'Title' and 'ISBN' columns. |
| *FROM books* | You're indicating that you're querying the 'books' table. |
| *WHERE Category = 'COMPUTER' AND PubDate > '2001-01-01'* | You're filtering the results to only include rows where the Category is 'COMPUTER' and the publication date is after January first of 2001. |
| *ORDER BY PubDate* | You're sorting the results in ascending order of publication date (*notice that you do not have to display the publication date to order the results by that criteria*). |

Significance of the Query

The constructed query carries significant implications. By extracting this specific subset of data, you can now provide customers with a list of computer-related books published since a specified date which are currently in-stock or available to order. This information can guide acquisitions, marketing strategies, and help patrons discover new releases.

Executing the Query

With the query in hand, you send it to the database using a compatible SQL tool or interface. The database engine processes your query. It locates the **books** table, applies the conditions specified in the **WHERE** clause, and sorts the results as indicated in the **ORDER BY** clause. Finally, the engine presents the refined data to you in a structured format. The figure below illustrates this query being executed using a SQL Server Database via the SQL Server Management Studio query client, along with its results:

# Single Table Queries

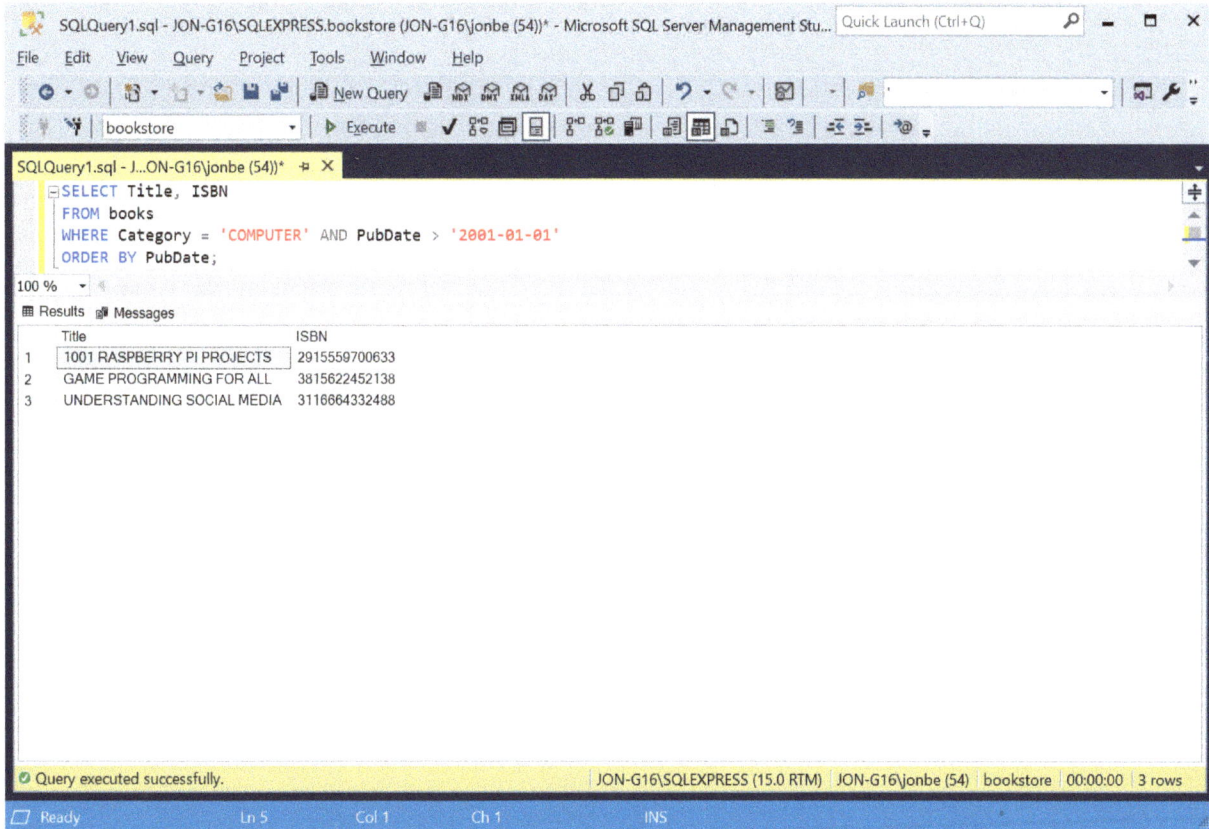

*Figure 11 - Single Table Query Example*

## The SELECT Statement

Understanding the **SELECT** statement is fundamental, as it forms the backbone of retrieving data from a single table in a relational database. Let's break down the syntax of the **SELECT** statement and provide an example to illustrate its usage.

**Syntax of the SELECT Statement:**

The basic syntax of the **SELECT** statement for retrieving data from a single table is as follows:

```
-- COMMON SQL
SELECT column1, column2, ...
FROM table_name
WHERE condition;
```

Now, let's explain each part of this syntax:

- **SELECT**: This keyword is used to specify which columns you want to retrieve data from. You can either list specific column names or use an asterisk * to select all columns.
- **FROM**: This keyword is used to specify the table from which you want to retrieve data. You need to provide the name of the table where the data is stored.
- **WHERE** (optional): This clause is used to filter the rows returned from the table based on a specific condition. It allows you to retrieve only the rows that meet certain criteria.

*Select Statement Example:*

Suppose we have a table called **Students** with the following columns: **StudentID**, **FirstName**, **LastName**, **Age**, and **Department**. We want to retrieve the first and last names of all students who are older than 20 years and belong to the "Computer Science" department.

Here's how we can construct the SQL query:

```
-- COMMON SQL
SELECT FirstName, LastName
FROM Students
WHERE Age > 20 AND Department = 'Computer Science';
```

In this example:

- We use the **SELECT** clause to specify that we want to retrieve the **FirstName** and **LastName** columns.
- We use the **FROM** clause to indicate that we are retrieving data from the **Students** table.
- We use the **WHERE** clause to filter the results. It specifies that we only want rows where the **Age** is greater than 20 and the **Department** is "Computer Science."

When this SQL query is executed, it will return a result set containing the first and last names of students who meet the specified criteria.

Understanding the **SELECT** statement is crucial for querying data in SQL, and it forms the foundation for more complex database operations. It allows you to retrieve and manipulate data in a structured and efficient manner from a single table or multiple tables using **JOIN** operations.

Specifying Selected Columns, or All Columns Using the Wildcard Operator

# Single Table Queries

The **SELECT** clause also allows you to specify which columns you want to retrieve from a table. It allows you to control the presentation of data in your query results. You can use it to display only selected columns, or you can employ the wildcard operator to select all columns.

*Using the SELECT Clause to Display Selected Columns*

When you want to retrieve specific columns from a table, you list those column names in the **SELECT** clause. Here's a breakdown of how to use it:

```
-- COMMON SQL
SELECT column1, column2, ...
FROM table_name
WHERE condition;
```

- **column1, column2, ...**: In this part of the statement, you specify the names of the columns you want to include in the query result. You can list one or more column names separated by commas.

SELECT Clause Displaying Selected Columns Example:

Suppose you have a table called **Employees** with columns **EmployeeID**, **FirstName**, **LastName**, **Salary**, and **Department**. If you want to retrieve only the first and last names of employees, your SQL query would look like this:

```
-- COMMON SQL
SELECT FirstName, LastName
FROM Employees;
```

This query will return a result set containing only the **FirstName** and **LastName** columns for all employees in the **Employees** table.

*Using the Wildcard Operator (*) to Select All Columns*

If you want to retrieve all columns from a table without specifying them individually, you can use the wildcard operator (*). Here's how it works:

```
-- COMMON SQL
SELECT *
FROM table_name
WHERE condition;
```

- **\*:** The asterisk (\*) is used as a placeholder for all columns in the table specified in the ***FROM*** clause.

Wildcard Operator Selecting All Columns Example:

Using the same ***Employees*** table, if you want to retrieve all columns for employees who belong to the "Marketing" department, you can use the wildcard operator like this:

```
-- COMMON SQL
SELECT *
FROM Employees
WHERE Department = 'Marketing';
```

This query will return all columns (***EmployeeID***, ***FirstName***, ***LastName***, ***Salary***, and ***Department***) for employees in the "Marketing" department.

It's important to note that while using the wildcard operator (\*) is convenient for selecting all columns, it may not be the most efficient approach in situations where you only need a subset of columns. Retrieving unnecessary data can result in increased network and processing overhead. Therefore, it's often best practice to explicitly specify the columns you need using the ***SELECT*** clause when writing SQL queries, especially in production scenarios.

*Filtering rows using the Where clause*

The ***SELECT*** clause in SQL allows you to retrieve data from a table, and the ***WHERE*** clause complements it by enabling you to filter the rows you want to include in the query result. When used together, these two clauses provide a powerful way to extract specific data that meets certain criteria from a table. Let's delve deeper into how to use the ***SELECT*** and ***WHERE*** clauses together to filter rows effectively:

# Single Table Queries

*Syntax of SELECT and WHERE together*

```
-- COMMON SQL
SELECT column1, column2, ...
FROM table_name
WHERE condition;
```

Here's a breakdown of how to use each of these components:

1. **SELECT** clause: In this part of the SQL statement, you specify the columns you want to retrieve data from. You can list one or more column names separated by commas, or you may use the wildcard operator (*) to select all columns.
2. **FROM clause**: This specifies the table from which you're retrieving data.
3. **WHERE clause**: This is where you specify the conditions that rows must meet to be included in the result set. The **WHERE** clause is essential for filtering rows based on specific criteria.

*Using the WHERE Clause to Filter Rows*

The **WHERE** clause is used to filter rows based on one or more conditions. These conditions are specified after the **WHERE** keyword, and rows that satisfy these conditions are included in the result set.

Common operators and constructs used in the **WHERE** clause include:

- **Comparison operators** (e.g., =, <, >, <=, >=, !=, <>): Used to compare values in columns against specific values or expressions.
- **Logical operators** (e.g., **AND**, **OR**, **NOT**): Used to combine multiple conditions in more complex expressions.
- **Wildcards** (e.g., % for pattern matching): Used to match partial strings within columns.

*Where Clause Example:*

Suppose you have a table called **Products** with columns **ProductID**, **ProductName**, **Category**, and **Price**. You want to retrieve all products that belong to the "Electronics" category and have a price greater than $500. You can use the **SELECT** and **WHERE** clauses together to achieve this:

```
-- COMMON SQL
SELECT ProductID, ProductName, Price
FROM Products
WHERE Category = 'Electronics' AND Price > 500;
```

In this example:

- The **SELECT** clause specifies that we want to retrieve the **ProductID**, **ProductName**, and **Price** columns.
- The **FROM** clause specifies the **Products** table as the data source.
- The **WHERE** clause filters the rows based on two conditions: products must have the "Electronics" category, and their price must be greater than $500.

The result of this query will be a list of products that meet these criteria.

Using the **WHERE** clause in conjunction with the **SELECT** statement allows you to extract specific data subsets from your database, making SQL a versatile tool for data retrieval and analysis. It's essential for customizing your query results to match your specific needs.

Sorting and Ordering Results

The **ORDER BY** clause in SQL is used to specify the order in which the query results should be displayed. It allows you to sort the rows in the result set based on one or more columns, either in ascending (ASC) or descending (DESC) order. This clause is especially useful when you want to present the data in a more meaningful and organized way.

*Basic Syntax of the ORDER BY Clause*

The basic syntax of the **ORDER BY** clause is as follows:

```
--COMMON SQL
SELECT column1, column2, ...
FROM table_name
WHERE condition
ORDER BY column1 [ASC | DESC], column2 [ASC | DESC], ...;
```

Here's what each part of the **ORDER BY** clause does:

- **column1, column2, ...**: These are the columns by which you want to sort the result set. You can specify one or more columns separated by commas.
- **ASC** (optional): This stands for ascending order (the default order if not specified). It sorts the result set in ascending alphabetical or numerical order.
- **DESC** (optional): This stands for descending order. It sorts the result set in descending alphabetical or numerical order.

*Ordering Results in Ascending Order*

When you want to sort your query results in ascending order, you can use the **ASC** keyword or omit it, as ascending order is the default behavior. Here's an example:

```
-- COMMON SQL
SELECT ProductName, Price
FROM Products
ORDER BY Price;
```

In this query, the result set will contain the product names and prices sorted in ascending order based on the **Price** column.

*Ordering Results in Descending Order*

To sort your results in descending order, you use the **DESC** keyword. Here's an example:

```
-- COMMON SQL
SELECT LastName, FirstName
FROM Employees
ORDER BY LastName DESC;
```

In this query, the result set will contain employee last names and first names sorted in descending order based on the **LastName** column.

*Sorting by Multiple Columns:*

You can also sort query results by multiple columns to achieve more precise ordering. When sorting by multiple columns, SQL first sorts the data based on the first column specified in the **ORDER BY** clause. If there are ties (rows with the same values in the first column), it then sorts those rows based on the second column specified, and so on.

Here's an example of sorting by multiple columns:

```
-- COMMON SQL
SELECT FirstName, LastName, Salary
FROM Employees
ORDER BY Salary DESC, LastName ASC;
```

In this query:

- The result set is first sorted in descending order by the **Salary** column.
- If two employees have the same salary, they are then sorted in ascending order by the **LastName** column

*Minor and Major Sort Keys*

When you sort by multiple columns, you can think of the first column specified as the major sort key, and subsequent columns as minor sort keys. The major sort key determines the primary order, and the minor sort keys are used to further refine the order of rows with identical values in the major sort key column.

In the previous example, **Salary** is the major sort key, and **LastName** is the minor sort key. This means that the primary sorting is done by salary, and for employees with the same salary, they are then sorted by last name.

The **ORDER BY** clause is a powerful tool in SQL, allowing you to control the presentation of query results by specifying the sorting criteria. Whether you need ascending or descending order, or if you want to sort by multiple columns, the **ORDER BY** clause helps you customize the order of your data to meet your specific needs.

# Single Table Queries

String and Date Functions

SQL provides a variety of string and date functions that allow you to manipulate and format strings and work with date and time values effectively. For your convenience, a list of commonly used SQL Server functions is provided in Appendix A, and commonly used MySQL functions in Appendix B. Let's explore some commonly used SQL string and date functions:

*String Functions:*

**Concatenation (*CONCAT* or +):** You can combine two or more strings into a single string using the **CONCAT** function or the + operator.

Example:

```
-- COMMON SQL
SELECT CONCAT(FirstName, ' ', LastName) AS FullName
FROM Employees;
```

**Substring (*SUBSTRING* or *SUBSTR*):** This function allows you to extract a portion of a string based on a specified starting position and length.

Example:

```
-- COMMON SQL
SELECT SUBSTR(Description, 1, 20) AS ShortDescription
FROM product;
```

**Changing Case (*UPPER* and *LOWER*):** SQL provides functions to change the case of strings. **UPPER** converts a string to uppercase, while **LOWER** converts it to lowercase.

Example:

```
-- COMMON SQL
SELECT UPPER(FirstName) AS UppercaseName
FROM employees;
```

*Date and Time Functions*

**DATEFORMAT (*FORMAT* in some SQL databases):** This function allows you to format date and time values into a specific format for presentation.

53

Example:

```
-- SQL Server
SELECT FORMAT(OrderDate, 'dd/MM/yyyy') AS FormattedDate
FROM Orders;
```

```
-- MySQL
SELECT DATE_FORMAT(OrderDate, '%d/%m/%Y') AS FormattedDate
FROM orders;
```

***DATEADD/DATE_ADD***: It lets you add or subtract a specific time interval (such as days, months, or years) from a date.

Example:

```
-- SQL SERVER
SELECT OrderDate, DATEADD(MONTH, 3, OrderDate) AS ReturnByDate
FROM orders;
```

```
-- MySQL
SELECT OrderDate,
DATE_ADD(OrderDate, INTERVAL 3 MONTH) AS ReturnByDate
FROM orders;
```

***DATEDIFF***: This function calculates the difference between two dates or times, returning the result in a specified unit (e.g., days, months, years).

Example:

```
-- SQL SERVER
SELECT  DATEDIFF(DAY, OrderDate, GETDATE()) AS DaysSinceOrder
FROM orders;
```

```
-- MySQL
SELECT DATEDIFF(CURDATE(), OrderDate) AS DaysSinceOrder
FROM orders;
```

***GETDATE*** (***CURRENT_TIMESTAMP*** in some SQL databases): It retrieves the current date and time from the system.

# Single Table Queries

Example:

```
-- SQL SERVER
SELECT GETDATE() AS CurrentDateTime;
```

```
-- MySQL
SELECT current_timestamp() AS CurrentDateTime;
```

***DATEPART/(YEAR/MONTH/DAY*** in some SQL databases): This function extracts a specific part (e.g., year, month, day) from a date or time value.

Example:

```
-- SQL SERVER
SELECT DATEPART(YEAR, OrderDate) AS OrderYear
FROM Orders;
```

```
-- MySQL
SELECT YEAR(OrderDate) AS OrderYear
FROM Orders;
```

These are just a few examples of SQL string and date functions. The availability and syntax of these functions may vary depending on the specific database system you are using (e.g., SQL Server, MySQL, PostgreSQL). It's essential to consult the documentation for your database system to understand the full range of functions and their usage. String and date functions are powerful tools that can help you manipulate and format data to meet your application's requirements in SQL queries.

## Aggregation and Grouping

Aggregation and grouping in SQL are essential concepts for summarizing and analyzing data in a database. These operations allow you to perform calculations on groups of rows and obtain summary information from your data. Let's delve into aggregation, grouping, and the use of aggregate functions along with the *HAVING* clause in SQL.

Understanding Aggregation and Grouping:

- ***Aggregation***: Aggregation refers to the process of applying an aggregate function to a set of values. Aggregate functions perform calculations on a group of rows and return a single result. Common aggregate functions in SQL include SUM, AVG, COUNT, MIN, and MAX.

- **_Grouping_**: Grouping involves dividing the rows of a table into groups based on the values in one or more columns. You can then apply aggregate functions to these groups to obtain summary data for each group.

*Aggregate Functions*

**_SUM_**: Calculates the sum of a numeric column's values within each group.

```
-- COMMON SQL
SELECT Department, SUM(Salary) AS TotalSalary
FROM Employees
GROUP BY Department;
```

**_AVG_**: Computes the average of numeric values within each group.

```
-- COMMON SQL
SELECT Department, AVG(Salary) AS AvgSalary
FROM Employees
GROUP BY Department;
```

**_COUNT_**: Counts the number of rows within each group.

```
-- COMMON SQL
SELECT Department, COUNT(*) AS EmployeeCount
FROM Employees
GROUP BY Department;
```

**_MIN_**: Finds the minimum value within each group.

```
-- COMMON SQL
SELECT Department, MIN(Salary) AS MinSalary
FROM Employees
GROUP BY Department;
```

*MAX*: Finds the maximum value within each group.

```
-- COMMON SQL
SELECT Department, MAX(Salary) AS MaxSalary
FROM Employees
GROUP BY Department;
```

*The HAVING Clause*

The **HAVING** clause is used in conjunction with the **GROUP BY** clause to filter the results of a grouped query based on a condition involving aggregate functions. Unlike the **WHERE** clause, which filters rows before grouping, the **HAVING** clause filters groups after the grouping and aggregation has occurred. It allows you to specify conditions on the aggregated data.

*HAVING Clause Example:*

Suppose you want to find departments with an average salary greater than $50,000:

```
-- COMMON SQL
SELECT Department, AVG(Salary) AS AvgSalary
FROM Employees
GROUP BY Department
HAVING AVG(Salary) > 50000;
```

In this query:

- The **GROUP BY** clause groups employees by department.
- The *AVG(Salary)* calculates the average salary for each department.
- The **HAVING** clause filters the result, ensuring that only departments with an average salary greater than $50,000 are included in the final result.

Without the **HAVING** clause, you couldn't filter the result based on the result of the *AVG* aggregate function because **WHERE** is used to filter individual rows, not groups.

In summary, aggregation and grouping, along with aggregate functions like *SUM*, *AVG*, *COUNT*, *MIN*, and *MAX*, allow you to summarize and analyze data in SQL. The **HAVING** clause plays a crucial role in filtering aggregated results, helping you focus on specific groups of data that meet your criteria for analysis.

The DISTINCT Statement

The **DISTINCT** statement in SQL is used to eliminate duplicate rows from the result set of a query. It ensures that only unique values are displayed in the output. The primary purpose of the **DISTINCT** statement is to retrieve distinct (unique) values from one or more columns within a table. Here's how it works and why it's useful:

*Operation of the DISTINCT Statement*

Consider a scenario where you have a table with duplicate values in one or more columns, and you want to retrieve a list of unique values from those columns. The **DISTINCT** statement allows you to achieve this by instructing the database to filter out duplicate rows based on the specified columns.

*Syntax of the DISTINCT Statement*

The basic syntax of the **DISTINCT** statement is as follows:

```
-- COMMON SQL
SELECT DISTINCT column1, column2, ...
FROM table_name
WHERE condition;
```

Here's what each part of this syntax does:

- **SELECT DISTINCT**: This clause instructs the database to return only unique values for the specified columns.
- **column1, column2, ...**: These are the columns for which you want to retrieve distinct values. You can specify one or more columns separated by commas.
- **FROM table_name**: This part specifies the table from which you want to retrieve data.
- **WHERE condition** (optional): You can include a **WHERE** clause to filter the rows before applying the **DISTINCT** operation. This clause is not required, but it can be useful for further refining your query.

# Single Table Queries

*Use Cases of the DISTINCT Statement*

**Removing Duplicates**: The primary use of **DISTINCT** is to remove duplicate rows from query results. For example, if you have a table of customer orders and you want to retrieve a list of unique customer names:

```
-- COMMON SQL
SELECT DISTINCT CustomerName
FROM Orders;
```

This query will return a list of unique customer names, removing any duplicate entries.

**Retrieving Unique Values**: **DISTINCT** is also useful when you need to find unique values within a single column or multiple columns. For instance, if you have a table of products and you want to know the unique categories available:

```
-- COMMON SQL
SELECT DISTINCT Category
FROM Products;
```

This query will return a list of unique product categories from the **Products** table.

It's important to note that while **DISTINCT** is effective in removing duplicate rows, it does not give you control over which specific row with duplicate values is retained. It simply returns one instance of each unique value found in the specified columns.

A word of caution: The author has observed both students new to SQL as well as experienced Database Administrators (DBAs), who have acquired the poor practice of habitually using the **DISTINCT** statement, without considering either the effect or necessity of its use. Perhaps this was a consequence of working with data sets of poor integrity and substantial duplication of data. But whatever its cause, this habit will lead to unintended consequences, and should be avoided. Always give due consideration to the objective of the SQL query you are composing and use or omit the **DISTINCT** key word by intention rather than habit!

In summary, the **DISTINCT** statement in SQL is a valuable tool for eliminating duplicate rows and retrieving unique values from one or more columns. It helps you clean up query results and obtain a concise, distinct list of values that meet your data analysis or reporting needs.

Chapter 3

Working with NULL Values

Working with **NULL** values in SQL is an essential aspect of database query development because **NULL** represents the absence of a value or an unknown value. SQL provides several operators and functions to handle **NULL** values effectively. Here, we'll discuss using **IS NULL**, **IS NOT NULL**, and the **COALESCE** function to work with **NULL** values:

*IS NULL and IS NOT NULL*

**IS NULL**: This operator is used to filter rows where a particular column contains NULL values.

```
-- COMMON SQL
SELECT FirstName, LastName
FROM Employees
WHERE MiddleName IS NULL;
```

In this example, the query retrieves employees whose middle names are NULL.

**IS NOT NULL**: Conversely, this operator is used to filter rows where a particular column does not contain NULL values.

```
-- COMMON SQL
SELECT ProductName, UnitPrice
  FROM Products
  WHERE UnitPrice IS NOT NULL;
```

This query retrieves products with non-null unit prices.

COALESCE Function

The **COALESCE** function is used to return the first non-null value in a list of expressions. It's particularly useful when you want to replace NULL values with a default or alternative value.

# Single Table Queries

*Syntax of COALESCE*

```
-- COMMON SQL
COALESCE(expression1, expression2, ...);
```

***expression1, expression2, ...:*** These are the expressions or values to be evaluated. The function returns the first non-null expression from left to right.

*Replacing NULL with a Default Value Example:*

Suppose you have a table of orders with a ***Discount*** column that may contain ***NULL*** values. You want to retrieve the order IDs and apply a default discount of 0% to orders with ***NULL*** discounts.

```
-- COMMON SQL
SELECT OrderID, COALESCE(Discount, 0) AS Discount
FROM Orders;
```

In this query, ***COALESCE(Discount, 0)*** replaces ***NULL*** discounts with 0% for the result set.

*Finding the First Non-NULL Value Example:*
You have a table of employees with three columns for different types of contact information: ***Email***, ***Phone***, and ***AlternatePhone***. You want to retrieve a single contact method for each employee, prioritizing ***Email*** over ***Phone*** and ***AlternatePhone***.

```
-- COMMON SQL
SELECT EmployeeID, COALESCE(Email, Phone, AlternatePhone) AS
ContactMethod
FROM Employees;
```

In this query, ***COALESCE*** returns the first non-null contact method from the list, effectively prioritizing email addresses over phone numbers and alternate phone numbers.

The ability to handle ***NULL*** values is crucial in SQL, as they often represent missing or incomplete data. ***IS NULL*** and ***IS NOT NULL*** operators allow you to filter rows based on the presence or absence of ***NULL*** values, while the ***COALESCE*** function helps you handle ***NULL*** values by providing default values or selecting the first non-null value from a list of expressions. These tools are essential for effective data manipulation and reporting in SQL.

# Chapter 3

Pattern Matching with LIKE and Wildcards

Pattern matching in SQL queries is a powerful way to search for data based on specific patterns within text values. SQL provides the **LIKE** operator and wildcard characters, such as % and _, to facilitate pattern matching in query conditions. Here's an explanation of how to use the **LIKE** operator and examples of its usage:

*The LIKE Operator*

The **LIKE** operator is used to match patterns in string data. It is typically combined with wildcard characters to specify a pattern to search for within a column's values.

*Wildcard Characters*

- %: Represents zero or more characters.
- _ (underscore): Represents a single character.

*Using the LIKE Operator with Wildcards:*

Matching a Prefix

To find all employees whose last names start with "S," you can use the % wildcard at the end of the pattern:

```
-- COMMON SQL
SELECT FirstName, LastName
FROM Employees
WHERE LastName LIKE 'S%';
```

This query retrieves employees whose last names start with "S."

# Single Table Queries

## Matching a Suffix

To find all email addresses ending with "@company.com," you can use the % wildcard at the beginning of the pattern:

```
-- COMMON SQL
SELECT Email
FROM Contacts
WHERE Email LIKE '%@company.com';
```

This query retrieves email addresses with the specified domain.

## Matching a Specific Character in a Position

You can use the _ wildcard to match a single character at a specific position. For example, to find all names with "e" as the third character:

```
-- COMMON SQL
SELECT FirstName
FROM Employees
WHERE FirstName LIKE '__e%';
-- For clarity, that is two underscores preceding e%
```

This query retrieves first names where "e" is the third character.

## Matching Any Character

To find all products with names containing "shirt" followed by any character(s), you can use %:

```
-- COMMON SQL
SELECT ProductName
FROM Products
WHERE ProductName LIKE '%shirt%';
```

This query retrieves products with names containing "shirt" anywhere in the name.

# Chapter 3

Matching Specific Patterns

To find all phone numbers with the format "123-45X-6789," where "X" can be any digit, you can use multiple _ wildcards:

```
-- COMMON SQL
SELECT PhoneNumber
FROM Contacts
WHERE PhoneNumber LIKE '123-45_-%';
```

This query matches the specified phone number pattern.

Escaping Wildcard Characters

If you need to search for actual wildcard characters like % and _, you can use the ESCAPE clause to escape them. For example, to find names containing "%shirt%":

```
-- SQL Server
SELECT ProductName
FROM Products
WHERE ProductName LIKE '\%shirt\%' ESCAPE '\';
```

```
-- MySQL
SELECT ProductName
FROM Products
WHERE ProductName  LIKE '\\%shirt\\%' ESCAPE '\\';

-- Note: In MySQL
-- LIKE '\\%shirt\\%' ESCAPE '\\'
-- ensures that the % characters are treated as literals rather
-- than wildcards, because \\ is the escape character.
```

The **ESCAPE** clause allows you to search for literal wildcard characters.

The *LIKE* operator with wildcard characters is a valuable tool for performing flexible pattern matching in SQL queries. It allows you to search for data that matches specific text patterns, making it useful for tasks like data validation, data extraction, and reporting.

# Single Table Queries

## Subqueries and Nested Queries

Subqueries, also known as nested queries, are a fundamental concept in SQL. They allow you to use the result of one query (the inner query) as a condition or value in another query (the outer query). Subqueries are useful for retrieving data based on results from other queries and can be particularly powerful for complex data retrieval and manipulation. Let's discuss how to use subqueries and provide examples of their incorporation in SQL statements.

### Incorporating Subqueries within SELECT Statements

You can use subqueries within the **SELECT** statement to retrieve data based on the results of an inner query. These subqueries can return single values or result sets that are then used in calculations or conditions in the outer query.

### Subquery to Retrieve the Maximum Salary Example:

Suppose you want to find the employee(s) with the highest salary. You can use a subquery to find the maximum salary and then retrieve the employee(s) with that salary:

```
-- COMMON SQL
SELECT FirstName, LastName, Salary
FROM Employees
WHERE Salary = (SELECT MAX(Salary) FROM Employees);
```

In this example, the subquery *(SELECT MAX(Salary) FROM Employees)* retrieves the maximum salary, and the outer query retrieves the employee(s) with that salary.

### Subqueries for Data Retrieval

Subqueries can also be used to retrieve specific data based on conditions defined in the subquery. For example, you can use a subquery to find customers who have placed orders:

*Subquery to Retrieve Customers with Orders Example:*

```
-- COMMON SQL
SELECT FirstName, LastName
FROM Customers
WHERE CustomerID IN (SELECT DISTINCT CustomerID FROM Orders);
```

Here, the subquery *(SELECT DISTINCT CustomerID FROM Orders)* retrieves a list of unique customer IDs from the **Orders** table, and the outer query retrieves customer names based on those IDs.

*Correlated Subqueries*

Correlated subqueries are subqueries where the inner query references columns from the outer query. They are executed for each row processed by the outer query, making them a powerful tool for performing row-level calculations or comparisons.

*Correlated Subquery to Find Employees with Salaries Above Average Example:*

```
-- COMMON SQL
SELECT FirstName, LastName, Salary
FROM Employees e
WHERE Salary > (SELECT AVG(Salary) FROM Employees WHERE
DepartmentID = e.DepartmentID);
```

In this correlated subquery, for each employee (represented as *e*), the inner query calculates the average salary within the same department as that employee (*e.DepartmentID*). The outer query then retrieves employees whose salaries are greater than the average salary within their respective departments.

Correlated subqueries are particularly useful when you need to make row-level comparisons or calculations based on related data.

In summary, subqueries in SQL are powerful tools for retrieving data based on the results of other queries. They can be used within **SELECT** statements to fetch values for use in calculations or conditions. Correlated subqueries, in particular, provide a way to perform row-level operations and comparisons based on related data in the database.

# Single Table Queries

## CASE Expressions

The *CASE* expression in SQL is a powerful tool for adding conditional logic to your queries. It allows you to create conditional statements within your SQL queries, making it possible to customize the results based on various conditions. *CASE* expressions are often used to assign values or perform calculations dynamically, depending on the data or specific criteria. Let's explore how to use *CASE* expressions and provide examples for better understanding.

### Basic Syntax of a CASE Expression

The basic syntax of a *CASE* expression is as follows:

```
-- COMMON SQL
CASE
    WHEN condition1 THEN result1
    WHEN condition2 THEN result2

    ...
    ELSE resultN
END
```

- ***WHEN condition1 THEN result1***: If *condition1* is true, the *CASE* expression returns *result1*.
- ***WHEN condition2 THEN result2***: If *condition2* is true, the *CASE* expression returns *result2*.
- ***ELSE resultN*** (optional): If none of the previous conditions are true, the *CASE* expression returns *resultN*. This part is optional.

### CASE Expression Examples:

### Assigning a Custom Category

Suppose you have a table of products, and you want to create a new column called *Category* based on the product's price. You want products with prices above $100 to be categorized as "High-End," and those below or equal to $100 as "Standard."

```
-- COMMON SQL
SELECT ProductName, Price,
    CASE
        WHEN Price > 100 THEN 'High-End'
        ELSE 'Standard'
    END AS Category
FROM Products;
```

In this example, the **CASE** expression checks the product's price, and if it's greater than $100, it assigns "High-End" as the category; otherwise, it assigns "Standard."

Custom Result Values

Suppose you have a table of orders, and you want to create a new column called *OrderStatus* based on the order's status code. You want to display user-friendly status names.

```
-- COMMON SQL
SELECT OrderID, StatusCode,
    CASE StatusCode
        WHEN 'P' THEN 'Pending'
        WHEN 'S' THEN 'Shipped'
        WHEN 'C' THEN 'Cancelled'
        ELSE 'Unknown'
    END AS OrderStatus
FROM Orders;
```

In this example, the **CASE** expression checks the order's status code and assigns a custom order status based on the code. If the code doesn't match any specified conditions, it assigns "Unknown" as the status.

Handling Multiple Conditions

You can use multiple **WHEN** clauses within a **CASE** expression to handle more complex conditions. Suppose you have a table of students, and you want to categorize their grades as "Excellent," "Good," "Satisfactory," or "Needs Improvement" based on their scores.

```
-- COMMON SQL
SELECT StudentName, Score,
    CASE
        WHEN Score >= 90 THEN 'Excellent'
        WHEN Score >= 80 THEN 'Good'
        WHEN Score >= 70 THEN 'Satisfactory'
        ELSE 'Needs Improvement'
    END AS Grade
FROM Students;
```

In this example, the *CASE* expression checks the student's score and assigns a grade based on multiple conditions, from "Excellent" for scores greater than or equal to 90, to "Needs Improvement" for scores below 70.

The *CASE* expression is a versatile tool in SQL, allowing you to apply conditional logic, assign custom values, and handle various conditions within your queries. It's particularly useful when you need to create calculated or derived columns based on specific criteria, enhancing the readability and usability of your query results.

---

Arithmetic and Mathematical Operations

In SQL, you can perform arithmetic and mathematical operations to manipulate numeric values within your queries. These operations include basic arithmetic operators (+, -, *, /) as well as mathematical functions that allow you to perform more complex calculations. Let's explore both aspects:

*Basic Arithmetic Operators:*

SQL supports the following basic arithmetic operators for performing mathematical operations on numeric values:

- + *(Addition)*: Adds two numeric values together.
- - *(Subtraction)*: Subtracts one numeric value from another.
- * *(Multiplication)*: Multiplies two numeric values.
- / *(Division)*: Divides one numeric value by another.

# Chapter 3

Further notes on mathematical, Boolean, logical operators, and operator precedence in the SQL language may be found in Appendix C.

*Basic Arithmetic Operation Examples:*

Addition (+)

```
SELECT 5 + 3 AS Sum;
```

Result: ***Sum: 8***

Subtraction (-)

```
SELECT 10 - 4 AS Difference;
```

Result: ***Difference: 6***

Multiplication (*)

```
SELECT 6 * 7 AS Product;
```

Result: ***Product: 42***

Division (/)

```
SELECT 15 / 3 AS Quotient;
```

Result: ***Quotient: 5***

Mathematical Functions

SQL databases provide a variety of mathematical functions that allow you to perform more complex mathematical calculations. Here are some commonly used mathematical functions:

- ***ROUND***: Rounds a numeric value to a specified number of decimal places.

- **CEIL** (or **CEILING**): Rounds a numeric value up to the nearest integer or specified number of decimal places.
- **FLOOR**: Rounds a numeric value down to the nearest integer or specified number of decimal places.
- **ABS**: Returns the absolute (positive) value of a numeric expression.

Mathematical Function Examples:

ROUND

```
-- SQL Server
SELECT ROUND(123.456, 2); -- Result: 123.46
SELECT ROUND(123.456, 2, 1); -- Result: 123.45 (truncated)
```

```
-- MySQL
SELECT ROUND(123.456, 2); -- Result: 123.46
```

CEIL (CEILING) and FLOOR

```
-- COMMON SQL
SELECT CEIL(4.25) AS CeilingValue, FLOOR(4.75) AS FloorValue;
```

Result: *CeilingValue: 5, FloorValue: 4*

ABS

```
    SELECT ABS(-7) AS AbsoluteValue;
```

Result: *AbsoluteValue: 7*

Combining Operators and Functions

You can also combine arithmetic operators and mathematical functions in your queries to perform complex calculations. For example, you can calculate the square root of a value:

```
SELECT SQRT(25) AS SquareRoot;
```

Result: ***SquareRoot: 5.00***

These are just a few examples of how you can use arithmetic operators and mathematical functions in SQL queries. Depending on your database system, you may have access to additional mathematical functions and capabilities for handling numeric data. These tools are crucial for performing calculations, aggregations, and transformations on numeric data within your database.

---

Date Arithmetic and Manipulation

Date arithmetic and manipulation are important aspects of SQL when dealing with date and time data. SQL provides date arithmetic operators and date functions to perform various tasks related to date calculations and manipulations. Let's explore how to use date arithmetic operators and date functions in SQL with examples.

*Date Arithmetic Operators*

SQL supports several date arithmetic operators to perform calculations with date and time values:

- + (Addition): Adds a specified number of days to a date or combines date and time values.
- - (Subtraction): Subtracts a specified number of days from a date or calculates the difference between two dates.

*Date Arithmetic Operator Examples:*

Adding Days to a Date (+)

```
-- SQL Server
SELECT DATEADD(day, 7, OrderDate) AS NewDeliveryDate
FROM Orders
```

```
WHERE OrderNum = 51619;
```

```
-- MySQL
SELECT OrderDate + 7 AS NewDeliveryDate
FROM Orders
WHERE OrderNum = 51619;
```

This query adds 7 days to the **OrderDate** and returns a new delivery date.

Subtracting Days from a Date (-)

```
-- SQL Server
SELECT DATEADD(day, -2, DueDate) AS NewDueDate
FROM Tasks
WHERE TaskID = 456;
```

```
-- MySQL
SELECT DueDate - 2 AS NewDueDate
FROM Tasks
WHERE TaskID = 456;
```

This query subtracts 2 days from the **DueDate** and returns a new due date.

Calculating Date Differences (-)

```
-- SQL SERVER
SELECT DATEDIFF(day, StartDate, EndDate) AS DaysBetween
FROM Projects
WHERE ProjectID = 789;
```

```
-- MySQL
SELECT DATEDIFF(EndDate, StartDate) AS DaysBetween
FROM Projects
WHERE ProjectID = 789;
```

This query calculates the number of days between **StartDate** and **EndDate** in the **Projects** table.

# Chapter 3

*Date Functions*

SQL provides a variety of date functions for manipulating date and time values. Some commonly used date functions include:

- **DATEADD**: Adds or subtracts a specified time interval (such as days, months, or years) from a date.
- **DATEDIFF**: Calculates the difference between two dates in terms of a specified time interval.
- **GETDATE** (or **CURRENT_TIMESTAMP**): Retrieves the current date and time from the system.

*Date Function Examples:*

Using DATEADD

```
-- SQL Server
SELECT DATEADD(month, 3, HireDate) AS ThreeMonthsLater
FROM Employees
WHERE EmployeeID = 101;
```

```
-- MySQL
SELECT DATEADD(month, 3, HireDate) AS ThreeMonthsLater
FROM Employees
WHERE EmployeeID = 101;
```

This query adds 3 months to the **HireDate** of the employee with ID 101.

Using DATEDIFF

```
SELECT DATEDIFF(day, OrderDate, ShippedDate) AS DaysToShip
FROM Orders
WHERE OrderID = 123;
```

This query calculates the number of days it took to ship an order with ID 123.

# Single Table Queries

Using GETDATE, CURRENT_TIMESTAMP, or NOW()

```
-- SQL SERVER
-- Using GETDATE() to get the current date and time
SELECT GETDATE() AS CurrentDateTime;

-- Using CURRENT_TIMESTAMP to get the current date and time
SELECT CURRENT_TIMESTAMP AS CurrentDateTime;
```

```
-- MySQL
-- Using NOW() to get the current date and time
SELECT NOW() AS CurrentDateTime;

-- Using CURRENT_TIMESTAMP to get the current date and time
SELECT CURRENT_TIMESTAMP AS CurrentDateTime;
```

This query retrieves the current date and time.

These examples demonstrate how to perform date arithmetic and manipulation using date arithmetic operators and date functions in SQL. Depending on your specific database system, additional date functions may be available for more advanced date and time operations. These tools are essential for tasks like calculating date differences, setting future dates, and extracting specific date components from datetime values.

---

Looking Ahead

Our introductory exploration of single table queries concludes here, but the journey has just begun. As you progress to intermediate and advanced study of SQL programming you will explore advanced concepts such as:

- Common Table Expressions
  Common Table Expressions (CTEs) in SQL programming serve as temporary result sets that are defined within the scope of a SELECT, INSERT, UPDATE, or DELETE statement. CTEs enhance the readability and maintainability of SQL queries by allowing the creation of named, self-contained queries that can reference and build upon each other. CTEs are typically employed for complex queries, recursive operations, or when

breaking down a larger query into more manageable and understandable parts. They provide a concise and elegant way to structure SQL code, promoting modular design and facilitating the development of intricate database queries.

- Window Functions

  Window Functions in SQL programming operate within a specified window or subset of rows related to the current row, allowing computations and analyses to be performed over that defined range. Unlike traditional aggregate functions, window functions do not collapse rows into a single result but rather provide a computed value for each row based on its window. These functions are particularly useful for tasks such as calculating running totals, ranking rows within partitions, or determining moving averages, enabling developers to perform advanced analytics and gain insights into the distribution and patterns within their data sets.

- Query Performance and Optimization

  Query performance in SQL programming refers to the efficiency and speed with which a database system executes a given query. It encompasses the time taken to retrieve and process data, and it becomes a crucial aspect as databases grow in size and complexity. Query optimization, on the other hand, is the process of refining SQL queries to enhance their performance. This involves analyzing the query execution plan, index usage, and overall database structure to identify and implement improvements. Optimization strategies may include indexing, rewriting queries, or restructuring the database schema to reduce the computational load and execution time, ultimately ensuring that queries run more swiftly and resource-efficiently. The goal of query optimization is to strike a balance between retrieving accurate results and doing so in the most timely and resource-efficient manner possible.

Final Thoughts on Single-Table Queries

Constructing single-table queries is a fundamental skill. It empowers you to extract precise information from large datasets, enabling informed decision-making and efficient data analysis. Whether it's a library's book collection or a company's inventory, the ability to craft and execute queries efficiently is an essential tool in today's data-driven world.

# Chapter 4 – Multi-Table Queries

## Introduction to Multiple Table Queries

You now know that Structured Query Language (SQL) is the backbone of managing and manipulating data within relational database systems. While SQL's basic SELECT statement can retrieve data from a single table, real-world scenarios often require pulling information from multiple tables. This is where the art of multiple table queries comes into play, allowing you to unlock complex data relationships and join tables to extract meaningful insights.

## The Need for Multiple Table Queries

In day-to-day database work, often all of the required data needed does not reside within a single table. Imagine a database for an e-commerce platform: you have customers, products, orders, and payments. Each of these entities is typically stored in a separate table, interconnected by various relationships. To answer questions such as "Which products did a specific customer purchase?", or "What are the total sales by product category?", you need to combine data from multiple tables.

## Understanding Table Relationships

Before diving into multiple table queries, it's crucial to understand the relationships between tables:

- ***One-to-One (1:1)***: In a one-to-one relationship, each record in one table corresponds to exactly one record in another table. For example, you might have a ***User*** table with a ***Profile*** table, where each user has a single corresponding profile.
- ***One-to-Many (1:N)***: In a one-to-many relationship, each record in one table can relate to multiple records in another table. Consider an ***Author*** table linked to a ***Book*** table. An author can write many books, but each book has only one author.
- ***Many-to-Many (M:N)***: In a many-to-many relationship, records in one table can be associated with multiple records in another table, and vice versa. For instance, a ***Student*** table and a ***Course*** table in a school database. A student can enroll in multiple courses, and a course can have many students.

# Chapter 4

Mastering SQL Joins

To harness the power of multiple table queries, you need to grasp SQL's join operations:

**Inner Join**: An inner join combines rows from two or more tables based on a related column, returning only the rows that have matching values in both tables. This is the most used join.

```
-- COMMON SQL
SELECT Customers.CustomerName, Orders.OrderDate
FROM Customers
INNER JOIN Orders ON Customers.CustomerID = Orders.CustomerID;
```

This query combines the **Customers** and **Orders** tables, returning customer names and order dates where there's a matching **CustomerID**.

**Left Join (or Left Outer Join)**: A left join returns all rows from the left table (the first table mentioned) and the matched rows from the right table. If there are no matches in the right table, NULL values are returned.

```
-- COMMON SQL
SELECT Customers.CustomerName, Orders.OrderDate
FROM Customers
LEFT JOIN Orders ON Customers.CustomerID = Orders.CustomerID;
```

In this query, you'll get all customer names and order dates, even if some customers haven't placed orders (resulting in NULL values for order dates).

**Right Join (or Right Outer Join)**: A right join is similar to a left join but returns all rows from the right table and the matching rows from the left table.

```
-- COMMON SQL
SELECT Customers.CustomerName, Orders.OrderDate
FROM Customers
RIGHT JOIN Orders ON Customers.CustomerID = Orders.CustomerID;
```

This query retrieves all order dates and customer names, ensuring that even customers without orders are included in the result.

# Multi-Table Queries

***Full Outer Join (or Full Join)***: A full outer join returns all rows from both tables, including the ones without matching values. This results in NULL values where there are no matches.

```
-- COMMON SQL
SELECT Customers.CustomerName, Orders.OrderDate
FROM Customers
FULL OUTER JOIN Orders ON Customers.CustomerID =
Orders.CustomerID;
```

Here, you'll get a comprehensive list of customer names and order dates, covering all cases, whether there are matches or not.

By mastering these join operations and understanding the relationships between your tables, you can craft SQL queries that extract valuable insights from complex, interconnected data. Whether you're analyzing sales data, managing customer relationships, or conducting research, multiple table queries are your key to unlocking the full potential of your database.

---

## Basic Join Syntax

SQL's JOIN operation is a fundamental tool for querying data from multiple tables within a relational database. Whether you're managing customer information, analyzing sales transactions, or extracting insights from complex datasets, JOINs enable you to combine and consolidate data in a structured and efficient manner. In this guide, we'll explore the essential aspects of basic SQL JOIN syntax, including the use of JOIN clauses, specifying join conditions with the ON keyword, aliasing tables for concise queries, and handling duplicate column names using aliases.

## Understanding JOIN Clauses

The primary SQL JOIN syntax involves combining rows from two or more tables based on a related column between them. The most common JOIN types are INNER JOIN, LEFT JOIN (or LEFT OUTER JOIN), RIGHT JOIN (or RIGHT OUTER JOIN), and FULL JOIN (or FULL OUTER JOIN). Here's a brief overview of these JOIN types:

- ***INNER JOIN***: Returns only the rows where there is a match in both tables.

- *LEFT JOIN (LEFT OUTER JOIN)*: Returns all rows from the left table and the matched rows from the right table. If there's no match in the right table, it returns NULL values.
- *RIGHT JOIN (RIGHT OUTER JOIN)*: Similar to LEFT JOIN but returns all rows from the right table and the matched rows from the left table.
- *FULL JOIN (FULL OUTER JOIN)*: Returns all rows when there is a match in either the left or right table, filling in NULL values where there's no match.

*The Syntax of the SELECT Statement with JOIN Clauses*

The basic syntax of the SELECT statement with JOIN clauses is as follows:

```
-- COMMON SQL
SELECT columns
FROM table1
JOIN table2
ON table1.column = table2.column;
```

- *columns*: Specifies the columns you want to select from the combined tables.
- *table1* and *table2*: Are the names of the tables you want to join.
- *ON table1.column = table2.column*: Defines the join condition that specifies how the two tables are related.

Using the ON Keyword to Specify Join Conditions

The *ON* keyword is crucial for specifying the conditions under which the tables should be joined. You typically specify the columns from each table that should match for a successful join. Here's an example:

```
-- COMMON SQL
SELECT Customers.CustomerName, Orders.OrderDate
FROM Customers
JOIN Orders
ON Customers.CustomerID = Orders.CustomerID;
```

In this example, we're joining the *Customers* and *Orders* tables on the *CustomerID* column. This query will retrieve the customer names and order dates for cases where there's a match between the *CustomerID* columns in both tables.

# Multi-Table Queries

## Aliasing Tables for More Concise Queries

When working with multiple tables, especially when their names are lengthy, it's common to use aliases to simplify queries. Table aliases are short, alternative names for tables that make your SQL code more readable and concise. Here's how to use table aliases:

```
-- COMMON SQL
SELECT c.CustomerName, o.OrderDate
FROM Customers AS c
JOIN Orders AS o
ON c.CustomerID = o.CustomerID;
```

In this query, we've used "c" as an alias for the **Customers** table and "o" as an alias for the **Orders** table. These aliases are then used in the SELECT statement, making the query more compact and easier to read.

## Handling Duplicate Column Names Using Aliases

When you join tables, it's common to encounter columns with the same name in both tables. To avoid ambiguity, you can use table aliases to specify which table's column you want to select. Here's an example:

```
-- COMMON SQL
SELECT c.CustomerName, o.OrderDate
FROM Customers AS c
JOIN Orders AS o
ON c.CustomerID = o.CustomerID;
```

In this query, we have **CustomerName** columns in both the **Customers** and **Orders** tables. By using aliases (**c.CustomerName** and **o.OrderDate**), we make it clear which columns we're selecting, preventing any ambiguity.

In conclusion, mastering basic SQL JOIN syntax is essential for effectively querying data from multiple tables. By understanding the JOIN types, using the ON keyword to specify join conditions, aliasing tables for clarity, and handling duplicate column names with aliases, you can harness the full power of SQL JOINs to extract valuable insights and information from your relational databases.

# Chapter 4

Inner Joins

The inner join stands out as a workhorse for retrieving matching records from multiple tables. In this section, we'll look into inner joins, how they work, and what you need to consider when using them.

## The Essence of Inner Joins

*Inner joins*, often simply referred to as *joins*, are a SQL operation that combines rows from two or more tables based on a related column. The result of an inner join contains only the rows for which there is a match in both tables. In other words, if a row in one table has no corresponding match in the other table, it won't appear in the result set.

## The Syntax of Inner Joins

The basic syntax for an inner join is as follows:

```
-- COMMON SQL
SELECT columns
FROM table1
INNER JOIN table2
ON table1.column = table2.column;
```

- *columns*: Specifies the columns you want to retrieve from the combined tables.
- *table1* and *table2*: Are the names of the tables you want to join.
- *ON table1.column = table2.column*: Defines the join condition, specifying how the tables are related.

Inner Join Examples:

Let's explore a few real-world scenarios where inner joins shine:

# Multi-Table Queries

*Combining Customer and Order Data*

Imagine you're managing an e-commerce platform with two tables: **Customers** and **Orders**. Each order is associated with a customer through a common **CustomerID** field.

```
-- COMMON SQL
SELECT Customers.CustomerName, Orders.OrderDate
FROM Customers
INNER JOIN Orders
ON Customers.CustomerID = Orders.CustomerID;
```

In this query, the inner join combines the **Customers** and **Orders** tables, connecting them via the **CustomerID** column. The result will display the customer names along with their respective order dates, but only for customers who have placed orders.

*Unifying Employee and Department Information*

Consider a human resources database with **Employees** and **Departments** tables. You want to retrieve a list of employees and their respective department names.

```
-- COMMON SQL
SELECT Employees.EmployeeName, Departments.DepartmentName
FROM Employees
INNER JOIN Departments
ON Employees.DepartmentID = Departments.DepartmentID;
```

In this case, the inner join merges the **Employees** and **Departments** tables using the **DepartmentID** column. The result will contain employee names and their corresponding department names, provided that every employee is associated with a department.

*Performance Considerations and Potential Pitfalls*

While inner joins are powerful tools, they come with some considerations and potential pitfalls:

- **Performance**: Depending on the size of your tables and the complexity of your queries, inner joins can be resource intensive. Ensure that your database is properly indexed and consider using appropriate indexing strategies to optimize join performance.

- *Ambiguity*: When joining tables with columns of the same name, you may encounter column naming conflicts. To address this, use table aliases to specify which table's column you want to select, ensuring clarity and avoiding ambiguity.
- *Null Values*: Inner joins exclude rows with no corresponding match in both tables. If you need to include such rows, consider using outer joins (LEFT JOIN, RIGHT JOIN, or FULL JOIN) instead.
- *Complexity*: In cases with multiple tables and complex relationships, the use of inner joins can lead to intricate queries that are challenging to manage. Always strive for clarity and readability in your SQL code.

In conclusion, inner joins are an invaluable tool in SQL for extracting matched records from multiple tables. By mastering the syntax and understanding the principles behind inner joins, you can combine data from different sources to answer complex questions and gain valuable insights from your relational databases. However, be mindful of performance considerations and potential pitfalls, and use inner joins judiciously to strike a balance between data unification and query efficiency.

---

Outer Joins

Outer joins—comprising left, right, and full outer joins—are essential tools. In this section, we'll explore outer joins, how they work, provide examples, and delve into various use cases and scenarios for each type.

Understanding Outer Joins

Outer joins are SQL operations that combine rows from two or more tables based on a related column, like inner joins. However, unlike inner joins, outer joins include unmatched rows from one or both tables in the result set, filling in with *NULL* values where no match exists. This makes outer joins particularly useful when you want to retain all records from one table while bringing in matched records from another.

# Multi-Table Queries

Left Outer Join

A *left outer join*, often referred to as a *left join*, retrieves all records from the left table and matching records from the right table. If there's no match in the right table, the result will contain *NULL* values for columns from the right table.

*Left Outer Join Example:*

```
-- COMMON SQL
SELECT Customers.CustomerName, Orders.OrderDate
FROM Customers
LEFT JOIN Orders
ON Customers.CustomerID = Orders.CustomerID;
```

In this query, we're retrieving customer names along with their order dates. Even if a customer has not placed an order, their name will still appear in the result set with a *NULL* value for the order date.

Right Outer Join

A *right outer join*, the counterpart of the left join, retrieves all records from the right table and matching records from the left table. If there's no match in the left table, the result will contain *NULL* values for columns from the left table.

*Right Outer Join Example:*

```
-- COMMON SQL
SELECT Customers.CustomerName, Orders.OrderDate
FROM Customers
RIGHT JOIN Orders
ON Customers.CustomerID = Orders.CustomerID;
```

In this query, we're retrieving customer names along with their order dates. Even if an order has no associated customer, the result will contain the order date with a *NULL* value for the customer name.

# Chapter 4

Full Outer Join

A *full outer join*, also known as a *full join*, retrieves all records from both tables, including unmatched rows from both sides. When there's no match, the result will have **NULL** values for columns from the table where no match exists.

*Full Outer Join Example:*

```
-- COMMON SQL
SELECT Customers.CustomerName, Orders.OrderDate
FROM Customers
FULL JOIN Orders
ON Customers.CustomerID = Orders.CustomerID;
```

In this query, we're combining customer names and order dates. The result will include all customers and all orders, and when there's no match, either the customer name or the order date will be **NULL**.

Use Cases and Scenarios for Outer Joins

Outer joins are incredibly versatile and come in handy in various scenarios, such as:

- *Analyzing Customer Data*: To examine customer data while including those who haven't made any purchases, use a left outer join between **Customers** and **Orders**.
- *Reviewing Product Inventory*: When assessing product stock levels and including discontinued items that may not have sales records, a right outer join between **Products** and **Sales** can be beneficial.
- *Merging Employee and Department Data*: To consolidate employee and department data, ensuring that departments without employees are not omitted, employ a full outer join.
- *Examining Web Traffic Logs*: For web analytics, when combining user data with page views and accounting for users who haven't visited any pages, a full outer join between **Users** and **PageViews** is essential.

In conclusion, outer joins—left, right, and full—add a new dimension to SQL query capabilities. They allow you to retain unmatched records from one or both tables, enabling comprehensive data analysis and reporting. By mastering outer joins and understanding their varied use cases, you can explore complex data relationships and extract valuable insights from your databases.

---

## Self-Joins and Aliases

There are times when you need to look within the same table to uncover valuable insights and relationships. Enter self-joins—a powerful technique that enables you to retrieve related information from the same table. To fully harness this capability, understanding aliases becomes crucial. In this section, we'll delve into self-joins, the significance of aliases, and explore practical applications of this dynamic duo.

### The Essence of Self-Joins

**Self-joins**, as the name suggests, are SQL operations where a table is joined with itself. This technique allows you to establish relationships between rows within the same table, just as you would with different tables. Self-joins are particularly useful when your data model includes hierarchical or nested structures.

### Exploring Self-Joins: Retrieving Related Information

Self-Join Example Scenario

Let's consider an organization with an employee database. Each employee has a unique ID and reports to another employee, identified by their manager's ID. To explore the hierarchy and find out who reports to whom, a self-join is required.

Self-Join Syntax

The basic syntax of a self-join (explicitly using the JOIN operator) looks like this:

```
-- COMMON SQL
SELECT t1.column, t2.column
FROM table AS t1
JOIN table AS t2
```

```
ON t1.relationship_column = t2.relationship_column;
```

- ***t1*** and ***t2***: Are aliases for the same table, making it possible to differentiate between the two instances.
- ***relationship_column***: Specifies the column used for the join, representing the relationship between rows in the table.

An equivalent self-join may be constructed using an implicit join (using the WHERE clause in lieu of the JOIN key word):

```
-- COMMON SQL
SELECT t1.column, t2.column
FROM table AS t1, table AS t2
WHERE t1.relationship_column = t2.relationship_column;
```

Self-Join Example:

Let's apply a self-join to our employee database scenario:

```
-- COMMON SQL
--Version 1, using an explicit JOIN:
SELECT E1.EmployeeName, E2.EmployeeName AS ManagerName
FROM Employees AS E1
JOIN Employees AS E2
ON E1.ManagerID = E2.EmployeeID;

--Version 2, using an implicit JOIN:
SELECT E1.EmployeeName, E2.EmployeeName AS ManagerName
FROM Employees AS E1, Employees AS E2
WHERE E1.ManagerID = E2.EmployeeID;

--Note that the implicit and explicit JOIN versions are
logically equivalent.
```

In this query, we've created two aliases, ***E1*** and ***E2***, for the ***Employees*** table. By joining the table with itself, we can identify each employee's manager and retrieve both the employee's name and the manager's name.

# Multi-Table Queries

*Understanding Aliasing and Its Significance*

Aliases are essential in self-joins to distinguish between the two instances of the same table. They act as alternate names for the table, allowing you to refer to different instances independently within the query.

Without aliases, SQL wouldn't know which instance of the table you're referring to, leading to ambiguity and errors. Aliases enhance code readability and clarity.

*Practical Applications of Self-Joins*

Hierarchical Data

One of the primary use cases for self-joins is handling hierarchical data. Examples include organizational structures, where employees report to managers, or product categories nested within broader categories.

Network Data

Self-joins are also valuable for network-related data, like social networks or organizational networks. You can use them to find connections or relationships between individuals or entities within the same dataset.

Historical Data

In historical data analysis, self-joins help identify trends or changes over time within the same dataset. For instance, tracking stock prices and comparing them to historical prices within the same table.

Recursive Queries

Recursive self-joins are a more advanced use of self-joins. They're employed when you need to traverse a hierarchy or relationship tree to retrieve data at different levels. Recursive self-joins are typically implemented using common table expressions (CTEs) in SQL.

# Chapter 4

*Final Thoughts on Self-joins*

Self-joins and aliases in SQL open up a world of possibilities when it comes to exploring relationships within the same dataset. They are indispensable for handling hierarchical, network, and historical data, as well as for constructing complex recursive queries. By mastering self-joins and adopting good practices with aliases, you can uncover valuable insights and gain a deeper understanding of your data structures.

---

## Cross Joins and Cartesian Products

When you need to explore every possible combination of rows between two tables, you turn to **cross joins**. These joins play a unique role in producing what's known as a **Cartesian product**. While they have their uses, it's essential to wield them carefully due to their potential to generate massive result sets. In this section, we'll dive into the world of cross joins and Cartesian products, understand their applications, and emphasize the need for caution.

## Unveiling Cross Joins and Cartesian Products

*Cross Joins*

A **cross join**, also called a **Cartesian join**, is a SQL operation that combines every row from one table with every row from another table, resulting in a Cartesian product of the two tables. Unlike other joins, cross joins don't rely on a specific condition or relationship between columns; they simply combine every possible pairing.

*Cartesian Products*

A **Cartesian product** is a set of all possible combinations of rows between two tables. It's named after the French mathematician René Descartes, who is also famous for introducing Cartesian coordinates for graphing points. In SQL, a Cartesian product is essentially the result of a cross join.

René Descartes, Father of Modern Philosophy

Figure 12 - René Descartes.

René Descartes, a renowned French mathematician, philosopher, and scientist, was born on March 31, 1596, in La Haye en Touraine, France. Often referred to as the "Father of Modern Philosophy," Descartes made groundbreaking contributions to a wide range of disciplines. He is best known for his groundbreaking work in mathematics, where he introduced Cartesian coordinates, which revolutionized geometry and laid the foundation for analytic geometry. His famous statement "Cogito, ergo sum" (I think, therefore I am) encapsulates his philosophical approach, emphasizing the power of individual reason and doubt as the basis for knowledge. Descartes' influence extended beyond mathematics and philosophy. He made significant contributions to physics, particularly in the study of optics, where he advanced the understanding of refraction and the formation of images. His works, including "Meditations on First Philosophy" and "Discourse on the Method," remain foundational texts in both philosophy and science. René Descartes passed away on February 11, 1650, in Stockholm, Sweden, but his ideas and legacy continue to shape the fields of mathematics, philosophy, and science to this day.

*Use Cases and Scenarios for Cross Joins*

While cross joins are relatively rare in everyday SQL, they have specific use cases and scenarios:

Generating Test Data

Cross joins are invaluable when you need to generate test data or permutations. For instance, if you're testing a product configuration system, you might use cross joins to combine different product options.

```sql
-- COMMON SQL
SELECT Products.ProductName, Colors.ColorName
FROM Products
CROSS JOIN Colors;
```

This query would produce every possible combination of product names and colors, which can be handy for testing purposes.

# Chapter 4

## Calculating Combinations

In mathematical and statistical analysis, cross joins are used to calculate combinations of items. For example, when analyzing survey responses, you might cross join the responses to questions about age and gender to explore demographic patterns.

```
-- COMMON SQL
SELECT AgeGroups.Age, Genders.Gender
FROM AgeGroups
CROSS JOIN Genders;
```

This query would give you all possible combinations of age groups and genders for analysis.

## *Proceed with Caution*

As powerful as cross joins can be, they come with a significant caveat: they can generate massive result sets. If you're not careful, you might inadvertently overwhelm your database and create queries that take forever to run.

## Cartesian Products as Potential Errors

One common pitfall with Cartesian products is that they can be the result of programming errors, often caused by omitting the requisite tables from a join clause. This can lead to unintentional cross joins and enormous result sets. This error is often referred to as a "blown" join.

## Self-Testing Queries

During query development, it's wise to self-test your queries on small datasets to ensure they produce the expected results. If the number of rows returned appears excessive, it could indicate an unintended Cartesian product.

# Multi-Table Queries

Sanity Checking

Before executing a cross join query on a large dataset, consider a sanity check. Review the query's logic and make sure it's what you intended. You can also limit the number of rows returned for testing purposes using the **LIMIT** clause.

## Final Thoughts on Cartesian Products

Cross joins and Cartesian products are valuable tools in SQL, especially for generating test data or exploring combinations of items. However, they must be used judiciously due to their potential to generate large result sets. Always double-check your queries during development, perform self-testing with small datasets, and apply sanity checks to avoid unintended Cartesian products that can cause performance issues and unexpected outcomes in your SQL queries.

---

## Using Joins for Data Aggregation

In working with SQL, the ability to aggregate and analyze data from multiple tables is a fundamental skill. Joins, coupled with aggregate functions, offer a potent combination for data aggregation, empowering you to gain valuable insights from complex datasets. In this section, we'll explore how to combine data from multiple tables for aggregate functions, group data using the **GROUP BY** clause in conjunction with joins, and filter grouped results using the **HAVING** clause.

## Combining Data for Aggregate Functions

Aggregate functions like SUM, AVG, COUNT, and others are essential for summarizing and analyzing data. When dealing with data scattered across different tables, joins are your ticket to combining and aggregating it effectively.

Combining Sales Data Example:

Consider a scenario where you have a **Sales** table containing order information and a **Products** table with product details. To calculate the total sales amount for each product category, you can join these tables and use the **SUM** function:

```
-- COMMON SQL
SELECT Categories.CategoryName, SUM(Sales.Amount) AS TotalSales
FROM Sales
JOIN Products ON Sales.ProductID = Products.ProductID
JOIN Categories ON Products.CategoryID = Categories.CategoryID
GROUP BY Categories.CategoryName;
```

In this query, we join the **Sales**, **Products**, and **Categories** tables, connecting them based on their respective keys. The SUM function aggregates the sales amount, and the GROUP BY clause groups the results by product category. This query produces a concise summary of total sales for each category.

*Grouping Data with GROUP BY and Joins*

The GROUP BY clause is essential for grouping data when aggregating information from multiple tables. It allows you to segment and analyze data based on specific columns or expressions.

Grouping by Time Period Example:

Imagine a situation where you have a **Sales** table with order data and a **Time** table containing information about time periods. To calculate total sales for each time period, you can use a join and GROUP BY clause:

```
-- COMMON SQL
SELECT Time.PeriodName, SUM(Sales.Amount) AS TotalSales
FROM Sales
JOIN Time ON Sales.TimeID = Time.TimeID
GROUP BY Time.PeriodName;
```

# Multi-Table Queries

In this query, we join the **Sales** and **Time** tables based on their common key, and then use **GROUP BY** to group the data by time periods. The **SUM** function aggregates the sales amount within each period, providing an insightful summary of sales over time.

*Filtering Grouped Results with HAVING Clause*

The **HAVING** clause is a powerful tool for filtering grouped results based on specific conditions. It allows you to focus on subsets of data that meet particular criteria after the aggregation has taken place.

Identifying High-Value Customers Example:

Suppose you have a **Customers** table and an **Orders** table, and you want to find customers with a total order value exceeding a certain threshold. You can achieve this by joining the tables, grouping the data, and using the **HAVING** clause:

```
-- COMMON SQL
SELECT Customers.CustomerName, SUM(Orders.OrderAmount) AS
TotalOrderValue
FROM Customers
JOIN Orders ON Customers.CustomerID = Orders.CustomerID
GROUP BY Customers.CustomerName
HAVING SUM(Orders.OrderAmount) > 10000;
```

In this query, we join the **Customers** and **Orders** tables, group the results by customer name, and calculate the total order value for each customer. The **HAVING** clause then filters the results, selecting only those customers whose total order value exceeds $10,000.

*Final Thoughts on Aggregation and the GROUP BY Clause*

Joins, combined with aggregate functions, the **GROUP BY** clause, and the **HAVING** clause, provide a robust framework for data aggregation in SQL. Whether you're analyzing sales data, summarizing customer behavior, or tracking trends over time, these tools enable you to derive valuable insights from complex datasets. By mastering these techniques, you can unlock the full potential of SQL for data aggregation and analysis.

# Chapter 4

## Subqueries and Nested Queries with Joins

You have learned about retrieving data from multiple tables using joins. Additional, powerful techniques to extract precise insights or solve complex problems involving multiple tables use subqueries and nested queries. These techniques involve joining two or more tables and offer the flexibility to incorporate subqueries within join statements, utilize them for filtering criteria or intermediate results, and harness nested queries to tackle intricate challenges efficiently. In this section, we'll explore the art of using subqueries and nested queries in multi-table joins through examples and explanations.

### Incorporating Subqueries within Join Statements

Subqueries, also known as inner queries or nested queries, are SQL queries nested within another query. When it comes to multi-table joins, subqueries can play a crucial role by providing additional filtering criteria or data for the join conditions.

*Utilizing Subqueries for Join Conditions Example:*

Let's consider a scenario with a ***Sales*** table and a ***Discounts*** table, where you want to calculate the total discounted sales amount. You can use a subquery to join these tables and compute the discount amount for each sale:

```
-- COMMON SQL
SELECT S.OrderID, S.ProductID, S.Quantity, S.UnitPrice,
       (S.Quantity * S.UnitPrice) AS TotalPrice,
       (S.Quantity * S.UnitPrice -
        (SELECT D.DiscountAmount
         FROM Discounts D
         WHERE D.ProductID = S.ProductID)) AS DiscountedAmount
FROM Sales S;
```

In this query, we join the ***Sales*** table with a subquery that retrieves the corresponding discount amount from the ***Discounts*** table based on the product ID. The subquery is used to subtract the discount from the total price, giving us the discounted amount for each sale.

# Multi-Table Queries

Subqueries with ALL and ANY

The ALL and ANY keywords are used in conjunction with subqueries to compare a value to a set of values returned by the subquery. They allow for more complex conditions within WHERE, HAVING, and other clauses.

*ALL Keyword*

The ALL keyword is used to compare a value to all values in a subquery. The condition will be true only if it holds true for **every** value returned by the subquery.

*Syntax:*

expression **operator ALL** (subquery)

*Example:*

Find all products whose price is higher than the price of all products in the 'Electronics' category.

```
-- COMMON SQL
SELECT product_name
FROM products
WHERE price > ALL (
    SELECT price
    FROM products
    WHERE category = 'Electronics'
);
```

**Explanation:**

- The subquery selects the prices of all products in the 'Electronics' category.

- The main query selects products whose price is higher than every price returned by the subquery.

*ANY Keyword*

The ANY keyword (or its synonym SOME) is used to compare a value to any value in a subquery. The condition will be true if it holds true for **at least one** of the values returned by the subquery.

*Syntax:*

expression **operator ANY** (subquery)

*Example:*

Find all products whose price is higher than the price of any product in the 'Electronics' category.

```
-- COMMON SQL
SELECT product_name
FROM products
WHERE price > ANY (
    SELECT price
    FROM products
    WHERE category = 'Electronics'
);
```

**Explanation:**

- The subquery selects the prices of all products in the 'Electronics' category.

- The main query selects products whose price is higher than at least one price returned by the subquery.

**Usage with Different Operators:**

- = ANY: True if the expression equals at least one value in the subquery result.

- <> ANY: True if the expression does not equal at least one value in the subquery result.

- > ANY, < ANY, >= ANY, <= ANY: True if the expression satisfies the condition with at least one value in the subquery result.

- = ALL: True if the expression equals all values in the subquery result.

- <> ALL: True if the expression does not equal any value in the subquery result.

- > ALL, < ALL, >= ALL, <= ALL: True if the expression satisfies the condition with every value in the subquery result.

**Examples with Different Operators:**

*Using ANY with < Operator:*

Find employees whose salary is less than any employee's salary in the 'Sales' department.

```
-- COMMON SQL
SELECT employee_name
FROM employees
WHERE salary < ANY (
```

```
    SELECT salary
    FROM employees
    WHERE department = 'Sales'
);
```

*Using ALL with >= Operator:*

Find products that have a price greater than or equal to all prices of products in the 'Books' category.

```
-- COMMON SQL
SELECT product_name
FROM products
WHERE price >= ALL (
    SELECT price
    FROM products
    WHERE category = 'Books'
);
```

**Key Points:**

- ALL requires the condition to be true for all values in the subquery result.

- ANY requires the condition to be true for at least one value in the subquery result.

- They are useful for comparing a single value against a set of values returned by a subquery, enhancing the ability to perform complex queries.

Subqueries with EXISTS

The **EXISTS** keyword is used to check if a subquery returns any rows. It is a logical operator that returns **TRUE** if the subquery returns one or more rows and **FALSE** if the subquery returns no rows. This can be particularly useful for checking the existence of certain conditions without having to retrieve the actual data from the subquery.

**Syntax**

```
-- COMMON SQL
SELECT column1, column2, ...
FROM table1
WHERE EXISTS (subquery);
```

## How EXISTS Works

- The subquery is typically a correlated subquery, meaning it references columns from the outer query.

- The EXISTS keyword stops processing as soon as it finds a matching row, making it potentially more efficient than other approaches in some scenarios.

## Examples

*Example 1: Simple Use of EXISTS*

Find all customers who have placed at least one order.

```
-- COMMON SQL
SELECT customerID, customerName
FROM customers c
WHERE EXISTS (
    SELECT 1
    FROM orders o
    WHERE o.customerID = c.customerID
);
```

## Explanation:

- The subquery checks if there is any order related to the customer.

- **SELECT** 1 is used because the actual data returned by the subquery is not needed; we only care if any row exists.

- The main query returns the customers who have at least one matching order.

*Example 2: EXISTS with Complex Conditions*

Find all products that have never been ordered by customers from 'NY'.

```
-- COMMON SQL
SELECT productID, productName
FROM products p
WHERE NOT EXISTS (
    SELECT 1
    FROM orders o
    JOIN customers c ON o.customerID = c.customerID
    JOIN order_details od ON o.orderID = od.orderID
    WHERE od.productID = p.productID AND c.state = 'NY'
);
```

**Explanation:**

- The subquery checks if there are any orders for the product by customers from 'NY'.

- NOT EXISTS is used to filter out products that have been ordered by customers from 'NY'.

- The main query returns products that have not been ordered by customers from 'NY'.

*Example 3: EXISTS for Data Validation*

Check if there are any products without any orders.

```
-- COMMON SQL
SELECT productID, productName
FROM products p
WHERE NOT EXISTS (
    SELECT 1
    FROM order_details od
    WHERE od.productID = p.productID
);
```

**Explanation:**

- The subquery checks if there are any entries in order_details for each product.

- NOT EXISTS is used to filter out products that have been ordered.

- The main query returns products that have never been ordered.

**Key Points:**

- **Performance**: EXISTS can be more efficient than IN or NOT IN because it stops processing as soon as it finds a match.

- **Readability**: Using EXISTS can make the intent of the query clearer, especially for existence checks.

- **Correlated Subqueries**: EXISTS is often used with correlated subqueries, where the subquery references columns from the outer query.

Using the EXISTS keyword is a powerful tool for performing existence checks in SQL, allowing for efficient and readable queries.

Utilizing Subqueries for Filtering Criteria or Intermediate Results

Subqueries can also be employed to filter data or retrieve intermediate results when performing multi-table joins. This allows you to refine your query and narrow down the dataset based on specific conditions.

*Using Subqueries for Filtering Example:*

Suppose you have a **Customers** table, an **Orders** table, and a **Countries** table, and you want to find customers who have placed orders from countries with a population above a certain threshold. You can use a subquery for this:

```
-- COMMON SQL
SELECT C.CustomerName, O.OrderDate, CO.CountryName
FROM Customers C
JOIN Orders O ON C.CustomerID = O.CustomerID
JOIN Countries CO ON C.CountryID = CO.CountryID
WHERE CO.Population > (SELECT AVG(Population) FROM Countries);
```

In this query, the subquery calculates the average population of all countries. The outer query then uses this result to filter customers who have placed orders from countries with populations greater than the average.

Using Nested Queries to Solve Complex Problems Efficiently

Nested queries, also known as subquery chains or correlated subqueries, are queries nested within other queries and linked to the outer query. In multi-table joins, nested queries can be instrumental in solving complex problems that require interrelated data.

*Solving Complex Problems with Nested Queries Example:*

Consider a scenario with an **Employees** table, a **Departments** table, and a **SalaryIncreases** table, and you want to find the employees who received salary increases greater than the department's average increase. You can achieve this with a nested query:

# Multi-Table Queries

```
-- COMMON SQL
SELECT E.EmployeeName, D.DepartmentName, SI.IncreaseAmount
FROM Employees E
JOIN Departments D ON E.DepartmentID = D.DepartmentID
JOIN SalaryIncreases SI ON E.EmployeeID = SI.EmployeeID
WHERE SI.IncreaseAmount >
    (SELECT AVG(IncreaseAmount)
     FROM SalaryIncreases SI2
     WHERE SI2.DepartmentID = D.DepartmentID);
```

In this query, we join the **Employees**, **Departments**, and **SalaryIncreases** tables and use a nested subquery to calculate the average salary increase for each department. The outer query then compares each employee's increase to their department's average, providing a concise list of employees who received above-average raises within their respective departments.

*Final thoughts on Nested Queries*

SQL subqueries and nested queries are potent tools in the arsenal of SQL developers, especially when dealing with multi-table joins. They offer the flexibility to incorporate subqueries within join statements, utilize them for filtering criteria or intermediate results, and leverage nested queries to tackle intricate challenges efficiently. By mastering these techniques, you can unlock the full potential of SQL for complex data analysis and problem-solving in multi-table environments.

---

## Many-to-Many Relationships and Junction Tables

Real-world relationships between entities often involve complex, many-to-many (M:N) relationships. In relational databases, implementing such relationships is computationally complex and inefficient. A practical solution to reduce this complexity is to use junction tables, also known as associative entities or bridging tables. Adding a junction table helps to resolve many-to-many relationships efficiently. You can intuitively grasp how this works by imagining all possible relationships between two tables *A*, and *C*, each containing 1000 records. There would be 1000 times 1000, or 1,000,000 potential combinations. However, if we insert a junction table, *B* between *A* and *C*, such that the relationship between *C* and *B* is 1:N, and the relationship between *A* and *B* is 1:N, we dramatically reduce the complexity. The math makes this clear. We now have two 1:N relations wherein N is 1000. This means we add the 1000 possible combinations from the first relation (1000) to the possible combinations from the second relation (1000), and the worst-case complexity is then a factor of 2000, instead of 1,000,000! If you consider how the original complexity grows if the tables in an M:N relationship are 10,000 each, instead of a worst case complexity factor of one million you will have a complexity of 100 million! Although the "real world" case is almost always better than the "worst case", it is still easy to see that the larger tables become, the larger the complexity. It is therefore well worth the time and effort to mitigate M:N relations into a pair of 1:N relations by use of a junction table. In this section, we'll explore many-to-many relationships, understand the challenges they pose, learn how to create and use junction tables, and master the art of querying data across these tables with joins.

## Understanding Many-to-Many Relationships and Their Challenges

A ***many-to-many relationship*** is a type of relationship between two entities where multiple records in one entity can be associated with multiple records in another entity, and vice versa. For example, consider the relationship between ***Students*** and ***Courses*** in an educational database. A student can enroll in multiple courses, and each course can have multiple students.

Challenges arise because traditional relational databases are designed for one-to-many relationships, not many-to-many. Directly representing many-to-many relationships in a database schema would require multiple columns, making it impractical. That's where junction tables come in.

## Creating and Using Junction Tables to Resolve Many-to-Many Relationships

***Junction tables*** are intermediary tables designed to resolve many-to-many relationships. They bridge the gap by breaking down a complex relationship into two one-to-many relationships. Each row in a junction table represents a unique combination of records from the two entities involved in the many-to-many relationship.

### *Students and Courses Junction Table Example:*

Let's create a junction table to resolve the many-to-many relationship between students and courses. We'll name it ***StudentCourses***.

# Multi-Table Queries

```sql
-- COMMON SQL
CREATE TABLE StudentCourses (
    StudentID INT,
    CourseID INT,
    PRIMARY KEY (StudentID, CourseID),
    FOREIGN KEY (StudentID) REFERENCES Students(StudentID),
    FOREIGN KEY (CourseID) REFERENCES Courses(CourseID)
);
```

In this example, the *StudentCourses* junction table links students and courses through their respective IDs. The **PRIMARY KEY** constraint ensures that each combination of *StudentID* and *CourseID* is unique, while the *FOREIGN KEY* constraints establish the relationships with the *Students* and *Courses* tables.

## Querying Data Across Junction Tables with Joins

Once you have a junction table in place, querying data across many-to-many relationships becomes straightforward using SQL joins. You can retrieve information about students and their enrolled courses or courses and their enrolled students effortlessly.

### Retrieving Student Enrollments Example:

To retrieve a list of students and the courses they're enrolled in, you can use a **JOIN** between the *Students* and *StudentCourses* tables, followed by another **JOIN** with the *Courses* table:

```sql
-- COMMON SQL
SELECT Students.StudentName, Courses.CourseName
FROM Students
JOIN StudentCourses ON Students.StudentID =
StudentCourses.StudentID
JOIN Courses ON StudentCourses.CourseID = Courses.CourseID;
```

In this query, the first **JOIN** connects students with their enrollments in the *StudentCourses* table, and the second **JOIN** connects those enrollments with the corresponding course information in the *Courses* table. The result will be a comprehensive list of students and the courses they're enrolled in.

# Chapter 4

Many-to-many relationships are a common challenge in relational databases, but with the aid of junction tables, they can be elegantly resolved. Junction tables, also known as associative entities or bridging tables, break down complex relationships into manageable one-to-many relationships. This approach not only simplifies data modeling but also enables efficient querying using SQL joins.

By understanding the essence of many-to-many relationships, creating well-designed junction tables, and mastering the art of querying data across these tables with joins, you can effectively model and manage complex relationships in your relational databases. Junction tables are a versatile tool that empowers you to tackle the intricacies of real-world scenarios with confidence and precision.

---

## Performance Optimization and Indexing

Performance optimization is a critical aspect of database management, particularly when dealing with complex multi-table queries. As data grows and queries become more intricate, developers and database administrators need to leverage indexing to ensure that queries execute efficiently. In this section, we'll delve into performance optimization and indexing in SQL for multiple table queries, discussing considerations, indexing strategies, analyzing query execution plans, and optimizing join operations with real-world examples.

### Query Performance Considerations with Multiple Table Queries

Multi-table queries are common in SQL, but they can introduce performance challenges, especially when dealing with large datasets. Some common performance bottlenecks in multi-table queries include:

- *Table Scans*: Without proper indexing, the database may need to scan entire tables to find matching rows, leading to slow query execution.
- *Join Overheads*: Joining multiple tables can be resource-intensive, particularly when joining large datasets, as it involves combining rows from different tables based on join conditions.
- *Data Skew*: Uneven distribution of data across tables or columns can impact query performance, as some joins may require more processing than others.

# Multi-Table Queries

## Identifying the Need for Proper Indexing on Join Columns

Proper indexing is a key strategy for optimizing multi-table queries. Indexes are data structures that provide quick access to rows in a table based on the values in one or more columns. To optimize join operations, it's crucial to index columns used in join conditions.

*Indexing Join Columns Example:*

Suppose you have two tables, **Orders** and **Customers**, and you often perform joins based on the **CustomerID** column. Creating an index on the **CustomerID** column in both tables can significantly improve query performance:

```
-- COMMON SQL
CREATE INDEX idx_CustomerID_Orders ON Orders (CustomerID);
CREATE INDEX idx_CustomerID_Customers ON Customers (CustomerID);
```

By indexing the **CustomerID** columns in both tables, the database engine can efficiently locate matching rows during join operations, reducing the need for full table scans.

## Analyzing Query Execution Plans and Optimizing Join Operations

Query execution plans provide insights into how the database engine processes a query. They show the sequence of operations, including joins, scans, and indexes used. Analyzing these plans can help identify bottlenecks and opportunities for optimization.

*Analyzing and Optimizing a Query Example:*

Consider a query that retrieves orders along with customer information:

```
-- COMMON SQL
SELECT Orders.OrderID, Customers.CustomerName
FROM Orders
JOIN Customers ON Orders.CustomerID = Customers.CustomerID
WHERE Orders.OrderDate BETWEEN '2023-01-01' AND '2023-12-31';
```

To analyze the query execution plan and identify optimization opportunities, you can use a command like **EXPLAIN** (MySQL) or query profiling tools provided by your database management system. The plan might reveal that indexes on the **CustomerID** columns are being used efficiently for the join, but there's a table scan on the **Orders** table due to the date filter.

Optimizations can include:

- Creating an index on the **OrderDate** column in the **Orders** table.
- Ensuring that the query filters are selective to reduce the number of rows processed.

*Final Thoughts on Optimization*

Performance optimization and indexing are crucial when dealing with multi-table queries in SQL. By identifying the need for proper indexing on join columns, creating relevant indexes, and analyzing query execution plans, you can streamline query performance, reduce execution times, and ensure efficient data retrieval from complex relational databases. Indexing is a powerful tool that can significantly enhance the efficiency of your SQL queries, enabling you to harness the full potential of your database systems.

---

Best Practices for Multi-Table Queries

Efficiently combining data from various tables requires finesse and understanding. Here we will examine best practices and common pitfalls of working with multi-table queries, providing insights into writing efficient and maintainable SQL code while steering clear of potential problems.

Best Practices for Writing Multi-Table Queries

Creating multi-table queries involves weaving intricate relationships into coherent narratives. Mastering the following best practices ensures your queries are both efficient and maintainable:

**Tip - Use Explicit Joins**: Some SQL programmers feel that explicitly stating the type of join (INNER, LEFT, RIGHT) enhances query readability and prevents accidental cross joins (*Nota bene: the author favors implicit joins which the author feels provides enhanced code readability due to its brevity*).

```
-- COMMON SQL
-- Good Practice: Explicit INNER JOIN
SELECT Orders.OrderID, Customers.CustomerName
FROM Orders
INNER JOIN Customers ON Orders.CustomerID =
Customers.CustomerID;
```

**Tip - Alias Tables for Clarity**: Alias tables using meaningful names for brevity and readability.

```
-- COMMON SQL
-- Good Practice: Table Aliases
SELECT o.OrderID, c.CustomerName
FROM Orders AS o
INNER JOIN Customers AS c ON o.CustomerID = c.CustomerID;
```

**Tip - Use Indexes**: Indexing the columns used in join conditions improves query performance, especially on large datasets. But remember, indexes impose an efficiency "tax" as well. Each time a record is created, updated, or deleted the corresponding index(es) must also be updated. Moreover, indexes perform best when they are entirely cached in RAM. RAM is a precious and finite commodity in computer systems, so the DBA must be judicious in creating indexes, carefully considering whether they benefit the most frequently executed or the slowest/longest running queries.

```
-- COMMON SQL
-- Good Practice: Indexed Columns in JOIN
CREATE INDEX idx_CustomerID ON Orders (CustomerID);
CREATE INDEX idx_CustomerID ON Customers (CustomerID);
```

Common Pitfalls to Avoid in Multi-Table Queries

Multi-table queries, if not crafted meticulously, can lead to a variety of pitfalls. Avoiding these common mistakes ensures the accuracy and efficiency of your SQL code:

**Pitfall - Accidental Cross Joins**: Forgetting to specify join conditions can lead to unintentional cross joins, resulting in massive result sets.

```
-- COMMON SQL
-- Pitfall: Accidental Cross Join
SELECT * FROM Orders, Customers;
```

**Pitfall - Overusing SELECT:** Selecting all columns without necessity can strain resources, especially on large datasets.

```
-- COMMON SQL
-- Pitfall: Selecting All Columns
SELECT * FROM Orders
INNER JOIN Customers ON Orders.CustomerID =
Customers.CustomerID;
```

**Pitfall - Neglecting Indexing**: Failing to index join columns can significantly slow down query performance.

```
-- COMMON SQL
-- Pitfall: Unindexed Join Columns
SELECT * FROM Orders
INNER JOIN Customers ON Orders.CustomerID =
Customers.CustomerID;
```

Challenges of Multi-Table Joins on Large Datasets

Working with multi-table joins on large datasets introduces unique challenges. Here's how to tackle them:

**Challenge - Efficient Pagination**: Implement efficient pagination techniques, such as using OFFSET and FETCH NEXT (for SQL Server) or LIMIT and OFFSET (for MySQL and PostgreSQL), to handle large result sets without overloading the server.

```
-- COMMON SQL
-- Example: Pagination with OFFSET and FETCH NEXT (SQL Server)
SELECT * FROM Orders
ORDER BY OrderID
OFFSET 10 ROWS
FETCH NEXT 10 ROWS ONLY;
```

# Multi-Table Queries

## Final Thoughts on Multi-Table Queries

Mastering multi-table queries is essential for harnessing the full potential of relational databases. By adhering to best practices, avoiding common pitfalls, and addressing challenges specific to large datasets, you can craft queries that are not only efficient and accurate but also maintainable and scalable.

With these skills, you can confidently navigate the complexities of multi-table joins, ensuring that your SQL applications perform optimally and provide valuable insights from the vast seas of interconnected data. Armed with this knowledge, you are well-equipped to tackle real-world scenarios, transforming complex datasets into meaningful and actionable information, thereby enriching your professional SQL programming.

---

# Chapter 5 – Updating Data with SQL

## Introduction to Data Modification

Data modification in SQL is a fundamental operation that allows you to make changes to existing data in your database tables. Whether you need to correct errors, update outdated information, or implement changes in response to evolving business requirements, understanding the art of updating data in SQL is crucial. In this section, we'll delve into the world of data modification, explore how to update data effectively, discuss best practices, and highlight potential consequences and other considerations.

## Updating Data: The Basics

The SQL *UPDATE* statement is the primary tool for modifying data in a database table. It allows you to specify which records to update and what changes to make. Here's a basic syntax of the *UPDATE* statement:

```
-- COMMON SQL
UPDATE table_name
SET column1 = value1, column2 = value2, ...
WHERE condition;
```

- *table_name*: The name of the table you want to update.
- *column1, column2, ...*: The columns you want to update and the new values you want to set.
- *condition*: The condition that specifies which rows to update. If omitted, all rows in the table will be updated.

*Updating Employee Salaries Example:*

Let's say you have an *Employees* table, and you want to give a 10% salary increase to all employees with a job title of "Manager." Here's how you can do it:

```
-- COMMON SQL
UPDATE Employees
SET Salary = Salary * 1.10
WHERE JobTitle = 'Manager';
```

In this example, the **UPDATE** statement modifies the **Salary** column for all employees with the job title **Manager** by multiplying their current salary by 1.10 (adding a 10% increase).

Best Practices for Updating Data

Updating data is a powerful operation that should be performed carefully to ensure data integrity and consistency. Here are some best practices to follow:

- **Backup Data**: Before making significant updates, it's advisable to create a backup of the data or work with a copy of the table to avoid accidental data loss.
- **Use Transactions**: Wrap your **UPDATE** statements in transactions when making multiple updates. Transactions ensure that either all updates are applied or none at all, maintaining data consistency.
- **Be Precise with WHERE Clause**: Always include a well-defined **WHERE** clause to specify which records should be updated. Omitting the **WHERE** clause can lead to unintended updates.
- **Test Queries**: Run **SELECT** queries with the same conditions first to verify which records will be affected by the **UPDATE** statement.
- **Avoid Mass Updates**: Be cautious when performing updates that affect a large number of records, as they can impact database performance.

Potential Consequences and Considerations

When updating data in SQL, there are several potential consequences and considerations to keep in mind:

- **Data Integrity**: Ensure that your updates maintain data integrity and do not violate constraints or relationships with other tables.
- **Concurrency**: Be aware of concurrent updates by multiple users. Use locking mechanisms or optimistic concurrency control to prevent conflicts.
- **Logging**: Many databases log changes, so be mindful of the storage and performance impact of updates, especially in high-transaction environments.
- **Rollback**: Plan for the possibility of rolling back updates in case of errors or unforeseen issues.
- **Auditing**: Implement audit trails or logging mechanisms to track changes made to critical data.

# Updating Data with SQL

*Final thoughts on Update Best Practices*

Updating data in SQL is a vital operation in database management, but it should be executed with care and precision. Understanding the **UPDATE** statement, adhering to best practices, and considering potential consequences are essential steps to ensure data accuracy, integrity, and consistency. By mastering the art of updating data in SQL, you can maintain a well-maintained and reliable database system that supports your organization's evolving data needs.

---

## Basic UPDATE Statement

The **UPDATE** statement is the essential tool for modifying data within a single table. It empowers you to make changes to existing records, correct errors, or adapt your database to evolving requirements. In this section, we'll explore the syntax of the SQL **UPDATE** statement, understand how to specify the target table and columns to be updated, and discover how the **WHERE** clause filters the rows that undergo transformation—all illustrated with real-world examples.

## The Anatomy of an SQL UPDATE Statement

The SQL **UPDATE** statement follows a clear and structured syntax, ensuring precise modifications to your data:

```
-- COMMON SQL
UPDATE table_name
SET column1 = value1, column2 = value2, ...
WHERE condition;
```

- ***table_name***: The name of the table you intend to update.
- ***column1, column2, ...***: The columns you wish to modify, along with the new values you want to assign.
- ***WHERE condition***: An optional clause that defines the criteria to identify the rows you want to update. Without this clause, all rows in the table will be affected.

# Chapter 5

Specifying the Target Table and Columns to Be Updated

Let's explore the **UPDATE** statement through a practical example. Imagine you're managing a database of products, and you need to update the price and stock quantity of a specific product. Here's how you can use the **UPDATE** statement to accomplish this task:

```
-- COMMON SQL
UPDATE Products
SET Price = 19.99, StockQuantity = 100
WHERE ProductID = 123;
```

In this example:

- **Products** is the target table.
- **Price** and **StockQuantity** are the columns you intend to update, with new values of 19.99 and 100, respectively.
- The **WHERE** clause filters the rows to update, ensuring that only the product with a **ProductID** of 123 is modified.

Using the WHERE Clause to Filter Rows to Be Updated

The **WHERE** clause plays a pivotal role in controlling which rows undergo modification. It allows you to filter records based on specific conditions, ensuring that only the desired subset of data is updated. Let's consider another scenario—you want to increase the price of all products in a specific category. Here's how you can do it:

```
-- COMMON SQL
UPDATE Products
SET Price = Price * 1.1
WHERE CategoryID = 5;
```

In this case:

- The **SET** clause multiplies the **Price** column by 1.1, effectively increasing all prices by 10%.
- The **WHERE** clause filters the rows to be updated, ensuring that only products in **CategoryID** 5 receive the price increase.

# Updating Data with SQL

*Final Thoughts on the Update Statement*

The SQL **UPDATE** statement is an indispensable tool for modifying data within a single table. By mastering its syntax and understanding how to specify the target table, columns to be updated, and how to use the **WHERE** clause to filter rows, you gain the ability to efficiently manage and adapt your database to evolving needs. Whether you're correcting errors, updating records, or making adjustments in response to changing requirements, the **UPDATE** statement is your key to maintaining accurate and up-to-date data in your SQL database.

---

## Updating with Expressions and Functions

Updating data in SQL is not limited to simple value assignments—you can harness the power of expressions and functions to perform complex modifications on column values. Whether you need to apply arithmetic operations, manipulate strings, or work with dates, SQL provides a plethora of functions and capabilities to transform your data. Recall that a reference for commonly used SQL Server functions is found in Appendix A, and a reference for commonly used MySQL functions in Appendix B. In this section, we'll explore how to update data using expressions and functions, covering arithmetic operations and various string and date functions, all illustrated with practical examples.

## Applying Arithmetic Operations to Modify Column Values

Arithmetic operations are incredibly useful when you want to perform mathematical calculations on column values while updating records. These operations can be as simple as adding or subtracting values or as complex as performing calculations with multiple columns. Let's dive into some examples.

*Increasing Product Prices by a Percentage Example:*

Suppose you have a table of products, and you want to increase the prices of all products by 10%. You can achieve this using a straightforward arithmetic operation:

```
-- COMMON SQL
UPDATE Products
SET Price = Price * 1.10;
```

In this SQL statement, we multiply the **Price** column by 1.10 to increase all prices by 10%.

*Calculating and Updating Total Sales Amount Example:*

Consider a sales table where you have order quantities and unit prices. To calculate the total sales amount for each order and update the table accordingly:

```
-- COMMON SQL
UPDATE Sales
SET TotalAmount = Quantity * UnitPrice;
```

Here, we use the expression **Quantity \* UnitPrice** to calculate the total amount for each order and update the **TotalAmount** column.

Utilizing String and Date Functions for Data Manipulation

SQL provides a rich set of functions for manipulating strings and dates, making it versatile for a wide range of data transformations.

*Changing String Case Example:*

Let's say you have a **Customers** table with customer names in mixed or lower case, and you want to convert them to all upper case:

```
-- COMMON SQL
UPDATE Customers
SET CustomerName = UPPER(CustomerName);
```

In this example, we use the **UPPER()** function to convert the **CustomerName** values to all upper case.

*Updating Dates Using Date Functions Example:*

Suppose you have an **Orders** table with an **OrderDate** column, and you need to adjust all order dates by adding three days:

# Updating Data with SQL

```
-- SQL SERVER
UPDATE Orders
SET OrderDate = DATEADD(DAY, 3, OrderDate);
```

```
-- MySQL
UPDATE Orders
SET OrderDate = DATE_ADD(OrderDate, INTERVAL 3 DAY);
```

Here, we use the **DATEADD()** function (the name may vary by database system) to add three days to each **OrderDate** value.

*Final Thoughts on Updating with Expressions and Functions*

Updating data in SQL goes beyond basic assignments; it involves using expressions and functions to perform a wide array of transformations. Whether you need to apply arithmetic operations for numerical updates or utilize string and date functions for data manipulation, SQL offers a robust set of tools to cater to your data modification needs. By mastering these capabilities, you can efficiently and accurately update data, ensuring that your database remains accurate and aligned with your evolving requirements.

---

## Batch Updating and Transaction Management

In SQL programming, efficiency and data integrity are paramount. Managing large volumes of data and ensuring that updates occur reliably are challenges often encountered in real-world applications. Let's explore the techniques of batch updating and transaction management, two vital skills for database professionals aiming for precision and speed.

### The Need for Batch Updating

Imagine managing an inventory system with thousands of products. Updating each record individually could be laborious and time-consuming. Batch updating, the practice of updating multiple records in a single operation, offers a solution to this challenge.

**Consideration**: Batch updating optimizes performance by reducing the number of transactions and interactions with the database server.

```
-- COMMON SQL
-- Example: Batch Update
UPDATE Products
SET StockQuantity = StockQuantity - 10
WHERE Category = 'Electronics';
```

In this example, a batch update reduces the stock quantity of all electronics products by 10 units.

Understanding Transactions

SQL Transactions are like most banking transactions - they involve multiple operations and must be completed as a whole or not at all. For example, when a merchant deposits a check you issued to pay for a product you purchased, the bank must BOTH deduct (debit) the amount from your account, and deposit (credit) the amount to the merchant's account. The concept of atomicity, ensuring that all steps of a transaction are executed completely or all are rolled back entirely in case of failure, is fundamental.

**Consideration**: Transactions ensure data integrity by preserving the consistency and reliability of your database even in the face of errors.

```
-- COMMON SQL
-- Example: Transaction Management
BEGIN TRANSACTION;

UPDATE Orders
SET Status = 'Shipped'
WHERE OrderID = 123;

INSERT INTO ShipmentHistory (OrderID, ShippedDate)
VALUES (123, GETDATE());

COMMIT;
```

# Updating Data with SQL

In this example, a transaction begins, updating the order status and inserting a shipment record. If any step fails, the entire transaction is rolled back, preserving data integrity.

## Final Thoughts on Batch Updates and Transactions

In SQL programming, mastering batch updating and transaction management is akin to becoming a skilled conductor orchestrating a complex symphony. Batch updating optimizes performance by minimizing individual interactions with the database, while transactions ensure data integrity by ensuring the reliability and completeness of operations.

By understanding the nuances of batch updating, the concept of transactions, and the fundamental principle of atomicity, you empower yourself to handle large datasets efficiently and maintain the consistency and reliability of your database. These skills are invaluable for database professionals navigating the complexities of data management, ensuring that their applications not only perform optimally but also maintain the highest standards of data integrity and reliability.

---

## Updating with Subqueries

The ability to manipulate and update data efficiently is vital. Subqueries, a powerful tool in SQL, allow for sophisticated data manipulation and retrieval. Let's explore the art of updating data using subqueries, both within UPDATE statements and in conjunction with other queries, unveiling their potential for complex, yet elegant, data transformations.

## Subqueries Within UPDATE Statements

Imagine a master conductor guiding an orchestra, where each musician plays their part in harmony. Subqueries within UPDATE statements operate similarly, orchestrating multiple actions into a cohesive performance.

**Consideration**: Subqueries within UPDATE statements allow for precise updates based on dynamic, context-specific conditions.

```
-- COMMON SQL
```

```
-- Example: Updating Based on Subquery Result
UPDATE Employees
SET Salary = Salary * 1.1
WHERE DepartmentID IN (SELECT DepartmentID FROM Departments
WHERE Category = 'Sales');
```

In this example, the subquery identifies departments belonging to the 'Sales' category, and the main UPDATE statement increases the salary of employees in those departments by 10%.

Using Subqueries to Update Data Based on Results from Other Queries

Think of subqueries as artisans creating detailed patterns, which, when combined, form a magnificent mosaic. When used to update data based on results from other queries, subqueries craft tailored solutions.

**Consideration**: Subqueries can be used within UPDATE statements to draw upon the results of other queries, providing a dynamic foundation for data updates.

```
-- COMMON SQL
-- Example: Updating Based on Aggregate Subquery Result
UPDATE Orders
SET DiscountedTotal = Total * 0.9
WHERE OrderID IN
(
  SELECT OrderID
  FROM OrderItems
  GROUP BY OrderID
  HAVING SUM(Price) > 1000
);
```

In this example, the subquery calculates the total price for each order in the OrderItems table, and the UPDATE statement applies a 10% discount to orders with a total exceeding $1000.

# Updating Data with SQL

## Final Thoughts on Updating with Subqueries

Subqueries add depth and complexity to SQL code. By incorporating subqueries within UPDATE statements and leveraging their ability to update data based on results from other queries, you gain a nuanced understanding of data manipulation.

Subqueries offer a flexible and dynamic approach to updating data, allowing you to perform intricate transformations with ease. Whether orchestrating updates within specific subsets of data or tailoring updates based on aggregated results, subqueries empower you to craft precise and efficient solutions in the ever-evolving landscape of database management. With these skills, you can navigate the complexities of data manipulation, ensuring that your SQL applications not only perform optimally but also respond to the dynamic needs of your data-driven endeavors.

---

## Updating Joined Tables:

Databases rarely stand alone in isolation. Relationships between tables often necessitate updates that span multiple domains of data. Let's examine the art of updating joined tables, a task that requires finesse and precision. We will delve into the complexities of modifying data across multiple tables using various types of joins, unlocking the potential of INNER, LEFT, and other joins in the context of update operations.

## Modifying Data Across Multiple Tables

Consider a scenario where customers place orders, and these orders are associated with products stored in different tables. Updating these tables independently might lead to inconsistencies. The solution lies in updating joined tables, ensuring that changes ripple through the interconnected web of data.

**Consideration**: Updating joined tables involves strategically using joins to ensure the changes are applied consistently and accurately.

```
-- COMMON SQL
-- Example: Updating Joined Tables
UPDATE Orders
SET Status = 'Shipped'
```

```
FROM Orders
JOIN Customers ON Orders.CustomerID = Customers.CustomerID
WHERE Customers.Country = 'USA';
```

In this example, the UPDATE statement modifies the 'Status' column in the 'Orders' table for orders placed by customers from the USA.

Different Types of JOINs in Update Operations

Join operations are like relationships in real life—they come in various forms. In the realm of SQL, INNER, LEFT, RIGHT, and FULL OUTER joins offer different perspectives on data relationships.

**Consideration**: Choosing the right type of join is crucial for ensuring that update operations are executed accurately based on the relationships between the tables.

```
-- COMMON SQL
-- Example: Using LEFT JOIN in Update
UPDATE Customers
SET Status = 'Preferred'
FROM Customers
LEFT JOIN Orders ON Customers.CustomerID = Orders.CustomerID
WHERE Orders.OrderID IS NOT NULL;
```

In this example, the LEFT JOIN ensures that all customers who placed orders have their 'Status' updated to 'Preferred', while customers without orders are unaffected.

Final Thoughts on Updating Through Joins

By mastering the art of updating tables through joins, you can maintain the integrity and consistency of your database, even in the face of complex relationships.

Each join offers a unique perspective, allowing you to tailor your updates precisely according to the relational patterns within your data.

With these skills, you can navigate the intricacies of updating joined tables, ensuring that your SQL applications not only function efficiently but also reflect the rich interconnections inherent in complex data structures. Armed with this knowledge, you are well-equipped to handle the challenges of modern database management, creating robust, harmonious systems that reflect the complexity and beauty of real-world relationships.

---

## Handling NULL Values in Update Queries

Null values signify missing or unknown data, presenting unique challenges when updating database records. Here we will examine the nuances of handling null values in update queries, and using techniques that ensure data accuracy and consistency.

### Updating NULL Values Using the UPDATE Statement

Imagine managing a database where some records lack critical information like customer addresses or product prices. Updating these records without introducing errors requires finesse.

**Consideration**: Handling null values in update queries demands precision to avoid inadvertently erasing valuable data.

```
-- COMMON SQL
-- Example: Updating NULL Values in Customers Table
UPDATE Customers
SET Address = 'Unknown Address'
WHERE Address IS NULL;
```

In this example, the UPDATE statement assigns the placeholder 'Unknown Address' to records where the address is missing (NULL) in the 'Customers' table.

### Using the COALESCE Function

The COALESCE function is a powerful tool that transforms null values into known entities. It replaces null values with specified alternatives, ensuring consistency and reliability in your data.

**Consideration**: COALESCE provides a dynamic way to handle null values, allowing for customization and flexibility.

```
-- COMMON SQL
-- Example: Using COALESCE to Handle Null Values
UPDATE Products
SET Price = COALESCE(Price, 0)
WHERE Category = 'Electronics';
```

In this example, the COALESCE function ensures that if the 'Price' of products in the 'Electronics' category is null, it is replaced with 0, preventing calculation errors or inconsistencies.

## Final Thoughts on Handling Nulls in Update Queries

Null values present both a challenge and an opportunity. Mastering the art of handling null values in update queries ensures that missing or unknown data does not disrupt the integrity of your database.

By using the **UPDATE** statement judiciously and harnessing the power of functions like **COALESCE**, you can navigate the complexities of null values with grace. These techniques not only safeguard your data from inaccuracies but also allow you to transform potential pitfalls into opportunities for enhanced data quality and consistency.

With these skills, you can confidently handle null values in your SQL applications, ensuring that your databases remain reliable, accurate, and resilient even in the face of missing or unknown data. Armed with this knowledge, you are well-equipped to navigate the challenges of real-world data management, creating robust and reliable database systems that stand the test of time.

## Using CASE Expressions for Updates

The ability to conditionally update data is a skill that elevates your database management capabilities. CASE expressions, akin to decision-making tools, empower you to modify data based on specific conditions. Here we will explore using CASE expressions to perform updates, offering insights into their flexibility and precision in transforming data according to custom criteria.

# Updating Data with SQL

The Power of Conditional Updates

Imagine managing a database of products where prices need to be adjusted based on categories or customer types. Conditionally updating this data necessitates a nuanced approach.

**Consideration**: **CASE** expressions serve as your toolset for crafting specific and precise updates, ensuring that modifications align with your tailored criteria.

```
-- COMMON SQL
-- Example: Using CASE Expression for Conditional Update
UPDATE Products
SET Price =
    CASE
        WHEN Category = 'Electronics' THEN Price * 1.1
        WHEN Category = 'Clothing' AND
          CustomerType = 'Wholesale' THEN Price * 0.9
        ELSE Price
    END;
```

In this example, the **CASE** expression modifies product prices. If the category is 'Electronics', the price is increased by 10%. For 'Clothing' items with 'Wholesale' customers, the price is decreased by 10%. For all other products, the price remains unchanged.

Modifying Data Based on Specific Conditions

**CASE** expressions offer a dynamic approach to data transformation. They allow you to apply complex rules and conditions to update data, ensuring flexibility and accuracy.

**Consideration**: Leverage CASE expressions to implement business rules and custom logic for updating data, providing a tailored approach to modification.

```
-- COMMON SQL
-- Example: Using CASE Expression for Custom Data Modification
UPDATE Employees
SET Salary =
    CASE
        WHEN ExperienceYears >= 10 THEN Salary * 1.2
        WHEN ExperienceYears >= 5 THEN Salary * 1.1
```

```
        ELSE Salary
    END;
```

In this example, the CASE expression updates employee salaries based on their experience. Employees with 10 or more years receive a 20% increase, while those with 5 or more years get a 10% raise. Other employees remain unaffected.

### Final Thoughts on Case Expressions

The CASE expression is a precision tool. By understanding the nuances of CASE expressions, you empower yourself to apply complex logic and rules to data modifications, ensuring that your updates align with specific criteria and business requirements.

With these skills, you can confidently navigate the complexities of data transformation, tailoring your SQL applications to meet the dynamic needs of your organization. Armed with this knowledge, you are well-equipped to handle real-world scenarios, transforming data based on custom conditions, and thus enriching your SQL programming journey.

---

### Updating Data While Upholding Integrity Constraints

In database work, data integrity is paramount. Databases rely on a network of constraints, such as primary keys and foreign keys, to maintain the reliability and coherence of the data they hold. Let's delve into the art of updating data while ensuring strict adherence to these constraints, highlighting methods for modifying data without jeopardizing the integrity of the entire database structure.

### Upholding Data Integrity: A Delicate Balance

Consider a scenario where a company's database tracks customers, orders, and products. Updating customer information or order details while preserving the relationships between them demands meticulous care.

**Consideration**: When updating data, it's crucial to ensure that the changes do not violate established constraints, preserving the integrity and reliability of the entire database system.

# Updating Data with SQL

```
-- COMMON SQL
-- Example: Updating Customer Information with Primary Key
Constraint
UPDATE Customers
SET CustomerName = 'New Customer Name'
WHERE CustomerID = 1;
```

In this example, the UPDATE statement modifies the customer's name while preserving the primary key constraint, ensuring the uniqueness of the CustomerID field.

Handling Constraint Violations and Error Management

When dealing with constraints, errors can arise due to data modifications that violate the established rules. Proper error management is essential to address these challenges without compromising the database's integrity.

**Consideration**: Handling constraint violations requires a proactive approach to identify issues and rectify them while providing meaningful feedback to users.

```
-- SQL SERVER
CREATE PROCEDURE UpdateOrderCustomerID
AS
BEGIN
    BEGIN TRY
        BEGIN TRANSACTION;

        -- Attempt to update Orders table
        UPDATE Orders
        SET CustomerID = 1000
        -- Assuming this CustomerID doesn't exist...
        WHERE OrderID = 1;

        -- Commit the transaction if no errors
        COMMIT;

        -- Indicate success
        PRINT 'Update successful.';
    END TRY
    BEGIN CATCH
        -- Rollback transaction in case of error
```

```
        ROLLBACK;

        -- Handling Constraint Violation Error
        PRINT 'Error: Foreign Key Constraint Violation.
            CustomerID does not exist.';
    END CATCH
END;
```

```
-- MySQL
DELIMITER //

CREATE PROCEDURE UpdateOrderCustomerID()
BEGIN
    -- Declare exit handler for SQLEXCEPTION
    DECLARE EXIT HANDLER FOR SQLEXCEPTION
    BEGIN
        -- Handling Constraint Violation Error
        SELECT 'Error: Foreign Key Constraint Violation.
            CustomerID does not exist.' AS ErrorMessage;
    END;

    -- Start a transaction
    START TRANSACTION;

    -- Attempt to update Orders table
    UPDATE Orders
    SET CustomerID = 1000
    -- Assuming this CustomerID doesn't exist
    WHERE OrderID = 1;

    -- Commit the transaction if no errors
    COMMIT;

    -- Indicate success
    SELECT 'Update successful.' AS SuccessMessage;
END //

DELIMITER ;
```

# Updating Data with SQL

In this example, an attempt is made to update the ***CustomerID*** in the ***Orders*** table to a non-existing value. By "non-existing value", we specifically mean that the value is not found in the ***CustomerID*** field of any record in the ***Customers*** table, which is on the primary key side of this primary key - foreign key relation. This constitutes a foreign key constraint violation, as we cannot permit an "orphaned" foreign key value to exist. The **TRY...CATCH** block (SQL Server) or the **EXIT HANDLER FOR SQL EXCEPTION** (MySQL) captures the error and provides a descriptive message, allowing for informed troubleshooting.

## Final Thoughts on Updating Data and Data Integrity

Updating data while upholding data integrity constraints is akin to walking a tightrope. It requires a delicate balance between making necessary modifications and preserving the relationships and rules that define the database's structure.

By understanding the interplay of constraints, applying meticulous care when updating data, and implementing robust error management strategies, you can navigate the challenges of maintaining data integrity with confidence. These skills ensure that your SQL applications not only perform optimally but also maintain the highest standards of reliability and consistency.

Armed with this knowledge, you are well-equipped to handle real-world scenarios, ensuring that your database systems remain resilient and trustworthy even in the face of complex data modifications. Thus, you enrich your SQL programming journey, becoming a proficient steward of data integrity in the ever-evolving landscape of database management.

---

## Updating Data with Transactions

Managing data modifications demands precision and reliability. Transactions, the bedrock of database management, ensure the integrity, consistency, and reliability of data modifications. Let's explore updating data using transactions, the fundamental concepts, practical implementation, and the critical role transactions play in maintaining data integrity.

## The Essence of Transactions: Data Modifications with Integrity

Consider a scenario where a banking system processes fund transfers. A transaction ensures that when money is debited from one account, it is simultaneously credited to another, or neither operation occurs. Transactions encapsulate this concept of atomicity, ensuring that all changes happen as a cohesive whole.

**Consideration**: Transactions are the guardians of data integrity, guaranteeing that database modifications occur atomically, preserving the consistency of the database.

```
-- COMMON SQL
-- Example: Fund Transfer Transaction
BEGIN TRANSACTION;

UPDATE Accounts
SET Balance = Balance - 100
WHERE AccountID = 123;

UPDATE Accounts
SET Balance = Balance + 100
WHERE AccountID = 456;

COMMIT;
```

In this example, the **BEGIN TRANSACTION** statement initiates a transaction, updating two accounts atomically. If either update fails, the **ROLLBACK** statement ensures that the entire transaction is rolled back, maintaining the integrity of the accounts' balances.

The ABCs of Transactions: BEGIN, COMMIT, and ROLLBACK

Transactions follow a structured lifecycle, commencing with initiation, continuing through modifications, and concluding with a commitment or rollback, based on the success or failure of the operations.

**Consideration**: The **BEGIN TRANSACTION, COMMIT**, and **ROLLBACK** statements are the tools through which transactions are initiated, completed, or undone, ensuring data consistency.

```
-- SQL SERVER
-- Example: Nested Transactions
BEGIN TRANSACTION;

UPDATE Employees
SET Salary = Salary * 1.1
WHERE DepartmentID = 1;

BEGIN TRY
    -- Nested Transaction within a TRY-CATCH Block
    BEGIN TRANSACTION;
    -- Add Code FoR Any Additional Complex Operations Here
    COMMIT;
END TRY
BEGIN CATCH
    -- Rollback Nested Transaction on Error
    ROLLBACK;
END CATCH;

COMMIT;
```

In this example, nested transactions are used within a **TRY-CATCH** block. If the nested transaction encounters an error, the **ROLLBACK** statement within the **CATCH** block ensures the nested transaction's atomicity, preserving the integrity of the database.

*MySQL does not support true nested transactions. Instead, MySQL uses SAVEPOINTs to allow partial rollback within a transaction. SAVEPOINTs enable you to mark specific points within a transaction, which you can later roll back to without affecting the entire transaction. This allows you to handle complex operations and errors more flexibly within a single transaction.*

```
-- MySQL
DELIMITER //

CREATE PROCEDURE UpdateEmployeeSalaries()
BEGIN
    DECLARE EXIT HANDLER FOR SQLEXCEPTION
    BEGIN
        -- Rollback the entire transaction on error
        ROLLBACK;
        SELECT 'Error: An error occurred, transaction rolled
```

```
                back.' AS ErrorMessage;
    END;

    -- Start the transaction
    START TRANSACTION;

    -- Update Employees table
    UPDATE Employees
    SET Salary = Salary * 1.1
    WHERE DepartmentID = 1;

    -- Create a SAVEPOINT
    SAVEPOINT before_complex_operations;

    -- Begin complex operations
    BEGIN
        DECLARE EXIT HANDLER FOR SQLEXCEPTION
        BEGIN
            -- Rollback to the SAVEPOINT on error within
            -- the complex operations
            ROLLBACK TO SAVEPOINT before_complex_operations;
            SELECT 'Error: An error occurred in complex
                    operations, rolled back to SAVEPOINT.'
            AS ErrorMessage;
        END;

        -- Add Code FoR Any Additional Complex Operations Here

        -- If all is well, release the SAVEPOINT
        RELEASE SAVEPOINT before_complex_operations;
    END;

    -- Commit the transaction if no errors
    COMMIT;

    -- Indicate success
    SELECT 'Update successful.' AS SuccessMessage;
END //

DELIMITER ;
```

# Updating Data with SQL

In this example, **START TRANSACTION** begins a new transaction. The**UPDATE** statement updates the *Employees* table. **SAVEPOINT** sets a savepoint named ***before_complex_operations*** before starting complex operations. The **BEGIN Block** uses a block with an error handler to manage errors within complex operations. If an error occurs, it rolls back to the savepoint. Next, **ROLLBACK TO SAVEPOINT** rolls back to the specified savepoint if an error occurs within the complex operations. The **RELEASE SAVEPOINT** releases the savepoint if all operations within the block succeed, indicating that this point in the transaction is now a stable state. If no errors occur throughout the entire process, the **COMMIT** statement commits the transaction. Finally, the **SELECT** statement outputs messages indicating the result of the transaction.

## Final Thoughts on Updating with Transactions

Transactions are a critical method for safeguarding data integrity against incomplete and interrupted modifications. Understanding the essence of transactions, mastering the use of **BEGIN TRANSACTION, COMMIT**, and **ROLLBACK** statements, and appreciating the concept of atomicity empower you to handle data modifications with finesse and reliability.

With these skills, you can confidently navigate the complexities of updating data, ensuring that your SQL applications not only perform optimally but also maintain the highest standards of data consistency and reliability. Armed with this knowledge, you are well-equipped to handle real-world scenarios, managing data modifications with precision and ensuring the integrity of your database systems. Thus, you enrich your SQL programming journey, becoming a skilled architect of data integrity in the ever-evolving landscape of database management.

---

## Rolling Back Changes

In database work, errors and unexpected events will occasionally crop up. Enter the hero of the hour: the **ROLLBACK** statement. This section delves into the art of rolling back changes, exploring the scenarios where it becomes essential and demonstrating how this powerful tool ensures data consistency and integrity even in the face of adversity.

## The Imperative of Rollbacks: A Shield Against Errors

Imagine a scenario where a batch of erroneous updates is accidentally executed, altering critical records. Such situations demand an immediate response to restore data integrity.

**Consideration**: Rollbacks act as a time-traveling tool, reverting the database to its original state before the erroneous changes, ensuring data remains untarnished.

```sql
-- SQL Server
-- Example: Rolling Back Changes After Error
BEGIN TRY
    BEGIN TRANSACTION;

    -- Erroneous Updates
    UPDATE Accounts
    SET Balance = Balance - 100
    WHERE AccountID = 123;

    -- Error Occurs
    -- ROLLBACK to Undo Changes
    ROLLBACK;
END TRY
BEGIN CATCH
    -- Handle Error
    PRINT 'Error: Transaction Rolled Back';
END CATCH;
```

```sql
-- MySQL
DELIMITER //

CREATE PROCEDURE UpdateAccountBalance()
BEGIN
    DECLARE EXIT HANDLER FOR SQLEXCEPTION
    BEGIN
        -- Rollback the transaction on error
        ROLLBACK;
        SELECT 'Error: Transaction Rolled Back' AS ErrorMessage;
    END;

    -- Start the transaction
    START TRANSACTION;

    -- Erroneous Updates
    UPDATE Accounts
    SET Balance = Balance - 100
    WHERE AccountID = 123;
```

```
    -- Rollback to simulate an error occurring
    ROLLBACK;

    -- If no error, select success message
    SELECT 'Update successful, but should not reach here due to
rollback.' AS SuccessMessage;
END //

DELIMITER ;
```

In this example, the **ROLLBACK** statement within the **CATCH** block (SQL Server) or in the **EXIT HANDLER FOR SQLEXCEPTION** (MySQL) undoes any changes made during the transaction, preserving the data integrity of the affected accounts.


The Art of Rolling Back: Maintaining Data Consistency


Rollbacks serve as the guardians of data consistency, ensuring that in the face of errors, the database can revert to a stable state, unmarred by unintended modifications.


**Consideration**: Rollbacks are crucial in scenarios where operations need to be aborted due to errors, preventing partial modifications and preserving the atomicity of transactions.

```
-- COMMON SQL
-- Example: Rolling Back a Failed Transaction
BEGIN TRANSACTION;

-- Series of Updates
UPDATE Employees
SET Salary = Salary * 1.1
WHERE DepartmentID = 1;

-- Error Occurs
-- ROLLBACK to Undo Changes
ROLLBACK;
```

In this example, if an error occurs during the transaction, the **ROLLBACK** statement ensures that all updates made within the transaction are reverted, preserving the original state of the affected records.

# Chapter 5

## Final Thoughts on RollBacks

The ability to roll back changes serves as the principal tool for avoiding loss of data integrity in the face of unexpected errors. Understanding the imperative of rollbacks, and mastering the art of employing the **ROLLBACK** statement, empowers you to navigate the complexities of database management with grace and precision.

With these skills, you can confidently handle scenarios where data integrity is threatened, ensuring that your SQL applications not only perform optimally but also maintain the highest standards of consistency and reliability. Armed with this knowledge, you are well-equipped to handle real-world scenarios, mitigating the impact of errors and ensuring the sanctity of your database systems. Thus, you enrich your SQL programming journey, becoming a steadfast guardian of data integrity in the ever-evolving landscape of database management.

---

## Triggers for Data Modification

Triggers provide a sophisticated mechanism for automating and responding to specific data modifications. This section explores the conceptual underpinnings of triggers, elucidating their role in automating data updates, and guides readers through the creation and implementation of triggers to seamlessly respond to nuanced changes in the database.

## Understanding Triggers

Triggers, at their essence, are specialized stored procedures that automatically execute in response to predefined events, often data modifications. This section introduces the conceptual framework of triggers, exploring their significance in automating routine tasks, enforcing business rules, and maintaining data integrity. Real-world examples illuminate the diverse scenarios where triggers prove invaluable in streamlining database management.

## Creating Triggers

Delving into the practical realm, this section navigates through the syntax and intricacies of creating triggers in SQL databases. Readers gain insights into the types of triggers, such as **BEFORE** and **AFTER** triggers (MySQL), and **AFTER** and **INSTEAD OF** triggers (SQL Server), and the events triggering their execution. Step-by-step examples guide readers through the process of crafting triggers tailored to specific requirements, laying the foundation for hands-on proficiency.

## Responding to Data Changes

Triggers shine brightest when responding to specific data changes. This section delves into the art of crafting triggers that react dynamically to modifications in the database. Whether it be updating related tables, enforcing referential integrity, or logging changes for audit purposes, triggers provide a versatile toolset. Real-world case studies showcase the strategic application of triggers to address nuanced data scenarios.

## Best Practices and Considerations

As with any powerful tool, the effective use of triggers demands a nuanced understanding of best practices and considerations. This section navigates through strategies for optimizing trigger performance, managing dependencies, and avoiding common pitfalls. Practical advice from seasoned professionals imparts valuable insights for crafting triggers that seamlessly integrate into a robust database architecture.

## SQL Server (T-SQL) Triggers and MySQL Triggers Compared

Coding SQL triggers in Transact-SQL (T-SQL) for SQL Server and SQL for MySQL DBMS involves several differences due to variations in syntax, capabilities, and the procedural language constructs supported by each system. Here are key differences with examples:

**1. Trigger Creation Syntax**

**SQL Server (T-SQL):**

- Uses **AFTER, INSTEAD OF**, and **FOR** keywords to specify when the trigger should fire.
- Supports **INSERTED** and **DELETED** virtual tables to access the affected rows.

**MySQL:**

- Uses **BEFORE** and **AFTER** keywords to specify when the trigger should fire.
- Uses **NEW** and **OLD** keywords to reference the affected rows.

**Example: Insert Trigger**

```
-- SQL SERVER
CREATE TRIGGER trgAfterInsert
ON Employees
AFTER INSERT
AS
BEGIN
    -- Inserted is a virtual table holding the newly inserted
rows
    INSERT INTO AuditTable (EmployeeID, Action)
    SELECT EmployeeID, 'INSERT'
    FROM INSERTED;
END;
```

```
-- MySQL
CREATE TRIGGER trgAfterInsert
AFTER INSERT ON Employees
FOR EACH ROW
BEGIN
    -- NEW references the new row being inserted
    INSERT INTO AuditTable (EmployeeID, Action)
    VALUES (NEW.EmployeeID, 'INSERT');
END;
```

## 2. Referencing Modified Rows

**SQL Server (T-SQL):**

- Uses **INSERTED** and **DELETED** tables to access new and old values, respectively.

**MySQL:**

- Uses **NEW** and **OLD** keywords for new and old values.

**Example: Update Trigger**

```
-- SQL Server
CREATE TRIGGER trgAfterUpdate
ON Employees
AFTER UPDATE
AS
BEGIN
```

```
    -- INSERTED holds the new values, DELETED holds the old
values
    INSERT INTO AuditTable (EmployeeID, OldSalary, NewSalary)
    SELECT D.EmployeeID, D.Salary, I.Salary
    FROM DELETED D
    JOIN INSERTED I ON D.EmployeeID = I.EmployeeID;
END;
```

```
-- MySQL
CREATE TRIGGER trgAfterUpdate
AFTER UPDATE ON Employees
FOR EACH ROW
BEGIN
    -- OLD references the old values, NEW references the new
values
    INSERT INTO AuditTable (EmployeeID, OldSalary, NewSalary)
    VALUES (OLD.EmployeeID, OLD.Salary, NEW.Salary);
END;
```

### 3. Conditional Logic and Flow Control

Both SQL Server and MySQL support procedural constructs, but there are differences in syntax and available features.

**SQL Server (T-SQL)**:

- Uses **BEGIN ... END** for block statements.

- Supports **IF ... ELSE** for conditional logic.

**MySQL**:

- Uses **BEGIN ... END** for block statements.

- Supports **IF ... THEN ... ELSE** for conditional logic.

**Example: Conditional Logic in a Trigger**

```
-- SQL SERVER
CREATE TRIGGER trgBeforeInsert
ON Employees
INSTEAD OF INSERT
AS
BEGIN
```

141

```
    -- Insert only if the salary is greater than 30000
    IF EXISTS (SELECT * FROM INSERTED WHERE Salary > 30000)
    BEGIN
        INSERT INTO Employees (EmployeeID, Name, Salary)
        SELECT EmployeeID, Name, Salary
        FROM INSERTED
        WHERE Salary > 30000;
    END;
END;
```

```
-- MySQL
CREATE TRIGGER trgBeforeInsert
BEFORE INSERT ON Employees
FOR EACH ROW
BEGIN
    -- Insert only if the salary is greater than 30000
    IF NEW.Salary > 30000 THEN
        -- Allow insert to proceed
    ELSE
        SIGNAL SQLSTATE '45000' SET MESSAGE_TEXT = 'Salary must
be greater than 30000';
    END IF;
END;
```

**Summary**

While the fundamental concepts of triggers are similar in SQL Server and MySQL, the syntax and certain features differ. SQL Server uses **INSERTED** and **DELETED** tables for row references and has specific keywords like **AFTER, INSTEAD OF**, and **FOR**. MySQL uses **NEW** and **OLD** for row references and employs **BEFORE** and **AFTER** keywords. Understanding these differences is crucial for writing effective triggers in each DBMS.

Triggers in Industry Applications

Mastery of triggers empowers the DBA to orchestrate intelligent and automated responses to data modifications. The passages presented here serve to equip readers with the theoretical understanding, practical skills, and strategic insights needed to leverage triggers effectively and elevate their proficiency in SQL database management.

# Updating Data with SQL

Let us examine how triggers find application in a real-world scenario. From e-commerce platforms ensuring inventory accuracy to financial systems enforcing transactional integrity, triggers play a crucial role in diverse domains.

---

Trigger Update Scenario

Imagine an e-commerce database where there is a need to track inventory changes and send notifications when the stock of a product falls below a certain threshold.

In this scenario:
1. **Problem:** The database needs to ensure that the inventory level for each product is updated whenever a new order is placed, or a product is restocked. Additionally, if the inventory falls below a certain threshold, notifications should be sent to alert the relevant stakeholders.
2. **Solution using Triggers:**
   - **Trigger for Updating Inventory:** A trigger can be created that automatically updates the inventory level in the product table whenever a new order is placed or when a restocking operation occurs. For example:

```sql
-- SQL Server
CREATE TRIGGER update_inventory
ON order_details
AFTER INSERT
AS
BEGIN
    SET NOCOUNT ON;
    -- Prevents message indicating number of row
affected
    -- by a SQL statement from being returned as part
of the
    -- the result set and messing up results

    UPDATE p
    SET p.stock_quantity = p.stock_quantity -
i.quantity
    FROM products p
    INNER JOIN inserted i ON p.product_id =
i.product_id;
END;
```

```sql
-- MySQL
CREATE TRIGGER update_inventory
AFTER INSERT ON order_details
FOR EACH ROW
```

```
BEGIN
    UPDATE products
    SET stock_quantity = stock_quantity - NEW.quantity
    WHERE product_id = NEW.product_id;
END;
```

This trigger ensures that the inventory is updated in real-time as orders are processed.

- **Trigger for Notification:** Another trigger can be implemented to check the inventory level after each update and send a notification if it falls below a specified threshold:

```
-- SQL Server
CREATE TRIGGER low_inventory_notification
ON products
AFTER UPDATE
AS
BEGIN
    SET NOCOUNT ON;

    IF EXISTS (SELECT 1
                FROM inserted
                WHERE stock_quantity < 10)
    BEGIN
        -- Send notification (e.g., email) to
        -- relevant stakeholders
        -- This action depends on the specific
        -- notification mechanism.
        -- The details of the notification action
        -- may vary based on the database system in use.
    END;
END;
```

```
-- MySQL
CREATE TRIGGER low_inventory_notification
AFTER UPDATE ON products
FOR EACH ROW
BEGIN
    IF NEW.stock_quantity < 10 THEN
        -- Send notification (e.g., email) to
        -- relevant stakeholders
        -- This action depends on the specific
        -- notification mechanism.
        -- The details of the notification action
```

```
                    -- may vary based on the database system in use.
          END IF;
END;
```

This trigger monitors changes to the inventory and triggers a notification if the stock quantity falls below 10 units.

In this way, triggers help automate and enforce specific actions based on database events, ensuring that inventory levels are accurately maintained, and relevant notifications are sent when necessary.

## Best Practices for Data Modification

The quest for efficient and secure data modification practices stands as a cornerstone of database management. This section explores some best practices essential for crafting update queries that are not only efficient but also safeguard the integrity of the database. The following material presents guidelines for writing robust and optimized update queries while steering clear of common pitfalls and potential issues that may arise.

## Crafting Efficient Update Queries

Efficiency lies at the heart of effective data modification. This section explores the art of crafting update queries that optimize performance and resource utilization. Guidelines for utilizing indexes judiciously, leveraging appropriate join strategies, and minimizing unnecessary computations form the foundation. Real-world examples showcase the tangible impact of these practices on the speed and reliability of update operations, providing readers with actionable insights.

# Chapter 6 – Elementary Database Administration Tasks and Concepts

## The Role of the Database Administrator

The Database Administrator (DBA) holds a challenging, multifaceted role in database management. The key responsibilities of this role are wide-ranging, from designing and implementing database structures to monitoring performance, ensuring data security, and devising backup and recovery strategies. The DBA's strategic decisions impact the efficiency, reliability, and accessibility of the database, underscoring their role as stewards of valuable organizational assets. When we consider even a partial list of the responsibilities of the DBA role, it becomes obvious why comprehensive coverage of this topic requires a dedicated textbook in itself:

1. **Database Design and Schema Management**: Designing database schemas, tables, indexes, and relationships to meet application requirements while ensuring data integrity and performance. This includes creating and maintaining views to provide customized data access for applications and users.

2. **Backup and Recovery**: Implementing backup and recovery strategies to protect data against loss or corruption and performing regular backups according to defined schedules.

3. **Security Management**: Setting up user accounts, roles, and permissions to control access to databases and ensuring compliance with security policies and regulations. This involves managing authentication mechanisms, encryption, and auditing.

4. **Performance Tuning and Optimization**: Monitoring database performance, identifying bottlenecks, and optimizing queries, indexes, and configuration settings to improve overall performance and scalability. This includes creating and maintaining indexes to speed up data retrieval and manipulation operations.

5. **Installation and Configuration**: Installing and configuring database software on servers, ensuring optimal performance and security settings.

6. **Monitoring and Alerting**: Implementing monitoring tools and alerts to proactively identify issues such as performance degradation, resource contention, or security breaches, and taking appropriate actions to resolve them.

7. **Capacity Planning and Resource Management**: Forecasting future resource requirements based on growth projections and usage patterns and planning for scalability by provisioning additional hardware or optimizing existing resources.

8. **Patch Management and Upgrades**: Applying patches, hotfixes, and upgrades to the database software to address security vulnerabilities, bugs, and performance improvements while minimizing downtime and impact on production systems.

9. **High Availability and Disaster Recovery**: Configuring and managing high availability solutions such as clustering, replication, or failover mechanisms to ensure uninterrupted access to data in case of hardware failure or disasters.

10. **Database Migration and Consolidation**: Planning and executing migrations of databases between different platforms or versions, as well as consolidating multiple databases onto a single platform for efficiency and cost savings.

11. **Documentation and Knowledge Sharing**: Maintaining documentation of database configurations, procedures, and best practices, and sharing knowledge with team members to ensure consistency and continuity in database management tasks.

12. **Compliance and Governance**: Ensuring compliance with regulatory requirements such as GDPR, HIPAA, or PCI DSS, and implementing policies and procedures to protect sensitive data and maintain data privacy and integrity.

13. **Troubleshooting and Incident Response**: Investigating and resolving database-related issues such as data corruption, performance degradation, or security breaches, and providing timely support to application developers and end-users.

14. **Disaster Recovery Planning and Testing**: Developing and testing disaster recovery plans to ensure business continuity in case of major outages or disasters, and regularly reviewing and updating these plans as needed.

15. **Vendor Management**: Interacting with database software vendors to understand product roadmaps, obtain support and assistance with critical issues, and stay informed about new features and technologies in the database ecosystem.

In this chapter, we will focus on specific aspects of the first four topics from this list, emphasizing practical skills over soft-skills, hands-on exploration, and some of the most common day-to-day tasks of the DBA: provisioning views, elementary database security, performance tuning with indexes, data integrity constraints, user management, backup, and recovery.

---

What is a View?

In SQL databases, a "view" is a virtual table derived from the result set of a **SELECT** query. It doesn't store any data itself but presents data from underlying tables in a structured manner, allowing users to query it as they would a regular table. Views are often used to simplify complex queries, hide sensitive data, or provide a customized perspective on the database for different users. For example, in a company database, a view called *EmployeeDetails* might combine data from the *Employees* and *Departments* tables, providing a convenient way for managers to access relevant employee information without needing to understand the underlying database schema.

## Creating and Dropping Views

DBAs are often called upon to provision and maintain views to facilitate and simplify end-user computing, as views are a useful mechanism to insulate the user of the view from the underlying complexity of the database schema. A view can present the related data from several tables as a single tabular view, very similar to a spreadsheet – a software application with which many users are already familiar and comfortable. Let's explore database views, their significance in simplifying complex queries, and enhancing security. From the syntax for creating and dropping views to real-world use cases, this section surveys the art of leveraging views within SQL databases.

### Syntax for Creating Views

The syntax for creating a view is very similar to a **SELECT** query but prefaced with the **CREATE VIEW** statement. Below is a SQL code example for creating a view called **EmployeeDetails** that combines data from two tables, **Employees** and **Departments**:

```
-- COMMON SQL
CREATE VIEW EmployeeDetails AS
SELECT e.EmployeeID, e.FirstName, e.LastName, e.DepartmentID,
d.DepartmentName
FROM Employees e JOIN Departments d
ON e.DepartmentID = d.DepartmentID;
```

Explanation: This SQL code creates a view named **EmployeeDetails** using the **CREATE VIEW** statement. It selects specific columns from the **Employees** table (**EmployeeID**, **FirstName**, **LastName**, **DepartmentID**) and the **Departments** table (**DepartmentName**), joining them on the **DepartmentID** column to associate each employee with their corresponding department. Once created, users can query the **EmployeeDetails** view as if it were a regular table, simplifying access to employee information combined with department details.

Syntax for Dropping Views

Below is a SQL code example for dropping the *EmployeeDetails* view:

```
-- COMMON SQL
DROP VIEW IF EXISTS EmployeeDetails;
```

Explanation: This SQL code uses the **DROP VIEW** statement to remove the **EmployeeDetails** view from the database. The **IF EXISTS** clause ensures that the view is only dropped if it exists in the database, preventing errors if the view has already been deleted or doesn't exist. While the **IF EXISTS** clause isn't strictly required, its use is a good "defensive programming" strategy, as a script that uses this approach will not stop due to an error if the view has previously been dropped or does not exist for some reason. This statement effectively eliminates the **EmployeeDetails** view, reverting the database to its state before the view was created.

Use Cases for Simplifying Complex Queries

Views serve as invaluable tools for simplifying complex queries and enhancing the efficiency of data retrieval. The following material explores a practical scenario where a view is instrumental. Whether consolidating information from multiple tables, aggregating data, or encapsulating complex joins, views offer a means of abstracting complexity, promoting modular query design, and fostering ease of maintenance.

Let us examine how views can be used to simplify query tasks in a real-world scenario.

View Use-Case Scenario

Consider a database for a university that tracks information about students, courses, and their enrollments. In this scenario, there is a need to simplify queries that involve joining multiple tables to retrieve information about students along with the courses they are enrolled in.

**Problem:**
Writing complex queries involving multiple joins can become cumbersome, especially when frequently retrieving information about students, courses, and their enrollments.

**Solution using a View:**
A view can be created to encapsulate the complex join operations and present a simplified, virtual table to users, making queries more straightforward.
**Create View:**

```
-- COMMON SQL
CREATE VIEW StudentCourseInfo AS
SELECT
  Students.StudentID,
  Students.StudentName,
  Courses.CourseID,
  Courses.CourseName,
  Enrollments.EnrollmentDate
FROM Students
JOIN Enrollments ON Students.StudentID =
Enrollments.StudentID
JOIN Courses ON Enrollments.CourseID = Courses.CourseID;
```

In this example, the **StudentCourseInfo** view combines information from the **Students**, **Courses**, and **Enrollments** tables, simplifying the query process.

**Sample Queries using the View:**

Now, querying information about students and their enrolled courses becomes much simpler using the view:

```
-- COMMON SQL
-- Query 1: Retrieve all students and their enrolled
courses
SELECT *
FROM StudentCourseInfo;

-- Query 2: Find courses in which a specific student is
enrolled
SELECT *
FROM StudentCourseInfo
WHERE StudentID = 123;

-- Query 3: List all students enrolled in a specific
course
SELECT *
FROM StudentCourseInfo
WHERE CourseID = 'CIS-117';
```

These queries are simpler and more intuitive compared to the equivalent queries that would be required without the view. The view encapsulates the complexity of joins and provides a more straightforward way to interact with the data, improving readability and maintainability of SQL queries.

# Chapter 6

# Elementary Database Administration Tasks and Concepts

## Enhancing Security with Views

Security, a paramount concern in database management, finds an ally in the form of views. The scenario below illustrates how views can be strategically employed to enhance data security. By restricting access to sensitive columns, concealing intricate table structures, and enforcing row-level security through views, administrators bolster the protective layers of their databases.

---

Scenario: Implementing Data Security Using a View

In a financial organization, the Database Administrator (DBA) is tasked with implementing security measures to restrict access to sensitive financial data. The DBA decides to create a view that allows only authorized users to access a subset of the data, masking sensitive information while providing necessary insights for reporting purposes.
**SQL Code to Create the View:**

---

```sql
-- COMMON SQL
-- Step 1: Create a table containing sensitive financial data
CREATE TABLE FinancialData (
    CustomerID INT,
    AccountNumber VARCHAR(20),
    Balance DECIMAL(10, 2),
    SSN VARCHAR(11) -- Social Security Number, sensitive
information );

-- Step 2: Populate the FinancialData table with sample data
INSERT INTO FinancialData (CustomerID, AccountNumber, Balance,
SSN)
VALUES
    (1, 'ACC123456', 5000.00, '123-45-6789'),
    (2, 'ACC654321', 7500.00, '987-65-4321'),
    (3, 'ACC987654', 3000.00, '456-78-9123');

-- Step 3: Create a view to restrict access to sensitive SSN
data
CREATE VIEW SecureFinancialView AS
SELECT
    CustomerID,
    AccountNumber,
    Balance
FROM
    FinancialData;
```

Explanation:

1. **Step 1:** The DBA creates a table named *FinancialData* to store sensitive financial information such as *CustomerID*, *AccountNumber*, *Balance*, and *SSN*.
2. **Step 2:** Sample data is inserted into the *FinancialData* table for demonstration purposes.
3. **Step 3:** The DBA creates a view named *SecureFinancialView* to restrict access to sensitive data. The view includes only non-sensitive columns (*CustomerID*, *AccountNumber*, and *Balance*) from the *FinancialData* table, excluding the *SSN* column.

By granting access to *SecureFinancialView* to "low-security" users, and revoking or denying their privilege to access the *FinancialData* table itself, these users can query the *SecureFinancialView*, but will only see non-sensitive information (customer ID, account number, and balance), while the sensitive *SSN* data remains hidden. This helps enforce security and control over data access and modification within the database.

## Working with Views

Let's explore further the practical aspects of working with views: retrieving, filtering, and sorting data.

## Retrieving Data from Views

Querying data from a view is very similar to querying data from a regular table. You can use *SELECT* statements to retrieve data, apply filtering conditions, sort the results, and choose specific fields to display. Below are examples demonstrating these operations on the *EmployeeDetails* view:

*Selecting all fields from the view:*

```
-- COMMON SQL
SELECT *
FROM EmployeeDetails;
```

# Elementary Database Administration Tasks and Concepts

This query retrieves all columns from the **_EmployeeDetails_** view, displaying information about each employee along with their corresponding department details.

*Filtering data from the view:*

```
-- COMMON SQL
SELECT *
FROM EmployeeDetails
WHERE DepartmentName = 'IT';
```

This query filters the data in the **EmployeeDetails** view to only include employees who belong to the IT department. It retrieves all columns for employees within the specified department.

*Sorting data from the view:*

The query defining a view cannot incorporate sorting or the ORDER BY clause, so any desired sorting on a view must be performed by a query against that view.

```
-- COMMON SQL
SELECT *
FROM EmployeeDetails
ORDER BY LastName ASC, FirstName ASC;
```

This query sorts the data in the **EmployeeDetails** view alphabetically by last name, and in case of identical last names, it further sorts by first name in ascending order. It retrieves all columns for all employees, displaying them in the specified order.

*Selecting specific fields from the view:*

```
-- COMMON SQL
SELECT EmployeeID, FirstName, LastName
FROM EmployeeDetails;
```

This query selects only the **EmployeeID**, **FirstName**, and **LastName** fields from the **EmployeeDetails** view, excluding other columns. It retrieves this reduced set of information for all employees.

# Elementary Database Administration Tasks and Concepts

Each of these examples demonstrates how SQL queries can be used to interact with a view just as with a regular table, providing flexibility in retrieving, filtering, and displaying data according to specific requirements.

## Modifying and Manipulating Data in Views

Thus far, we have learned that the SELECT operation on views works essentially the same as it does on tables. But what about INSERT, UPDATE, and DELETE operations on views? These operations are less straightforward where views are concerned.

## INSERTS and Views

Let's first consider the **INSERT** operation on views. Recall our earlier example of defining the **EmployeeDetails** view:

```
-- COMMON SQL
CREATE VIEW EmployeeDetails AS
SELECT e.EmployeeID, e.FirstName, e.LastName, e.DepartmentID,
d.DepartmentName
FROM Employees e
JOIN Departments d
ON e.DepartmentID = d.DepartmentID;
```

Notice that the **DepartmentID** from the **Departments** table is essential to the join, but that this field is not displayed as one of the columns visible in the view. In other words, although it was used in creating the view, it was not *preserved*. Further, notice that **DepartmentID** is the primary *key* of the Departments table. Thinking critically about this, you will realize that if you wish to perform an insert of a new record on the **EmployeeDetails** view, the data must actually be stored in the underlying table or tables of the view, as the view itself contains no data. All the data for the view comes from the underlying tables. Moreover, since the PK for the **Departments** table was not preserved, there is no way for the **INSERT** statement to provide the PK value (which must be unique and non-NULL). We can therefore conclude that **INSERT** operations on a view cannot update a non-*key preserved* constituent table. Even if the PK of all constituent tables is preserved, we may have additional difficulties. For example, imagine that the **Departments** table also contains a field for the department telephone number, **DeptTelNum**, which was not included in the view. Again, it would be impossible to insert a record containing a value for a field of a table not included in the **SELECT** clause of the view.

What about *INSERTS* on views constructed on single tables? Again, a moment's critical thought should lead to the realization that, provided the view is key preserved, an *INSERT* is possible (with the limitation that only the fields enumerated in the *SELECT* clause defining the view are available to receive data; you must be satisfied to allow absent fields to be created in the record with their value set to *NULL*). However, there can still be some quirky situations arising that may prove confusing to users (and even to DBAs)!

Consider the view created by the following code:

```
-- COMMON SQL
CREATE VIEW HiBalCustomer AS
SELECT *
FROM Customer
WHERE CustBalance >= 300;
```

Next, imagine that we execute the following *INSERT* query:

```
-- COMMON SQL
INSERT INTO HiBalCustomer
VALUES (9999, 'Rich', 'Richie', '123 Easy St.', 'Golden Valley',
'CA', 91500, 100.00)
```

However, if we then attempt to run this query:

```
-- COMMON SQL
SELECT * from HiBalCustomer
WHERE CustID = 9999;
```

We obtain no matching results. But, if we run this same query against the base table:

```
-- COMMON SQL
SELECT * from Customer
WHERE CustID = 9999;
```

We obtain the expected result:

| CustID | LName | FName | Address | City | State | Zip | Balance |
|--------|-------|-------|---------|------|-------|-----|---------|
| 9999 | Rich | Richie | 123 Easy St. | Golden Valley | CA | 91500 | 100.00 |

Do you see what happened here?

- The **INSERT** through the view worked correctly, as we would expect for a key-preserved view.
- However, this view filters out customer records with a customer balance of less than $300.
- So, even though this record was successfully inserted through this view, the view's own filter criteria prevents it from selecting the record it just inserted.
- However, running the query against the base table, **Customer**, displays the newly inserted record with no difficulty.

All of this is quite logical and correct, and yet the behavior can be completely baffling to a user (or even a distracted DBA) that does not fully understand it! And so, even though this view *can* be used to update its base table, a prudent User Experience (UX) design might elect not to offer the user the option to update through this view, due to the potential ensuing confusion. Alternatively, the UX design might automatically switch to an unfiltered view or direct use of the base table when a record is inserted. Details like this need to be implemented at the application level (by the application software engineers or programmers), rather than by the DBA on the database end of things.

In light of these considerations, most DBAs choose to avoid attempting to **INSERT** records through views involving joins, and many prefer to avoid performing **INSERTS** through views altogether.

*UPDATES and Views*

**UPDATE** operations have exactly the same limitations as **INSERTS** with respect to views. To summarize:

- An **UPDATE** can only make updates to a key-preserved table
- An **UPDATE** can only modify the values of key-preserved base table fields which are included in the **SELECT** clause of the query that defines the view.
- Updating any value of a field by which the view performs filtering will succeed but may cause the record(s) updated to "disappear" from the result set if the altered value(s) cause the updated record to be filtered out.

To observe this last point in action, consider the following sequence of SQL commands:

```
-- COMMON SQL
SELECT *
FROM HiBalCustomer;

UPDATE HiBalCustomer
SET CustBalance = CustBalance - 600
WHERE CustID = 1021;

SELECT *
FROM HiBalCustomer;
```

The following image shows the initial query results, which include the record for customer number 1021, whose account balance is $896.55.

A payment of $600.00 is then recorded to the account (causing the customer balance to fall below the $300 filter threshold of the view)

A subsequent **SELECT \*** query shows that the updated record has "disappeared:

| | CustID | CustLName | CustFName | CustAddress | CustCity | CustState | CustZip | CustBalance |
|---|---|---|---|---|---|---|---|---|
| 1 | 1014 | Hathaway | Jane | 9313 McBean Ave. | Canyon Country | CA | 91355 | 431.00 |
| 2 | 1018 | Christian | Shirley | 293 Columbus Ave. | Sherman Oaks | CA | 91412 | 535.75 |
| 3 | 1019 | Walters | Noel | 32123 Mobil Ave. | Pacoima | CA | 91403 | 382.00 |
| 4 | 1021 | Newmark | Muriel | 281 N. Main St. | West Hills | CA | 91416 | 896.55 |

| | CustID | CustLName | CustFName | CustAddress | CustCity | CustState | CustZip | CustBalance |
|---|---|---|---|---|---|---|---|---|
| 1 | 1014 | Hathaway | Jane | 9313 McBean Ave. | Canyon Country | CA | 91355 | 431.00 |
| 2 | 1018 | Christian | Shirley | 293 Columbus Ave. | Sherman Oaks | CA | 91412 | 535.75 |
| 3 | 1019 | Walters | Noel | 32123 Mobil Ave. | Pacoima | CA | 91403 | 382.00 |

*Figure 13 – Comparison of SELECT through base table and through view showing "disappearing" data*

*DELETES and Views*

**DELETE** operations have exactly the same limitations as **INSERTS** and **UPDATES** with respect to views. To summarize:

- A **DELETE** can only make deletions on a key-preserved table

- DELETING records from a key-preserved view permanently deletes those record from the base table (remember, all **UPDATE**, **INSERT**, and **DELETE** operations on a view effect the data in the base table, as a view does not have any data of its own!).
- Executing **DELETE** queries against a filtered view can be especially misleading and confusing to the unwary, as the scope of the deletion is limited to the filtered dataset defined by the view.

To understand this last point, consider what would happen if one were to execute the following **DELETE** query:

```
-- COMMON SQL
DELETE
FROM HiBalCustomer
WHERE CustState = 'CA';
```

If one fails to understand the scope of the filtered view, **HiBalCustomer**, one might mistakenly believe that one had deleted all customer records for customers residing in the state of California. In fact, this deletion would NOT delete records for California Customers whose customer account balance is under $300.00, as executing a **SELECT \*** query against the view (rather than the base table) would show that there are no California Customers remaining in the list returned from the **HiBalCustomer** view.

## Summary of Data Modifiable and Data Non-modifiable Views

The ability to **INSERT**, **UPDATE**, or **DELETE** data through a view depends on various factors, and understanding these factors is crucial for effective data management. In general, a view is updatable if it meets certain criteria, and it becomes non-updatable if it violates certain rules. Here are key considerations:

### Data Modifiable Views

Data in views is generally modifiable in these situations:

1. Key preserved single table views - views based on a single underlying table are often inherently updatable.
2. Column-complete views. Views that include all columns from underlying base tables, without any expressions or computations.

3. Views constructed without **DISTINCT**, **GROUP BY**, or **HAVING** clauses: Data in views that involve **DISTINCT**, **GROUP BY**, or **HAVING** clauses are typically non-modifiable.
4. Views created without a **JOIN**, **OUTER JOIN** or **UNION** clause. Views constructed with these clauses may have limited or no ability to modify data in the underlying base tables.

*Data Non-modifiable Views*

Data in views is generally non-modifiable in these situations:

1. Non-key preserved views
2. Fields with aliased names
3. Views omitting fields with **NOT NULL** or other data validation constraints
4. Views involving complex joins, especially outer joins, aggregates, or subqueries
5. Views constructed with **DISTINCT**, **GROUP BY**, or **HAVING** clauses
6. Views containing computed columns
7. Views containing aggregate functions (e.g., **SUM**, **AVG**)
8. Read-Only Views: Views created with the **WITH CHECK OPTION** clause, or views derived from read-only tables or complex queries
9. Views constructed with **JOIN**, **OUTER JOIN**, or **UNION** clauses may have limited or no ability to modify data in the underlying base tables.

It's important for database administrators and developers to be aware of these factors when designing views and to check the updatable status of a view based on the database system being used. Different database management systems may have specific rules and optimizations that impact the updatability of views.

---

## Managing Database Users and Privileges

Management of users and their privileges is a crucial aspect of database administration, and of security. We will explore creating users, deleting users, and granting and revoking user privileges—a nuanced process that empowers administrators to sculpt finely-tailored access permissions. From wielding the **GRANT** and **REVOKE** statements to controlling user permissions for data manipulation and database management, these are key concepts in user access control.

# Elementary Database Administration Tasks and Concepts

## Granular Security

Modern database management systems (DBMS) employ a granular security model to control access to sensitive data at a detailed level. This model allows administrators to define permissions at various levels, including database, table, column, and even row levels. Users or roles can be granted or revoked specific privileges, such as select, insert, update, delete, or execute, on specific objects within the database. Additionally, fine-grained access control mechanisms enable restrictions on viewing certain columns or rows based on user roles or conditions. Auditing and logging features track user activities for security and compliance purposes. Overall, the granular security model ensures that only authorized users have access to the data they need, minimizing the risk of unauthorized access or data breaches.

## The Power of GRANT and REVOKE Statements

The *Grant* and *Revoke* statements are essential features of modern database management systems (DBMS), facilitating the control and management of user privileges and access rights. *Grant* allows administrators to explicitly grant specific permissions, such as *select*, *insert*, *update*, *delete*, or *execute*, to users or roles on various database objects, including databases, tables, views, and procedures. This statement empowers administrators to define who can perform certain actions on specific data within the database. Conversely, *Revoke* enables administrators to revoke previously granted permissions from users or roles, restricting their access to database objects. Together, *Grant* and *Revoke* statements form the backbone of access control mechanisms in DBMS, ensuring data security and integrity by precisely managing user privileges.

## A User and Privilege Management Scenario

Let's explore user creation and privilege management via a simple business scenario. Because these processes are similar, but not identical across different DBMS systems, the scenario will present solutions for both MySQL and SQL Server (Transact SQL).

*Privileges Scenario: A Finance Manager account and Information Worker account*

In this scenario, we'll walk through the process of creating two users, "Pat" – a Finance Manager and "Ruby" -- an Information Worker, in both MySQL and Transact-SQL (T-SQL). We'll grant and revoke privileges to these users to control their access to the *Employee* table, with specific restrictions on certain fields. Finally, we'll demonstrate how to delete the "Ruby" user account.

## MySQL

### Creating Users

```
-- Creating users
CREATE USER 'Pat'@'localhost' IDENTIFIED BY ' Hard2Gue55';
CREATE USER 'Ruby'@'localhost' IDENTIFIED BY ' mine15TOO';
```

### Granting Privileges

```
-- Granting privileges to Pat
GRANT ALL PRIVILEGES
ON database_myDB.Employee
TO 'Pat'@'localhost';

-- Granting limited privileges to Ruby
GRANT SELECT (FirstName, LastName, Position)
ON database_myDB.Employee
TO 'Ruby'@'localhost';
```

### Revoking Privileges

```
-- Revoking specific privileges from Ruby
REVOKE SELECT (SSN, Salary)
ON database_myDB.Employee
FROM 'Ruby'@'localhost';
```

### Deleting User

```
-- Deleting user Ruby
DROP USER 'Ruby'@'localhost';
```

## Transact-SQL (T-SQL)

### Creating Users

```
-- Creating users
CREATE LOGIN Pat WITH PASSWORD = 'Hard2Gue55';
CREATE LOGIN Ruby WITH PASSWORD = 'mine15TOO';
```

**Creating Database User Mappings**

```
-- Creating user mappings
USE database_myDB;
CREATE USER Pat FOR LOGIN Pat;
CREATE USER Ruby FOR LOGIN Ruby;
```

**Granting Privileges**

```
-- Granting privileges to Pat
GRANT SELECT, INSERT, UPDATE, DELETE ON Employee TO Pat;

-- Granting limited privileges to Ruby
GRANT SELECT (FirstName, LastName, Position) ON Employee TO
Ruby;
```

**Revoking Privileges**

```
-- Revoking specific privileges from Ruby
DENY SELECT (SSN, Salary) ON Employee TO Ruby;
```

**Deleting User**

```
-- Deleting Ruby Infoworker user DROP USER Ruby;
```

**Summary**

- **Creating Users**: We create the users "Pat" and "Ruby" with their respective passwords.

- **Granting Privileges**: Pat is granted full privileges on the Employee table, while Ruby is granted only select privileges on specific columns.

- **Revoking Privileges**: We revoke the select privilege on sensitive columns from Ruby.

- **Deleting User**: Finally, we delete the user Ruby from the database.

By following these steps, you can effectively manage user access and permissions in both MySQL and Transact-SQL databases, ensuring data security and integrity.

# Chapter 6

Understanding Indexes

Of all the things a DBA can do to improve the performance of a database system, building useful indexes is among the most potent. Let's explore why. First consider what the query optimizer must do if no useful index is available. Let's imagine that we have one million records, represented by their ordinal position in a list:

**One Million Records**
1 2 3 ... 999998 999999 1000000

*Figure 14 - modelling a list of one million records.*

Let's further imagine that the data we are searching for resides in the record which happens to fall very last in this list. With no other recourse, the query optimizer will resort to a table scan. A table scan is simply a search in which the computer starts at the first record in the list and compares the value it is seeking with the value of the specified field in each record in turn. In this situation, our luck has been as bad as it could be – we must compare the target field value in each of the one million records, until we finally find the one we are seeking, in the very last row. Due to the inelegant, mindlessness of this approach, a table scan is sometimes referred to as a "brute force" search, or a "needle-in-a-haystack" search.

Now, the chances that our luck would be this bad are only one-in-a-million. With the best possible luck, we would have found the record we were seeking in the very first position. Alas, our chances of having luck this good are also one-in-a-million. Even without rigorous mathematical proof, we can intuitively discern that half of the time a record we are seeking will fall within the first 500,000 rows, and half of the time it will fall in the second 500,000 rows. So, on average, we can expect to have to scan 500,000 rows to find the record we seek (or go through the entire one million rows to determine that there is no matching record!).

Can we do better? Indeed, we can! Would you believe that, for a list of 1,000,000 records, we can find the record we are seeking, or prove that the record is not in the database, with not more than 21 tries? That sounds like a pretty far-fetched claim, doesn't it? But it's true – *if* we have the right index. Imagine we have a table of one million records, and each record contains a field named ***word*** which contains four lower-case letters:

*Table 1 – A record set viewed in its native (arbitrary) row order.*

| Record # | word |
|---|---|
| 1 | jgvu |
| 2 | blsj |
| 3 | nlob |
| … | … |
| 999997 | ylps |
| 999998 | tdyn |
| 999999 | pokk |
| 1000000 | wjwe |

We want to find the record containing the **word** "xxxx". It's just our bad luck that this record isn't found in the table, but our very good fortune that there is an index available on the **word** field. This index lets us search through the table on the sorted word list, instead of row-by-row from first to last, as if the table were ordered this way:

*Table 2 – a record set viewed in its indexed order, using index on the **word** field.*

| Record # | word |
|---|---|
| 2 | blsj |
| 1 | jgvu |
| 3 | nlob |
| … | … |
| 999999 | pokk |
| 999998 | tdyn |
| 1000000 | wjwe |
| 999997 | ylps |

*(Be honest: when you noticed the words are now arranged in alphabetic order, your eyes jumped toward the bottom of the list to see if "xxxx" was there, didn't they? Your eyes intuitively understand the power of an ordered or indexed list!)*

Equipped with this index, here is how the query optimizer might (using an algorithm known as the *binary search algorithm*) construct a query that determines the value "xxxx" is not found in the **word** field of this table in only twenty-one steps. On each try, the query optimizer will go to the middle of the list of remaining records to be searched, and compare the record found there with the value we are seeking: "xxxx". If the record compared is alphabetically less than "xxxx", it will discard the first half of the list, and repeat this process with the second half of the list. If the record compared is alphabetically greater than "xxxx", it would discard the second half of the list, and continue with the first half of the list. (If the value of the word field found at the tested record was equal to "xxxx", we would have found the record, and would stop, but in this case the value "xxxx" doesn't exist in the list). Here is a summary of how this search would proceed:

1.  Test the middle record from the whole list (1,000,000 items to start with)
2.  Test the middle record from 1/2 of the list (500,000 items)
3.  Test the middle record from 1/4 of the list (250,000 items)
4.  Test the middle record from 1/8 of the list (125,000 items)
5.  Test the middle record from 1/16 of the list (62,500 items)
6.  Test the middle record from 1/32 of the list (31,250 items)
7.  Test the middle record from 1/64 of the list (15,625 items)
8.  Test the middle record from 1/128 of the list (7,812 items)
9.  Test the middle record from 1/256 of the list (3,906 items)
10. Test the middle record from 1/512 of the list (1,953 items)
11. Test the middle record from 1/1024 of the list (976 items)
12. Test the middle record from 1/2048 of the list (488 items)
13. Test the middle record from 1/4096 of the list (244 items)
14. Test the middle record from 1/8192 of the list (122 items)
15. Test the middle record from 1/16348 of the list (61 items)
16. Test the middle record from 1/32768 of the list (30 items)
17. Test the middle record from 1/ 65536 of the list (15 items)
18. Test the middle record from 1/131072 of the list (7 items)
19. Test the middle record from 1/262144 of the list (3 items)
20. Test the middle record from 1/524288 of the list (1 items)
21. Test that last item. In this case, it does not match, so we know that "xxxx" is not found in the list!

Let's sum things up:

- Without an index, average comparisons needed to find something the list contains: 500,000 (for a list of 1,000,000 records), or 1,000,000 if it's not in the list.
- With an index: No more than 21 steps to either find the record, or prove the item is not in the list.

Let's see that again, as a ratio: Indexed Search vs. Table Scan of 1,000,000 records:

**21 vs. 500,000**

While there are many complex factors contributing to the total query processing time, an indexed search, which takes 21/500,000 the time (in other words, performs more than 23,000 times better!) is going to be much faster than a raw table scan. This gives rise to the notion of "query cost" as a useful idea. While the exact amount of time a query will take will vary from data set to data set, and from one set of hardware and software to another, it is clear that a lower query cost means improved performance, and a high query cost means degraded performance. The query cost can be calculated from the query execution plan, and DBMS systems such as MySQL and SQL Server typically provide report of query costs using built-in utilities that report or "explain" the query execution plan. Examples include the ***EXPLAIN*** command (MySQL), and the "Display Estimated Execution Plan" and "Include Actual Execution Plan" controls in SQL Server Management Studio.

The figure below shows a comparison of a simple SELECT query with WHERE filter on a table containing 100,000 records, with and without a usable index:

*Table 3 - Comparing Query Cost: table scan vs. index lookup.*

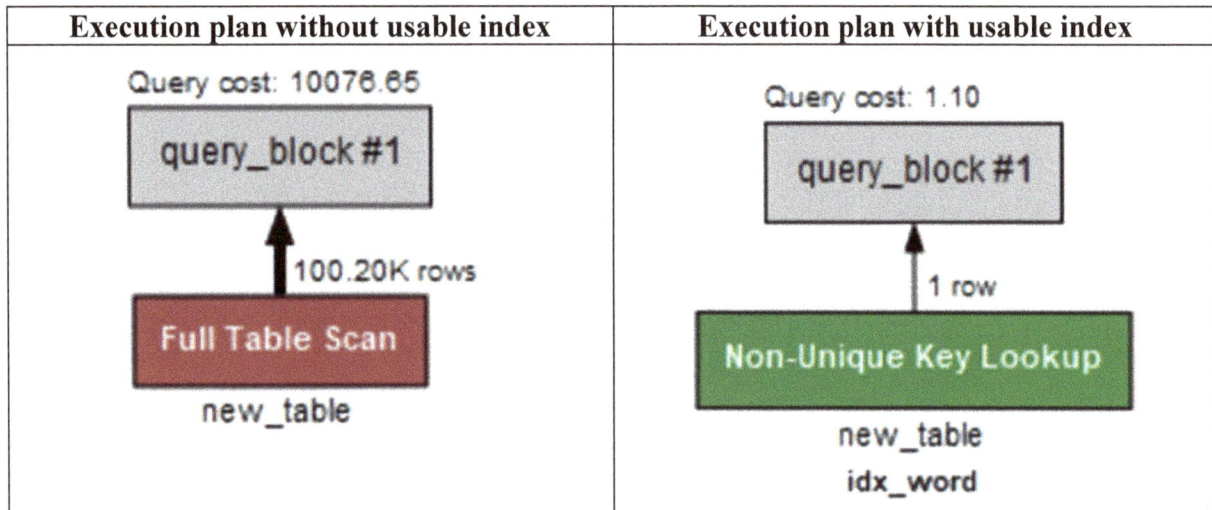

| Execution plan without usable index | Execution plan with usable index |
|---|---|
| Query cost: 10076.65 <br><br> query_block #1 <br><br> ↑ 100.20K rows <br><br> Full Table Scan <br><br> new_table | Query cost: 1.10 <br><br> query_block #1 <br><br> ↑ 1 row <br><br> Non-Unique Key Lookup <br><br> new_table <br> idx_word |

Indexes Are Not Free

Given that the benefits to performance can be so tremendous, you might be wondering why we don't just index everything? The problem here is that indexes come at a cost. For one thing, indexes perform at their best when they fit, and can be kept in RAM while the database is running. But RAM is more costly, and more limited in most computer architectures, than secondary storage (hard disk or solid-state disk). Consequently, it is impractical to have all our indexes completely loaded into RAM, if we simply index everything. And, though a non-RAM resident index may still perform better than a raw table scan, there is another cost to consider. Indexes must be updated each and every time that the indexed field(s) change in any way. Add a new record? You need to update all effected indexes. Delete an old record? Once again, it's time to update the indexes. Update a data value in a field? You guessed it – you need to update the indexes again. So, as you can imagine, a prudent DBA must balance the considerations of the benefits of a particular index, and the costs, in terms of both commitment of scarce RAM resources, for optimal performance, and the "performance tax" imposed by the need to frequently update each index. While the intricacies of this subject deserve an entire textbook to themselves (and many such books on database tuning and optimization have been written), Some of the most common strategies are fairly straightforward. One very common strategy is to examine the database logs to identify: 1) especially slow-running queries; and 2) very frequently executed queries. Each of these are obvious areas wherein optimization is likely to be both fruitful and cost-effective. Next, the DBA will analyze the performance of these queries to determine if additional or different indexes would likely improve performance, and then conduct tests to confirm and to quantify the improvement. This effort is typically informed by the database's query optimizer itself, which is usually capable of reporting the "query execution plan". The query execution plan is the program that the query optimizer generates in building the actual programmatic steps to be run in producing the result set described by the query's SQL code.

## Types of Indexes and Their Uses

SQL Database Management Systems support a variety of index types, and each is necessary or optimal in different use-cases. The material which follows provides a useful survey of index types and their uses.

### *Unique Index*

A unique index ensures that the values in the indexed column(s) are unique across the table, meaning no two rows can have the same value for the indexed column(s). This constraint guarantees data integrity by preventing the insertion of duplicate values into the indexed column(s).

Unique indexes are commonly used in two scenarios:

1. **Primary Key Constraint**: In many databases, a primary key is a unique identifier for each row in a table. A primary key constraint ensures that each row has a unique value in the specified column(s) or set of columns. Under the hood, a primary key constraint typically creates a unique index on the specified column(s) to enforce uniqueness. Primary keys are essential for uniquely identifying rows in a table and are often used as the basis for relationships between tables in a relational database schema.

2. **Non-Primary Key Fields**: Unique indexes can also be applied to columns that are not part of the primary key. In this case, the unique constraint ensures that the values in the indexed column(s) are unique across the table, but these columns are not necessarily the primary key of the table. Non-primary key unique indexes are useful when there's a business requirement for certain columns to contain unique values, even if they are not the primary means of identifying rows.

# Elementary Database Administration Tasks and Concepts

Here's an example scenario to illustrate the use of a unique index in a non-primary key situation:

Suppose you have a *Users* table in a database that tracks users' information, including their email addresses. While the primary key of the *Users* table might be an auto-incrementing *user_id*, you also want to ensure that each user's email address is unique to prevent multiple users from registering with the same email. In this case, you would create a unique index on the *email* column to enforce this constraint:

```
-- SQL SERVER
CREATE TABLE Users
(
  user_id INT IDENTITY(1,1) PRIMARY KEY,
  username VARCHAR(50),
  email VARCHAR(100) UNIQUE, -- Unique index on email column
  password VARCHAR(100)
  -- Other columns
);
```

```
-- MySQL
CREATE TABLE Users
(
  user_id INT PRIMARY KEY AUTO_INCREMENT,
  username VARCHAR(50),
  email VARCHAR(100) UNIQUE, -- Unique index on email column
  password VARCHAR(100)
  -- Other columns
);
```

In the above SQL statement, the *UNIQUE* constraint on the *email* column ensures that each email address stored in the *Users* table is unique. This unique constraint is implemented internally as a unique index on the *email* column. As a result, attempts to insert or update a row with a duplicate email address will be rejected by the database, maintaining data integrity.

*Composite Index*

A composite index, also known as a multi-column index or composite key, is an index created on multiple columns in a table. Unlike single-column indexes, which are created on a single column, composite indexes are created on two or more columns. This allows for more efficient querying when filtering, sorting, or joining based on multiple columns.

**Benefits of Composite Indexes:**

1. **Improved Query Performance**: Composite indexes can significantly improve query performance for queries that involve filtering, sorting, or joining based on multiple columns. By indexing multiple columns together, the database can quickly locate the relevant rows without having to perform a full table scan.

2. **Covering Indexes**: Composite indexes can serve as covering indexes for queries, where all the columns needed for a query are included in the index. This allows the database to satisfy the query entirely from the index without accessing the underlying table, leading to improved query performance.

3. **Reduced Disk Space**: While composite indexes index multiple columns, they often require less disk space compared to creating separate indexes on each individual column. This can lead to better disk space utilization and less overhead in index maintenance.

**Limitations of Composite Indexes:**

1. **Index Size**: Composite indexes can become larger in size compared to single-column indexes, especially when indexing multiple large columns. This may lead to increased storage requirements and slower index updates.

2. **Query Specificity**: Composite indexes are most effective for queries that use the indexed columns together in the *WHERE*, *ORDER BY*, or *JOIN* clauses. Queries that do not utilize all columns in the composite index may not benefit from the index.

3. **Index Maintenance Overhead**: Composite indexes require additional maintenance overhead compared to single-column indexes, especially when data in the indexed columns is frequently updated, inserted, or deleted.

**Example Use-Case Scenario:**

Suppose you have a *Sales* table in a database that stores information about sales transactions, including the *product_id*, *customer_id*, and *transaction_date*. You frequently query the table to retrieve sales data for a specific product within a certain date range. In this scenario, creating a composite index on the *product_id* and *transaction_date* columns can improve query performance.

Here's how you can create a composite index for this use-case scenario:

```
-- COMMON SQL
CREATE INDEX idx_product_transaction_date
ON Sales (product_id, transaction_date);
```

The above SQL statement creates a composite index named ***idx_product_transaction_date*** on the ***product_id*** and ***transaction_date*** columns of the ***Sales*** table. This composite index can efficiently handle queries that filter sales data based on the ***product_id*** and ***transaction_date***, providing improved query performance for such use cases.

*Covering Index*

As mentioned briefly in the discussion of composite indexes, a covering index is usually a composite index that includes all the columns needed to satisfy a query, allowing the database to fulfill the query's requirements directly from the index without accessing the underlying table (the exception would technically be a query on an indexed field that only needs to return that field, in which case the simple index on that single field is, in fact, a covering index). In other words, a covering index "covers" the query by providing all the necessary data, eliminating the need for the database to perform additional lookups in the table itself. This can lead to significant performance improvements, especially for queries that involve retrieving a subset of columns from a table. In essence, if all the fields required by a query are "covered" by the index, it may be unnecessary to consult the table at all, allowing the query to execute more efficiently.

**Benefits of Covering Indexes:**

1. **Improved Query Performance**: Covering indexes can significantly improve query performance by reducing the need for disk I/O operations. Since the index contains all the columns required by the query, the database engine can retrieve the necessary data directly from the index without accessing the table, resulting in faster query execution.

2. **Reduced Disk I/O**: By eliminating the need to access the underlying table, covering indexes can reduce disk I/O operations, leading to faster data retrieval and improved overall system performance, particularly for queries that access large datasets.

3. **Minimized Lock Contention**: Covering indexes can help minimize lock contention by reducing the time data pages are locked during query execution. This can improve concurrency and scalability in multi-user environments where multiple transactions may be accessing the same data concurrently.

**Limitations of Covering Indexes:**

1. **Index Size**: Covering indexes may be larger in size compared to traditional indexes, especially when including multiple columns. This can increase storage requirements and index maintenance overhead, particularly for tables with a large number of columns or frequently updated data.

2. **Index Maintenance Overhead**: Adding additional columns to an index increases the index maintenance overhead, as the database engine needs to update the index whenever

the indexed columns are modified. This can impact the performance of write operations, such as inserts, updates, and deletes.

3. **Query Specificity**: Covering indexes are most effective for queries that retrieve a specific subset of columns from a table. Queries that require a large number of columns or involve complex filtering conditions may not benefit from covering indexes.

**Example Use-Case Scenario:**

Suppose you have a *Products* table in a database that stores information about products, including their *product_id*, *name*, *price*, and *category*. You frequently run queries to retrieve the names and prices of products within a specific category. In this scenario, creating a covering index on the *category*, *name*, and *price* columns can improve query performance.

Here's how you can create a covering index for this use-case scenario:

```
-- COMMON SQL
CREATE INDEX idx_covering_products_category_name_price
ON Products (category, name, price);
```

The above SQL statement creates a covering index named *idx_covering_products_category_name_price* on the *category*, *name*, and *price* columns of the *Products* table. This covering index includes all the columns needed to satisfy queries that retrieve product names and prices within a specific category, allowing for efficient query execution without accessing the underlying table.

*Other Index Types*

We have so far discussed unique indexes, composite indexes, and covering indexes, which are common to both MySQL and SQL server database systems. However, there are numerous additional index types, which vary from system to system, and which have special purposes and/or superior performance characteristics in different use cases. Examples include index types such as spatial indexes, useful in Geographic Information Systems (GIS), and Columnstore indexes, which are special in-memory indexes that work well in data warehousing applications, and which can offer 10x query performance and 7x data compression, but which are intended for use with read-only queries and data. As this text focuses, to the extent possible, upon a non-proprietary/non-vendor centric treatment of topics, and moreover its intent is to serve as an *introduction* to SQL programming, we will defer deeper discussion of this worthy topic to other textbooks, other than to underscore their existence and importance, and to refer the reader to the documentation for their chosen DBMS system(s). Familiarity and fluency with the indexing technologies available in the database engines in one's care is essential to the professional DBA.

# Elementary Database Administration Tasks and Concepts

Dropping Indexes

Dropping an index in SQL databases involves removing the index definition from the database schema. This operation removes the index entirely, including any associated metadata and data structures, such as B-tree or hash structures used to organize and store the index data.

Here's how you can drop an index in SQL:

```
-- COMMON SQL
DROP INDEX index_name ON table_name;
```

In the above SQL statement:

- **DROP INDEX** is the command used to drop an index.

- **index_name** is the name of the index you want to drop.

- **table_name** is the name of the table on which the index is defined.

For example, to drop an index named **idx_product_category** from the **Products** table:

```
-- COMMON SQL
DROP INDEX idx_product_category ON Products;
```

**Common Reasons to Drop an Index:**

1. **Unused Indexes**: Indexes that are no longer being used by queries can consume storage space and add overhead to data modification operations (e.g., inserts, updates, deletes). Dropping unused indexes can help reduce storage requirements and improve overall database performance.

2. **Redundant Indexes**: Sometimes, multiple indexes are created on the same set of columns or provide redundant coverage for query patterns. Redundant indexes can waste resources and slow down data modification operations. Dropping redundant indexes can streamline index maintenance and improve query performance.

3. **Performance Optimization**: In some cases, dropping an index that is not being used or is inefficiently designed can lead to better query performance. For example, if a query is using a less selective index or if a covering index is not providing significant performance benefits, dropping the index may improve overall query execution times.

4. **Database Migration or Restructuring**: During database migrations or schema restructuring, certain indexes may become obsolete or unnecessary. Dropping such indexes can help simplify the database schema and reduce maintenance overhead.

5. **Temporary Indexes**: In some scenarios, temporary indexes may be created for specific tasks or queries. Once the task is completed or the query optimization is no longer needed, dropping the temporary index can free up resources and improve database performance.

6. **Space Management**: In environments with limited storage resources, dropping unnecessary indexes can help reclaim disk space and optimize storage utilization.

It's essential for database administrators (DBAs) to periodically review and evaluate the indexes in their databases to ensure they are serving their intended purposes efficiently. Dropping unnecessary or unused indexes is a common maintenance task performed by DBAs to optimize database performance and resource utilization. However, caution should be exercised to avoid dropping critical indexes that are still necessary for query performance.

---

Displaying and Retrieving Database Metadata in SQL

The ability to explore and understand the structure of your database is as crucial as crafting the data itself. This section introduces the tasks of displaying database and table definitions, querying system catalogs for metadata retrieval, utilizing both ANSI SQL standards-compliant (cross-platform) and DBMS vendor/dialect-proprietary commands to reveal table structures, and retrieving essential information about indexes, constraints, and keys. A reference comparing SQL Server and MySQL system catalog commands is provided in Appendix H.

What is Metadata?

In the context of a SQL database, metadata refers to data that provides information about other data within the database. It describes the structure, organization, and properties of the database objects, such as tables, columns, indexes, constraints, and stored procedures. Metadata plays a crucial role in managing and understanding the database schema, ensuring data integrity, and facilitating efficient query execution.

Common examples of metadata in a SQL database include:

1. **Table Metadata:** Information about tables, such as the table name, column names, data types, constraints (e.g., primary keys, foreign keys), and indexes.
2. **Column Metadata:** Details about individual columns within a table, including the column name, data type, size, constraints, and any other properties.
3. **Index Metadata:** Information about indexes, such as the indexed columns, uniqueness, and the type of index (e.g., clustered or non-clustered).
4. **Constraint Metadata:** Details about constraints defined on tables, such as primary key constraints, foreign key constraints, check constraints, etc.
5. **View Metadata:** Information about views, including the underlying query, columns, and any related constraints.
6. **Procedure and Function Metadata:** Information about stored procedures and functions, such as their names, parameters, and code.
7. **User Metadata:** Details about database users, roles, and permissions, including who has access to specific objects and what actions they are allowed to perform.
8. **Database Metadata:** General information about the database itself, such as its name, version, owner, and creation date.

SQL databases often provide system tables or views that store this metadata, and users can query these tables to retrieve information about the database schema and its objects. This metadata is essential for database administrators, developers, and analysts to understand the structure of the database and to interact with it effectively.

System Catalogs and Metadata: An Analogy

Imagine exploring the card catalog of a library with books neatly organized on shelves, each with a title, author, and genre tag. The library's card catalog is like a "book about the books", in the same way that the metadata in a database is like "data about the data". To effectively use the library, the ability to examine these tags and get a sense of what's available is vital. Similarly, in the realm of SQL databases, knowing how to retrieve and display metadata is fundamental for database management and development.

# Chapter 6

Understanding ANSI SQL Standards and System Catalogs:

The American National Standards Institute (ANSI) SQL standards lay down guidelines and specifications for relational databases, ensuring a common syntax and semantics across various implementations. When it comes to system catalogs, ANSI SQL defines a standardized way to access metadata, promoting consistency and ease of use across different database platforms. This means that it is possible for you to use the same SQL code to interrogate the system catalog of different ANSI-compliant databases, even though the underlying proprietary implementation of these different database engines my differ radically from one another.

System catalogs typically include tables containing metadata about the database schema, such as information about tables, views, columns, indexes, privileges, and constraints. By querying these catalogs, users and applications can dynamically retrieve information about the database structure without relying on vendor-specific commands or interfaces.

## Information_Schema Views: Features and Limitations

One of the key components of ANSI SQL standards for accessing system catalogs is the **information_schema** schema, which contains a set of read-only views providing metadata about the database objects. These views offer a standardized way to query metadata, irrespective of the underlying database management system.

**Features:**

1. **Standardized Interface: information_schema** views provide a uniform interface for querying metadata across different database platforms, ensuring portability and interoperability.

2. **Comprehensive Metadata:** These views offer a wide range of metadata, including information about tables, columns, indexes, constraints, privileges, and more, allowing users to gather comprehensive insights into the database schema.

3. **Simple Query Syntax:** Querying **information_schema** views involves using standard SQL syntax, making it easy for developers and administrators to retrieve metadata without needing to learn vendor-specific commands.

4. **Dynamic Updates: information_schema** views reflect real-time changes to the database schema, ensuring that users always access the latest metadata.

**Limitations:**

1. **Limited Scope:** While **information_schema** views provide essential metadata about the database schema, they may not cover all aspects of system catalogs. Some database-specific features or extensions may not be accessible through these views.

2. **Performance Overhead:** Querying **information_schema** views can sometimes incur a performance overhead, especially in large databases, as the metadata is dynamically generated at query time.

3. **Vendor-Specific Extensions:** Despite the standardized interface, vendors may introduce proprietary extensions or optimizations that are not supported by **information_schema** views, limiting their universality in certain scenarios.

## Vendor-Neutral Approach to Accessing System Catalogs:

To ensure a vendor-neutral approach to accessing system catalogs, developers and administrators can leverage **information_schema** views alongside vendor-specific catalog queries. By using **information_schema** views as the primary interface for metadata retrieval and supplementing them with vendor-specific queries for specialized requirements, users can achieve a balance between standardization and flexibility.

Additionally, some third-party tools and libraries provide abstraction layers that abstract away the differences between various database platforms, offering a unified interface for interacting with system catalogs. These tools often utilize **information_schema** views as the foundation for cross-platform compatibility while providing additional functionalities for specific use cases.

In the author's experience, while the unified approach and compatibility afforded by the provisioning of an ANSI-compatible information_schema schema is important and useful, there are areas of performance, completeness, and proprietary detail where it is essential to learn and utilize proprietary functions and stored procedures (e.g. "catalog stored procedures") unique to the DBMS engine being used. Specifically, neither MySQL nor Microsoft SQL Server are exceptions to this.

## Querying System Catalogs

SQL databases maintain a treasure trove of metadata about database objects like tables, columns, indexes, and constraints. This metadata is stored in system catalogs or data dictionaries. Querying these catalogs provides invaluable information about the database structure.

# Chapter 6

*System Catalog Commands: SQL Server vs. MySQL*

The design and details of the DBMS system catalog vary from database engine to database engine, so it is not surprising that the SQL commands and functions provided by a given DBMS for viewing and interrogating the system catalogs also varies. A quick reference listing equivalent frequently used system catalog commands for SQL Server DBMS and MySQL DBMS is found in Appendix H.

*Example of ANSI-Standard System Catalog Queries*

Let's examine some examples exploring system catalogs using an ANSI-Standard approach. These queries will produce materially identical results on different DBMS systems such as Microsoft SQL Server and MySQL. For instance, you can retrieve a list of all tables in a database named ***kandee*** using a query like:

```
-- COMMON SQL
SELECT table_name
FROM information_schema.tables
WHERE table_schema = 'kandee';
```

This query accesses the ***information_schema*** catalog, which contains metadata about tables, and returns the following results, irrespective of whether the DBMS being queried is SQL Server or MySQL:

| table_name |
|---|
| client |
| manufacturer |
| orderprod |
| orders |
| product |
| salesagent |

Similarly, we can retrieve the column metadata for the ***kandee.client*** table using this query, which will work across ANSI SQL-compliant databases:

```
-- COMMON SQL
SELECT COLUMN_NAME, DATA_TYPE, CHARACTER_MAXIMUM_LENGTH,
IS_NULLABLE
FROM INFORMATION_SCHEMA.COLUMNS
WHERE TABLE_SCHEMA = 'kandee' and
```

```
TABLE_NAME = 'client'
order by COLUMN_NAME;
```

This code generates the following results:

| COLUMN_NAME | DATA_TYPE | CHARACTER_MAXIMUM_LENGTH | IS_NULLABLE |
|---|---|---|---|
| Balance | decimal | NULL | YES |
| City | nchar | 15 | YES |
| ClientName | nchar | 35 | NO |
| ClientNum | nchar | 6 | NO |
| CreditLimit | decimal | NULL | YES |
| PostalCode | nchar | 5 | YES |
| SalesAgentNum | nchar | 4 | YES |
| State | nchar | 2 | YES |
| Street | nchar | 20 | YES |

*Example of Proprietary System Catalog Queries*

Let's contrast the ANSI SQL/vendor-neutral catalog queries above with proprietary commands for SQL Server and MySQL. For example, in SQL Server we can obtain the same column metadata as above, along with much, much more by using the SQL Server catalog stored procedure, ***sp_help***:

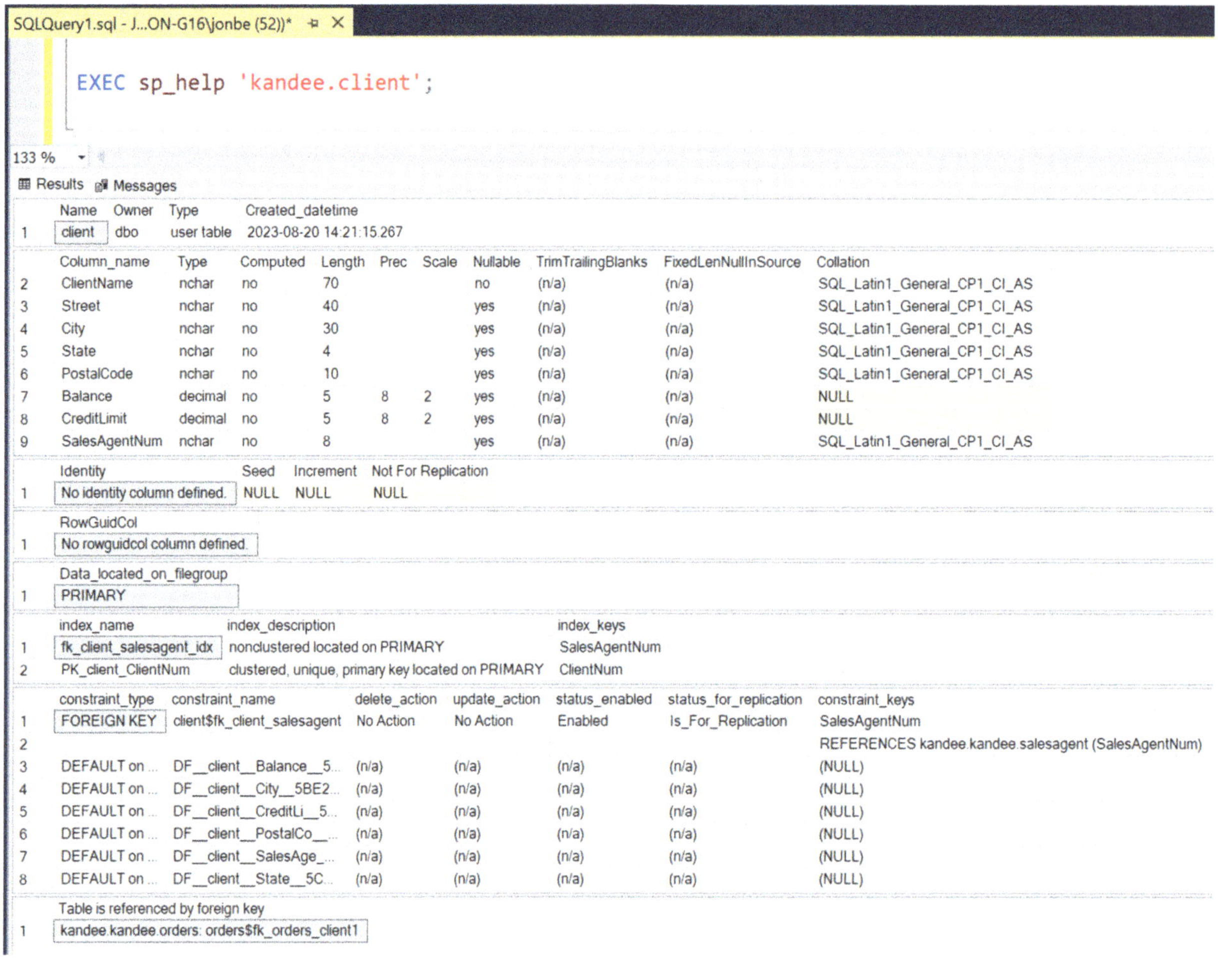
SQLQuery1.sql - J...ON-G16\jonbe (52))*

```
EXEC sp_help 'kandee.client';
```

133 %

Results | Messages

| | Name | Owner | Type | Created_datetime |
|---|---|---|---|---|
| 1 | client | dbo | user table | 2023-08-20 14:21:15.267 |

| | Column_name | Type | Computed | Length | Prec | Scale | Nullable | TrimTrailingBlanks | FixedLenNullInSource | Collation |
|---|---|---|---|---|---|---|---|---|---|---|
| 2 | ClientName | nchar | no | 70 | | | no | (n/a) | (n/a) | SQL_Latin1_General_CP1_CI_AS |
| 3 | Street | nchar | no | 40 | | | yes | (n/a) | (n/a) | SQL_Latin1_General_CP1_CI_AS |
| 4 | City | nchar | no | 30 | | | yes | (n/a) | (n/a) | SQL_Latin1_General_CP1_CI_AS |
| 5 | State | nchar | no | 4 | | | yes | (n/a) | (n/a) | SQL_Latin1_General_CP1_CI_AS |
| 6 | PostalCode | nchar | no | 10 | | | yes | (n/a) | (n/a) | SQL_Latin1_General_CP1_CI_AS |
| 7 | Balance | decimal | no | 5 | 8 | 2 | yes | (n/a) | (n/a) | NULL |
| 8 | CreditLimit | decimal | no | 5 | 8 | 2 | yes | (n/a) | (n/a) | NULL |
| 9 | SalesAgentNum | nchar | no | 8 | | | yes | (n/a) | (n/a) | SQL_Latin1_General_CP1_CI_AS |

| | Identity | Seed | Increment | Not For Replication |
|---|---|---|---|---|
| 1 | No identity column defined. | NULL | NULL | NULL |

| | RowGuidCol |
|---|---|
| 1 | No rowguidcol column defined. |

| | Data_located_on_filegroup |
|---|---|
| 1 | PRIMARY |

| | index_name | index_description | index_keys |
|---|---|---|---|
| 1 | fk_client_salesagent_idx | nonclustered located on PRIMARY | SalesAgentNum |
| 2 | PK_client_ClientNum | clustered, unique, primary key located on PRIMARY | ClientNum |

| | constraint_type | constraint_name | delete_action | update_action | status_enabled | status_for_replication | constraint_keys |
|---|---|---|---|---|---|---|---|
| 1 | FOREIGN KEY | client$fk_client_salesagent | No Action | No Action | Enabled | Is_For_Replication | SalesAgentNum |
| 2 | | | | | | | REFERENCES kandee.kandee.salesagent (SalesAgentNum) |
| 3 | DEFAULT on ... | DF__client__Balance__5... | (n/a) | (n/a) | (n/a) | (n/a) | (NULL) |
| 4 | DEFAULT on ... | DF__client__City__5BE2... | (n/a) | (n/a) | (n/a) | (n/a) | (NULL) |
| 5 | DEFAULT on ... | DF__client__CreditLi__5... | (n/a) | (n/a) | (n/a) | (n/a) | (NULL) |
| 6 | DEFAULT on ... | DF__client__PostalCo__... | (n/a) | (n/a) | (n/a) | (n/a) | (NULL) |
| 7 | DEFAULT on ... | DF__client__SalesAge__... | (n/a) | (n/a) | (n/a) | (n/a) | (NULL) |
| 8 | DEFAULT on ... | DF__client__State__5C... | (n/a) | (n/a) | (n/a) | (n/a) | (NULL) |

| | Table is referenced by foreign key |
|---|---|
| 1 | kandee.kandee.orders: orders$fk_orders_client1 |

*Figure 15 - Example of sp_help execution.*

Similarly, MySQL implements the DESCRIBE (DESC) and SHOW commands, which may be used to retrieve column metadata from a MySQL schema:

- ***DESCRIBE Command***:

```
-- MySQL
DESC kandee.client;
```

- ***SHOW Command***:

```
-- MySQL
SHOW COLUMNS FROM kandee.client;
```

Either of these commands yield the following results, providing information about the columns, their data types, and any constraints applied:

| | Field | Type | Null | Key | Default | Extra |
|---|---|---|---|---|---|---|
| ▶ | ClientNum | char(6) | NO | PRI | NULL | |
| | ClientName | char(35) | NO | | NULL | |
| | Street | char(20) | YES | | NULL | |
| | City | char(15) | YES | | NULL | |
| | State | char(2) | YES | | NULL | |
| | PostalCode | char(5) | YES | | NULL | |
| | Balance | decimal(8,2) | YES | | NULL | |
| | CreditLimit | decimal(8,2) | YES | | NULL | |
| | SalesAgentNum | char(4) | YES | MUL | NULL | |

*Figure 16 - DESCRIBE command results*

*Retrieving Index, Constraint, and Key Information*

Indexes, constraints, and keys are the backbone of a well-structured database, and understanding their details is vital. SQL provides mechanisms to retrieve this information programmatically.

- ***Indexes***:

To retrieve index information for a table, you can query system catalogs. For example, to list all indexes on the ***kandee.client*** table (MySQL):

```
-- MySQL
SHOW INDEX FROM kandee.client
```

Or (SQL Server):

```
-- SQL SERVER
sp_helpindex 'kandee.client';
```

# Chapter 6

- ***Constraints***:

To retrieve constraint information, you can query the ***information_schema***. To find all primary key constraints on a table:

```sql
-- COMMON SQL
SELECT constraint_name
FROM information_schema.table_constraints
WHERE table_name = 'Employees' AND
constraint_type = 'PRIMARY KEY';
```

- ***Keys***:

Keys, including primary and foreign keys, are crucial for maintaining data integrity. You can use queries to extract this information. To find foreign keys in a table (MySQL):

```sql
-- MySQL
SELECT constraint_name AS foreign_key_name,
table_name as parent_table, column_name as parent_column,
referenced_table_name as referenced_table,
referenced_column_name as referenced_column
FROM information_schema.key_column_usage
WHERE table_name = 'client' AND constraint_name LIKE 'fk%';
```

Or (SQL Server):

```sql
-- SQL SERVER
SELECT fk.name AS foreign_key_name,
OBJECT_NAME(fk.parent_object_id) AS parent_table,
COL_NAME(fkc.parent_object_id, fkc.parent_column_id) AS
parent_column,
OBJECT_NAME(fk.referenced_object_id) AS referenced_table,
COL_NAME(fkc.referenced_object_id, fkc.referenced_column_id) AS
referenced_column
FROM sys.foreign_keys AS fk
INNER JOIN sys.foreign_key_columns AS fkc
ON fk.object_id = fkc.constraint_object_id
WHERE OBJECT_NAME(fk.parent_object_id) = 'client';
```

*Final Thoughts on Querying Metadata*

The ANSI SQL standards pertaining to system catalogs and the **information_schema** views play a vital role in promoting interoperability and standardization in the world of relational databases. By adhering to these standards and adopting a vendor-neutral approach to accessing system catalogs, developers and administrators can ensure compatibility across different database platforms while retaining the flexibility to leverage vendor-specific features when needed. However, the **Information_schema** views implemented by vendors in their proprietary DBMS engines may not address desired performance nor provide insight into proprietary parameters, configuration and tuning options, and other elements essential to the DBA's tuning and operation of the database. Consequently, a DBA should expect to spend time and effort in learning the important proprietary aspects of the DBMS engines for which they are responsible. That said, in an era of increasing data proliferation and heterogeneous environments, a standardized approach to metadata access remains essential for seamless data management and application development.

---

Data Integrity and Constraints:

Effective data integrity controls ensure the reliability, accuracy, and consistency of the information stored within databases. We will discuss the concept of data integrity and the pivotal role played by integrity constraints—such as primary keys, foreign keys, unique constraints, and check constraints—in fortifying the database ecosystem. Through exploration, examples, and practical insights, readers will gain the knowledge needed to uphold data quality and prevent the infiltration of invalid data.

Understanding Data Integrity

Data integrity encompasses the trustworthiness and accuracy of data within a database. At its core, data integrity ensures that information remains consistent, coherent, and valid throughout its lifecycle. This section explores the importance of data integrity, emphasizing its role in fostering confidence among users, promoting accurate decision-making, and ensuring the long-term reliability of the database.

# Chapter 6

Integrity Constraints: Guardians of Consistency

Integrity constraints emerge as the guardians of data consistency, acting as rules that govern the permissible state of the database. This section introduces the key types of integrity constraints—primary key, foreign key, unique constraint, and check constraint—and elucidates their individual roles in maintaining the integrity of the database.

## Primary Key Constraint

The primary key constraint serves as a unique identifier for each record in a table, ensuring that no two records share the same key value. This section explores the significance of primary keys in establishing data uniqueness and provides examples that showcase how primary key constraints prevent duplicate and null values, reinforcing the integrity of the data.

## Foreign Key Constraint

Foreign key constraints establish relationships between tables, ensuring referential integrity. This section delves into the importance of foreign keys in maintaining the consistency of relationships between tables. Examples illustrate how foreign key constraints prevent the creation of orphaned records and enforce the coherence of data across related tables.

## Unique Constraint

The unique constraint ensures that values in a particular column or a combination of columns are unique across the table. This section explores how unique constraints prevent the duplication of data, fostering data consistency and accuracy. Practical examples showcase scenarios where unique constraints act as guardians against redundant information.

Consider a scenario where we have a table named employees with columns for employee information, including *employee_id*, *first_name*, and *last_name*. We want to ensure that combinations of *first_name* and *last_name* are unique. Here's an example of how you can use a unique constraint to achieve this:

```
-- COMMON SQL
-- Creating the employees table with a
```

```
-- Unique Constraint on first_name and last_name
CREATE TABLE employees (
    employee_id INT PRIMARY KEY,
    first_name VARCHAR(50),
    last_name VARCHAR(50),
    -- Adding a Unique Constraint on the combination of
    -- first_name and last_name
    CONSTRAINT unique_name_combination UNIQUE (first_name,
    last_name)
);

-- Inserting some sample data
INSERT INTO employees (employee_id, first_name, last_name)
VALUES
(1, 'John', 'Doe'),
(2, 'Jane', 'Smith'),
(3, 'John', 'Doe'); -- This insert would violate the
                    -- Unique Constraint

-- Attempting to insert data that violates the
-- Unique Constraint will result in an error
-- The constraint ensures that combinations of
-- first_name and last_name are unique
```

In this example:

- The employees table has three columns: *employee_id*, *first_name*, and *last_name*.
- The CONSTRAINT *unique_name_combination UNIQUE (first_name, last_name)* part specifies a unique constraint named *unique_name_combination* on the combination of *first_name* and *last_name*.
- The *INSERT INTO* statements demonstrate the insertion of data into the table. The third insert attempts to insert a duplicate combination of 'John' and 'Doe', which would violate the unique constraint and result in an error.

This unique constraint ensures that no two rows in the employees table can have the same combination of *first_name* and *last_name*. It's a powerful mechanism to maintain data integrity and prevent the insertion of duplicate information in specific columns or combinations of columns.

Check Constraint

Check constraints provide a mechanism for validating data based on specific conditions. This section navigates through the versatility of check constraints, illustrating how they prevent the insertion of invalid data into a table. Real-world examples showcase the role of check constraints in enforcing domain-specific rules and enhancing data quality.

Let's consider a scenario where we have a table named orders with a column for order quantities (quantity). We want to ensure that the quantity is always greater than zero. We can use a check constraint to enforce this condition. Here's an example:

```sql
-- COMMON SQL
-- Creating the orders table with a Check Constraint
-- on the quantity column
CREATE TABLE orders (
    order_id INT PRIMARY KEY,
    product_name VARCHAR(100),
    quantity INT,
    -- Adding a Check Constraint to ensure quantity is
    -- greater than zero
    CONSTRAINT check_quantity_positive CHECK (quantity > 0)
);

-- Inserting some sample data
INSERT INTO orders (order_id, product_name, quantity) VALUES
(1, 'Product A', 5),
(2, 'Product B', 10),
(3, 'Product C', -2); -- This insert would violate the
                      -- Check Constraint

-- Attempting to insert data that violates the
-- Check Constraint will result in an error
-- The constraint ensures that quantity is always
-- greater than zero
```

In this example:

- The orders table has three columns: *order_id*, *product_name*, and *quantity*.
- The *CONSTRAINT check_quantity_positive CHECK (quantity > 0)* part specifies a check constraint named *check_quantity_positive* on the quantity column, ensuring that the quantity is always greater than zero.

- The **INSERT INTO** statements demonstrate the insertion of data into the table. The third insert attempts to insert a negative quantity, which would violate the check constraint and result in an error.

This check constraint ensures that only values greater than zero can be inserted into the quantity column. It serves as a mechanism to enforce specific conditions on the data being inserted or updated, contributing to data quality and integrity.

## Ensuring Data Quality through Constraints

Integrity constraints collectively contribute to ensuring data quality. By preventing the introduction of inconsistent, duplicate, or invalid data, constraints serve as proactive measures that fortify the database against potential pitfalls. Best practices and considerations provide a roadmap for implementing constraints effectively in diverse database scenarios.

In the dynamic landscape of SQL databases, the concept of data integrity and the strategic application of integrity constraints stand as pillars in the pursuit of a reliable and consistent data ecosystem.

---

## Enforcing Referential Integrity

Enforcing referential integrity is a crucial task to ensure the consistency and coherence of relationships between tables. The deployment of foreign key constraints plays an important role in maintaining referential integrity. By exploring the role of foreign keys and delving into practical examples, you will strengthen your knowledge of constructing an effective framework of referential integrity controls.

## Understanding Referential Integrity

Referential integrity is a fundamental concept that governs the relationships between tables in a relational database. It ensures that relationships between tables remain valid and consistent, preventing scenarios where references to non-existent records or orphaned records could compromise the integrity of the database.

## Role of Foreign Key Constraints

# Chapter 6

Foreign key constraints emerge as the guardians of referential integrity. A foreign key is a field in a table that matches the primary key of another table, establishing a link between the two. The foreign key constraint serves as a set of rules that dictate how changes to the referenced table (the table with the primary key) are handled concerning the referencing table (the table with the foreign key).

Enforcing Referential Integrity with Foreign Keys

Let's consider an example to illustrate how foreign keys enforce referential integrity:

```
-- COMMON SQL
-- Creating the departments table
CREATE TABLE departments (
    department_id INT PRIMARY KEY,
    department_name VARCHAR(50)
);

-- Creating the employees table with a foreign key constraint
CREATE TABLE employees (
    employee_id INT PRIMARY KEY,
    employee_name VARCHAR(50),
    department_id INT,
    -- Adding a foreign key constraint referencing
    -- the departments table
    CONSTRAINT fk_department FOREIGN KEY (department_id)
    REFERENCES departments(department_id)
    ON DELETE CASCADE
    ON UPDATE CASCADE
);

-- Inserting some sample data
INSERT INTO departments (department_id, department_name) VALUES
(1, 'HR'),
(2, 'IT');

INSERT INTO employees
(employee_id, employee_name, department_id) VALUES
(101, 'Alice', 1),
(102, 'Bob', 2),
(103, 'Charlie', 1);
```

```
-- Attempting to insert data that violates
-- referential integrity will result in an error
-- The foreign key constraint ensures that department_id
-- in employees references a valid department_id in departments

-- Updating or deleting records in the referenced table triggers
actions defined in the foreign key constraint
```

In this example:

- The *departments* table contains information about different departments, with *department_id* as the primary key.
- The *employees* table has a foreign key constraint (*fk_department*) on the *department_id* column, referencing the *departments* table.
- The *ON DELETE CASCADE and ON UPDATE CASCADE* clauses specify actions to take if referenced records are deleted or updated. In this case, if a department is deleted or its *department_id* is updated, the corresponding changes are cascaded to the *employees* table.

Handling Actions on Delete or Update of Referenced Records

Foreign key constraints allow you to define actions to take when referenced records are deleted or updated. Common actions include:

- *CASCADE*: If a referenced record is deleted or updated, the changes are propagated to the referencing table.
- *SET NULL*: If a referenced record is deleted or updated, the foreign key columns in the referencing table are set to NULL.
- *SET DEFAULT*: Similar to SET NULL but sets the foreign key columns to their default values.
- *NO ACTION / RESTRICT*: Prevents the deletion or update of referenced records if there are dependent rows in the referencing table.

It's important to carefully choose the appropriate action based on the specific requirements and business logic of your application.

Enforcing referential integrity through foreign key constraints not only maintains data relationships but also contributes to the overall reliability and coherence of the database. As stewards of relational harmony, foreign keys play a pivotal role in upholding the integrity of the interconnected tables within the database ecosystem.

---

## Managing Database Security

Managing database security is a task of paramount importance, akin to fortifying a digital fortress against potential threats and vulnerabilities. This section introduces key topics and considerations essential to effective database security practice.

## Understanding Database Security

Database security encompasses a comprehensive set of measures designed to protect data from unauthorized access, manipulation, or destruction. It involves safeguarding the confidentiality, integrity, and availability of data, ensuring that only authorized users can interact with the database and perform specific actions.

## Security Considerations and Best Practices

- ***Authentication and Authorization***: Rigorous authentication mechanisms ensure that users are who they claim to be, while authorization defines the level of access granted to authenticated users. Best practices involve employing strong authentication methods and employing the principle of least privilege to restrict access based on roles and responsibilities.
- ***Encryption***: Encryption plays a pivotal role in securing data both in transit and at rest. Utilizing technologies like SSL/TLS for data in transit and Transparent Data Encryption (TDE) for data at rest adds an additional layer of protection.
- ***Regular Software Updates***: Keeping database software and associated systems up to date with the latest security patches is critical. Regularly applying patches and updates helps mitigate vulnerabilities and enhances the overall security posture.
- ***Auditing and Monitoring***: Robust auditing mechanisms allow organizations to track and review user activities. Monitoring tools provide real-time insights into potential security threats, enabling proactive responses to suspicious behavior.

# Elementary Database Administration Tasks and Concepts

## Auditing User Activities

- ***Database Auditing***: Enabling database auditing captures a trail of user activities, including logins, queries, modifications, and access attempts. This audit trail serves as a valuable resource for forensic analysis and compliance requirements.
- ***Log Management***: Effective log management involves the secure storage, retention, and analysis of audit logs. Utilizing dedicated log management solutions helps centralize log data and facilitates timely detection of anomalies or security incidents.

## Implementing Security Measures

- ***Firewalls and Network Security***: Configuring firewalls and implementing network security measures ensure that only authorized connections are permitted to access the database. Utilizing Virtual Private Networks (VPNs) and secure network protocols adds an additional layer of defense.
- ***Database Security Features***: Leveraging built-in database security features, such as role-based access control (RBAC), row-level security, and fine-grained access controls, enables administrators to finely tune access permissions and restrictions.
- ***Penetration Testing***: Regularly conducting penetration testing allows organizations to proactively identify vulnerabilities by simulating real-world attacks. Addressing the findings from penetration tests strengthens the database security posture.

## Continual Improvement and Training

Database security is an ever-evolving discipline. Continual improvement requires a sustained training and communications campaign in order to stay abreast of emerging threats, adopt new security technologies, and ensure security awareness of a well-trained community of database administrators and users. Security awareness programs ensure that all stakeholders are cognizant of security best practices and potential risks.

---

## Backup and Recovery

In professional database practice, the tasks of backup and recovery stand out as guardians of data resilience—shielding the digital fortress from the unforeseen storms of data loss and system failures. This section discusses database backup and recovery strategies, providing guiding principles for students and practitioners seeking to fortify the database ecosystem against potential disasters. We will survey key principles of full backups, incremental backups, and the orchestration of recovery plans.

Understanding Database Backup and Recovery

At its core, database backup involves creating copies of critical data, ensuring that in the face of adversity, a resilient system can be restored to a point of operational integrity. Recovery, on the other hand, is the orchestrated process of restoring the database to a valid and consistent state following a failure or data loss event.

Database Backup Strategies

- Full Backups: A full backup captures the entirety of the database, providing a comprehensive snapshot of the data at a specific point in time. Full backups serve as the foundation for recovery, offering a complete dataset to restore the database in its entirety.
- Incremental Backups: Incremental backups focus on capturing only the changes made since the last backup. These changes, often referred to as the database's delta, are smaller in size compared to full backups, leading to more efficient storage usage. Incremental backups are essential for reducing backup times and conserving resources.
- Differential Backups: Differential backups capture the changes made since the last full backup. Unlike incremental backups, which consider changes since the last backup (whether full or incremental), differential backups specifically focus on changes since the last full backup. While larger than incremental backups, differential backups are generally smaller than full backups.

Orchestration of Backup Strategies

- **Regular Scheduling:** Establishing a regular backup schedule is imperative. Full backups, depending on the criticality of the data, may be scheduled less frequently than incremental or differential backups. Consistent scheduling ensures that backup copies remain current and reliable.
- **Storage Considerations**: Choosing an appropriate storage solution for backups is critical. Whether leveraging on-premises storage solutions, cloud storage services, or a combination of both, the selected storage solution should align with the organization's recovery time objectives (RTO) and recovery point objectives (RPO).

- ***Testing Backups***: Regularly testing backups ensures their validity and recoverability. Conducting recovery drills helps verify the effectiveness of backup strategies, allowing organizations to identify and address potential issues before they become critical.

Database Recovery Strategies

- ***Point-in-Time Recovery***: Point-in-time recovery allows administrators to restore the database to a specific moment in time. This is crucial for scenarios where data corruption or errors need to be rolled back to a precise state, minimizing data loss.
- ***Rollback and Rollforward Operations***: Rollback operations involve undoing changes made since a specific point in time, reverting the database to a prior state. Conversely, rollforward operations apply changes from a given point in time to bring the database to a desired state. These operations are pivotal for fine-tuning the recovery process.
- ***Transaction Log Management***: Transaction logs play a pivotal role in recovery strategies. Regularly backing up transaction logs enables point-in-time recovery and provides a granular view of changes made to the database.

Best Practices for Backup and Recovery

- ***Offsite Backups***: Storing backups in an offsite location safeguards against the loss of data due to disasters affecting the primary data center.
- ***Versioning Backups***: Implementing versioning for backups allows for the retention of multiple historical backup copies. This facilitates the selection of specific backup points for recovery, addressing diverse recovery scenarios.
- ***Monitoring and Alerts***: Establishing monitoring mechanisms and alerts for backup and recovery processes ensures timely identification and resolution of issues. Proactive monitoring contributes to the overall reliability of backup and recovery strategies.

Mastering the tasks of backup and recovery is foundational to ensuring data resilience and operational continuity. By embracing best practices and leveraging strategic approaches, administrators and practitioners fortify the pillars of data resilience, ensuring that the digital fortress remains impervious to the unforeseen challenges that may arise.

---

# Chapter 6

Ensuring optimal performance of the database is a ranking priority for Database Administrators. Let us discuss some common practices that DBAs utilize in their performance analysis efforts.

## Monitoring and Analysis

To begin with, DBAs rely heavily on performance monitoring tools. Leading SQL database management systems include at least elementary tools to help address this, and the marketplace is crowded with additional offerings. Some examples of commonly used tools include SQL Server Profiler, which allows for the tracing of SQL Server events, and Dynamic Management Views (DMVs), which provide real-time insights into server health and performance. Additionally, DBAs will typically also develop a level of expertise in native Operating System monitoring tools, or partner with Systems Administrators in order to keep an eye on hardware resource usage. The Perfmon performance monitor built into Windows systems on one example; Linux administrators accomplish similar monitoring using command-line tools such as top, htop, vmstat, mpstat, and others, or use third-party consoles for this. Popular comprehensive monitoring systems include third-party tools such as SolarWinds Database Performance Analyzer, Redgate SQL Monitor, and New Relic.

When it comes to analyzing query performance, execution plans are invaluable. They reveal how SQL Server executes queries, highlighting inefficient operations. The Query Store feature is another critical tool, storing historical query execution data to assist in diagnosing performance issues. Moreover, Extended Events offer a lightweight monitoring system for tracking detailed system and application events.

As previously discussed, index analysis is another vital aspect of performance monitoring. By examining index usage statistics, DBAs can identify missing, unused, or inefficient indexes. Fragmentation analysis is also crucial, as it helps detect and address index fragmentation, ensuring that indexes operate optimally.

## Optimization Techniques

Query optimization is a core strategy in performance enhancement. DBAs often rewrite poorly constructed queries to improve efficiency. Addressing parameter sniffing issues, where SQL Server's parameter sniffing leads to suboptimal query plans, is another common task. Additionally, optimizing joins and subqueries can significantly enhance query performance.

Index optimization is equally important. This involves creating new indexes or dropping unnecessary ones based on analysis. Regular maintenance, such as rebuilding or reorganizing fragmented indexes, is essential to keep the database running smoothly.

## Resource Management

Effective memory management is crucial for database performance. Monitoring the buffer pool ensures sufficient memory allocation for caching data pages, while managing query workspace memory helps in handling sorting and hashing operations efficiently.

CPU and disk I/O management also play a significant role. By analyzing CPU usage, DBAs can identify and mitigate CPU-intensive operations. Similarly, monitoring and optimizing disk I/O operations helps in reducing bottlenecks and improving overall performance.

**Configuration and Maintenance**

Proper database configuration is fundamental to performance. Configuring database and storage system parameters (for example, TempDB in SQL Server) correctly is vital, as these components can profoundly enhance or degrade overall DBMS performance. Setting appropriate values for threads, processes, and similar elements that control the degree of query parallelism, such as SQL Server's Max Degree of Parallelism (MAXDOP) setting ensures that queries are executed with the right level of parallelism for a given systems size, load, and hardware resources.

Regular maintenance tasks are necessary to keep the database in top condition. For example, updating statistics helps in maintaining accurate query optimization data. Regularly running utilities that identify and fix corruption issues aid in ensuring database integrity. Additionally, testing backup and recovery processes is critical to guarantee that backups are performed regularly and can be restored quickly in case of failures.

**Diagnostics and Troubleshooting**

Identifying and resolving blocking and deadlocks is another key diagnostic task. Monitoring for blocking issues helps in pinpointing long-running blockages, while tools like SQL Servers SQL Server Profiler or Extended Events can capture and analyze deadlocks.

Wait statistics analysis is another crucial diagnostic activity. By examining wait types, such as PAGEIOLATCH or LCK_M_X, DBAs can determine the causes of performance bottlenecks and take appropriate action.

**Capacity Planning and Scaling**

Capacity planning is essential for anticipating future needs. Analyzing data growth trends allows DBAs to plan for storage and performance requirements proactively. Resource forecasting helps in predicting future demands based on usage patterns.

Scaling strategies are employed to handle increased loads. Vertical scaling involves upgrading hardware resources, such as CPU and memory, while horizontal scaling includes implementing sharding or partitioning to distribute load across multiple servers.

By undertaking these comprehensive tasks and strategies, DBAs can effectively analyze and optimize SQL database performance, ensuring that the systems they manage run efficiently and reliably. This multifaceted approach not only enhances performance but also ensures the integrity and security of the database environment.

# Chapter 7 – Introduction to SQL Functions and Procedures

## Introduction to SQL Functions and Procedures

Functions and procedures are indispensable tools in SQL programming, elevating the art of data manipulation and query capabilities. This section unveils the essence of SQL functions and procedures, exploring their roles in streamlining operations, enhancing query flexibility, and empowering practitioners to wield the full potential of the database ecosystem. As has been mentioned previously, you will find a convenient reference of commonly used SQL Server functions in Appendix A, and a reference of commonly used MySQL functions in Appendix B.

## SQL Functions

SQL functions are powerful constructs that encapsulate logic to perform specific operations on data, returning results based on input parameters. These functions can be categorized into two types: built-in functions provided by the database system and user-defined functions created by developers.

## Roles of SQL Functions

- Data Transformation: Functions excel in transforming data, enabling operations like string manipulation, date formatting, and mathematical calculations. For example:

```
-- COMMON SQL
-- Using the CONCAT function to concatenate strings
SELECT CONCAT(first_name, ' ', last_name) AS full_name
FROM employees;
```

- Aggregation: Functions play a pivotal role in aggregating data, summarizing information through functions like SUM, AVG, COUNT, MIN, and MAX. For example:

```
-- COMMON SQL
-- Using the AVG function to calculate the average salary
SELECT AVG(salary) AS average_salary
FROM employees;
```

- Date Manipulation: Functions simplify date-related operations, allowing for tasks such as extracting components, formatting, and arithmetic. For example:

```
-- SQL SERVER
-- Using the DATEADD function to add 7 days to the hire date
SELECT employee_id, hire_date, DATEADD(day, 7, hire_date) AS
new_hire_date
FROM employees;
```

```
-- MySQL
-- Using the DATEADD function to add 7 days to the hire date
SELECT employee_id, hire_date,
       DATE_ADD(hire_date, INTERVAL 7 DAY) AS new_hire_date
FROM employees;
```

Introduction to SQL Procedures

SQL procedures, also known as stored procedures, are precompiled and stored sets of one or more SQL statements that can be executed as a single unit. They enhance code modularity, reusability, and security by encapsulating logic on the server side.

Roles of SQL Procedures

- Code Modularity: Procedures promote modular programming by encapsulating specific functionalities within a named unit. This enhances code organization and readability.
- Transaction Management: Procedures facilitate transaction management by allowing multiple SQL statements to be executed as a single unit, ensuring atomicity, consistency, isolation, and durability (ACID properties).
- Enhanced Security: Procedures contribute to enhanced security by allowing controlled access to data and operations. Users can execute a procedure without direct access to underlying tables.

# Introduction to SQL Functions and Procedures

SQL Functions and Procedures Examples:

- **User-Defined Function**

```
-- SQL SERVER
-- Creating a user-defined function to calculate
-- the square of a number
CREATE FUNCTION CalculateSquare(@num INT)
RETURNS INT
AS
BEGIN
    RETURN @num * @num;
END;


-- Using the user-defined function
SELECT CalculateSquare(5) AS square_result;
```

```
-- MySQL
-- Creating a user-defined function to calculate
-- the square of a number
DELIMITER $$

CREATE FUNCTION CalculateSquare(num INT)
RETURNS INT
DETERMINISTIC
BEGIN
    RETURN num * num;
END$$

DELIMITER ;

-- Using the user-defined function
SELECT CalculateSquare(5) AS square_result;
```

- **Stored Procedure**

```
-- SQL SERVER
-- Creating a stored procedure to update employee salaries
-- by a percentage
CREATE PROCEDURE UpdateSalaries(@percentage DECIMAL)
AS
```

```
BEGIN
    UPDATE employees
    SET salary = salary * (1 + @percentage / 100);
END;

-- Executing the stored procedure
EXEC UpdateSalaries 10;
```

```
-- MySQL
-- Creating a stored procedure to update employee salaries
-- by a percentage
DELIMITER $$

CREATE PROCEDURE UpdateSalaries(IN percentage DECIMAL(5,2))
BEGIN
    UPDATE employees
    SET Salaries = Salaries * (1 + percentage / 100);
END$$

DELIMITER ;

-- Executing the stored procedure
CALL UpdateSalaries(10);
```

Enhancing Query Capabilities with Functions and Procedures

- Dynamic Queries with Functions

```
-- SQL SERVER
-- Using the CONCAT function to dynamically
-- construct SQL queries
DECLARE @column_name VARCHAR(50) = 'first_name';
DECLARE @query NVARCHAR(MAX);
SET @query = 'SELECT ' + @column_name + ' FROM employees;';
EXEC sp_executesql @query;
```

```
-- MySQL
-- Using the CONCAT function to dynamically
-- construct SQL queries
SET @column_name = 'first_name';
```

```
SET @query = CONCAT('SELECT ', @column_name, ' FROM
employees');
PREPARE stmt FROM @query;
EXECUTE stmt;
DEALLOCATE PREPARE stmt;
```

- Complex Operations with Procedures

```
-- SQL SERVER
-- Creating a procedure to calculate bonus based on
-- department performance
CREATE PROCEDURE CalculateBonus
AS
BEGIN
    DECLARE @total_sales DECIMAL;
    SELECT @total_sales = SUM(sales_amount) FROM sales;

    UPDATE employees
    SET bonus = salary * 0.1
    WHERE department_id = 1 AND sales > @total_sales;
END;
```

```
-- MySQL
-- Creating a procedure to calculate bonus based on
-- department performance
DELIMITER $$

CREATE PROCEDURE CalculateBonus()
BEGIN
    DECLARE total_sales DECIMAL(10,2);

    -- Assigning the sum of sales_amount to total_sales
variable
    SELECT SUM(sales_amount) INTO total_sales FROM sales;

    -- Updating employees' bonus
    UPDATE employees
    SET bonus = salary * 0.1
    WHERE department_id = 1 AND sales > total_sales;
END$$

DELIMITER ;
```

# Chapter 7

## Row Functions and Aggregate Functions

Row functions and aggregate functions are crucial in SQL programming because they allow for powerful data manipulation and analysis. Row functions perform operations on individual rows, enabling tasks such as data transformation, formatting, and extraction of specific values. Aggregate functions, on the other hand, summarize data across multiple rows, providing essential calculations like sums, averages, counts, and other statistical measures. Together, these functions enhance SQL's capability to efficiently handle and derive meaningful insights from large datasets.

## Introduction to Row Functions

Row functions, often referred to as scalar functions or single-row functions, operate on individual rows of data, transforming or manipulating values within each row independently. These functions allow for intricate data transformations, enhancing the flexibility of query results.

## Using Row Functions for Data Transformation

- String Functions:

```
-- COMMON SQL
-- Using the UPPER function to convert names to uppercase
SELECT UPPER(first_name) AS upper_case_name
FROM employees;
```

- Mathematical Functions:

```
-- COMMON SQL
-- Using the ROUND function to round salary values
SELECT employee_id, salary, ROUND(salary, 2) AS rounded_salary
FROM employees;
```

- Date Functions:

```
-- SQL SERVER
-- Using the DATEDIFF function to calculate the tenure
-- of employees in years
```

```
SELECT employee_id, hire_date, DATEDIFF(year, hire_date,
GETDATE()) AS tenure_years
FROM employees;
```

```
-- MySQL
-- Using the TIMESTAMPDIFF function to calculate the tenure
-- of employees in years
SELECT employee_id, hire_date, TIMESTAMPDIFF(YEAR, hire_date,
CURDATE()) AS tenure_years
FROM employees;
```

Introduction to Aggregate Functions

Aggregate functions, in contrast, operate on sets of rows, summarizing or aggregating values across multiple rows. These functions are pivotal for gaining insights into data distributions and deriving meaningful summaries.

Utilizing Aggregate Functions for Summarizing Data

- SUM Function:

```
-- COMMON SQL
-- Using the SUM function to calculate total sales
SELECT department_id, SUM(sales_amount) AS total_sales
FROM sales
GROUP BY department_id;
```

- AVG Function:

```
-- COMMON SQL
-- Using the AVG function to calculate average salary
-- by department
SELECT department_id, AVG(salary) AS average_salary
FROM employees
GROUP BY department_id;
```

# Chapter 7

- COUNT Function:

```
-- COMMON SQL
-- Using the COUNT function to count the number of employees
-- in each department
SELECT department_id, COUNT(employee_id) AS employee_count
FROM employees
GROUP BY department_id;
```

Differentiating Between Row and Aggregate Functions

- Scope of Operation:
  - Row functions operate on individual rows independently.
  - Aggregate functions operate on sets of rows, summarizing or aggregating values.
- Usage with GROUP BY:
  - Row functions can be used without the GROUP BY clause.
  - Aggregate functions often require the GROUP BY clause to specify the grouping criteria.
- Result Cardinality:
  - Row functions return a value for each row in the result set.
  - Aggregate functions return a single value or a set of values summarizing the entire group.

Row and Aggregate Functions Examples:

- Row Function

```
-- COMMON SQL
-- Using the CONCAT function to concatenate
-- first and last names
SELECT CONCAT(first_name, ' ', last_name) AS full_name
FROM employees;
```

- Aggregate Function

```
-- COMMON SQL
-- Using the MAX function to find the highest salary
-- in each department
SELECT department_id, MAX(salary) AS highest_salary
FROM employees
GROUP BY department_id;
```

# Introduction to SQL Functions and Procedures

Creating Row and Aggregate Functions:

Next, let's explore the SQL code needed to create these functions.

Syntax and Steps to Create User-Defined Row Functions

- Syntax:

```
-- SQL SERVER
CREATE FUNCTION function_name (@parameter1 data_type,
@parameter2 data_type, ...)
RETURNS return_type
AS
BEGIN
    -- Function logic
    RETURN result;
END;
```

```
-- MySQL
DELIMITER $$

CREATE FUNCTION function_name (parameter1 data_type,
parameter2 data_type, ...)
RETURNS return_type
DETERMINISTIC
BEGIN
    -- Function logic
    RETURN result;
END$$

DELIMITER ;
```

- Steps:
    - Create the Function:

```
-- SQL SERVER
CREATE FUNCTION CalculateTax(@salary DECIMAL)
RETURNS DECIMAL
AS
```

```
BEGIN
    DECLARE @tax DECIMAL;
    SET @tax = @salary * 0.1; -- Assuming a flat 10% tax
rate
    RETURN @tax;
END;
```

```
-- MySQL
DELIMITER $$

CREATE FUNCTION CalculateTax(salary DECIMAL(10, 2))
RETURNS DECIMAL(10, 2)
DETERMINISTIC
BEGIN
    DECLARE tax DECIMAL(10, 2);
    SET tax = salary * 0.1;
    -- Assuming a flat 10% tax rate
    RETURN tax;
END$$

DELIMITER ;
```

o Use the Function:

```
-- COMMON SQL
SELECT employee_id, salary, CalculateTax(salary)
  AS tax_amount
FROM employees;
```

Syntax and Steps to Create User-Defined Aggregate Functions

- Syntax:

```
-- SQL SERVER
CREATE AGGREGATE aggregate_function_name (@parameter
data_type)
RETURNS return_type
BEGIN
    -- Aggregate function logic
    RETURN result;
```

```
END;
```

```
-- MySQL
DELIMITER $$

CREATE FUNCTION aggregate_function_name (@parameter data_type)
RETURNS return_type
BEGIN
    -- Aggregate function logic
    DECLARE result return_type;

    -- Calculate result based on parameter
    -- Example: If the aggregate function is SUM
      -- SELECT SUM(column_name)
      -- INTO result
      -- FROM table_name
      -- WHERE some_condition;

    RETURN result;
END$$

DELIMITER ;
```

- Steps:
    o Create the Aggregate Function: (*note: the sample code is simplified; a needed improvement here would make certain that the employ count is not zero, or we will be dividing by zero!*)

```
-- SQL SERVER
CREATE AGGREGATE CalculateAverageSalary(@salary DECIMAL)
RETURNS DECIMAL
BEGIN
  DECLARE @total_salary DECIMAL;
  DECLARE @employee_count INT;
  SELECT @total_salary = SUM(@salary),
    @employee_count = COUNT(@salary);
  RETURN @total_salary / @employee_count;
END;
```

```
-- MySQL
DELIMITER $$
```

```
CREATE FUNCTION CalculateAverageSalary(salary
                DECIMAL(10,2))
RETURNS DECIMAL(10,2)
BEGIN
    DECLARE total_salary DECIMAL(10,2);
    DECLARE employee_count INT;
    SELECT SUM(salary), COUNT(*)
    INTO total_salary, employee_count
    FROM employees;

    RETURN total_salary / employee_count;
END$$

DELIMITER ;
```

- Use the Aggregate Function:

```
-- COMMON SQL
SELECT department_id, CalculateAverageSalary(salary) AS
avg_salary
FROM employees
GROUP BY department_id;
```

Defining Custom Functions to Meet Specific Requirements

- Row Function Example:
    - Creating a function to generate a full name from first and last names.

```
-- SQL SERVER
CREATE FUNCTION GenerateFullName(@first_name VARCHAR(50),
@last_name VARCHAR(50))
RETURNS VARCHAR(100)
AS
BEGIN
    RETURN CONCAT(@first_name, ' ', @last_name);
END;
```

```
-- MySQL
DELIMITER $$
```

```
CREATE FUNCTION GenerateFullName(first_name VARCHAR(50),
last_name VARCHAR(50))
RETURNS VARCHAR(100)
BEGIN
    DECLARE full_name VARCHAR(100);
    SET full_name = CONCAT(first_name, ' ', last_name);
    RETURN full_name;
END$$

DELIMITER ;
```

o Using the function:

```
-- COMMON SQL
SELECT employee_id, GenerateFullName(first_name,
last_name) AS full_name
FROM employees;
```

- Aggregate Function Example:
  o Creating an aggregate function to calculate the weighted average salary by department. *Note: the code presented is simplified. An appropriate improvement would ensure appropriate error handling if the employee count equals 0.*

```
-- SQL SERVER
CREATE AGGREGATE WeightedAverageSalary(@salary DECIMAL,
@employee_count INT)
RETURNS DECIMAL
BEGIN
    DECLARE @total_salary DECIMAL;
    SELECT @total_salary = SUM(@salary);
    RETURN @total_salary / @employee_count;
END;
```

```
-- MySQL
DELIMITER $$

CREATE FUNCTION WeightedAverageSalary(salary
DECIMAL(10,2), employee_count INT)
RETURNS DECIMAL(10,2)
BEGIN
```

```
    DECLARE total_salary DECIMAL(10,2);
    SELECT SUM(salary) INTO total_salary;
    RETURN total_salary / employee_count;
END$$

DELIMITER ;
```

o   Using the aggregate function:

```
-- COMMON SQL
SELECT department_id, WeightedAverageSalary(salary,
COUNT(employee_id)) AS weighted_avg_salary
FROM employees
GROUP BY department_id;
```

As you have seen, user-defined Row and Aggregate functions enable the DBA to sculpt bespoke functionalities tailored to their specific requirements, elevating the finesse and efficiency of their SQL programs.

---

Subqueries in Queries

Subqueries provide versatility, allowing DBAs to craft nested queries that provide nuanced data retrieval. This material will examine the incorporation of subqueries at various points within outer queries: within SELECT, WHERE, and HAVING clauses.

Introduction to Subqueries

A subquery, also known as a nested query or inner query, is a query nested within another query. Subqueries are used to retrieve data that will be used in the main query's conditions or expressions, enabling complex and dynamic data extraction.

# Introduction to SQL Functions and Procedures

Incorporating Subqueries within SELECT Clause

- Example: Retrieving Average Salary per Department with Subquery in SELECT:

```
-- COMMON SQL
SELECT department_id,
        (SELECT AVG(salary)
         FROM employees
         WHERE department_id = d.department_id)
         AS avg_salary
FROM departments d;
```

Incorporating Subqueries within WHERE Clause

- Example: Filtering Employees with Salaries Above Department Average:

```
-- COMMON SQL
SELECT employee_id, first_name, last_name, salary,
        department_id
FROM employees
WHERE salary > (SELECT AVG(salary)
                FROM employees
                WHERE department_id =
                        employees.department_id);
```

Incorporating Subqueries within HAVING Clause

- Example: Filtering Departments with Average Salary Above Global Average:

```
-- COMMON SQL
SELECT department_id, AVG(salary) AS avg_salary
FROM employees
GROUP BY department_id
HAVING AVG(salary) > (SELECT AVG(salary)
                      FROM employees);
```

Using Subqueries to Retrieve Data Based on Results from Other Queries

- Example: Finding Employees with Maximum Salary in Each Department:

```
-- COMMON SQL
SELECT employee_id, first_name, last_name, salary,
       department_id
FROM employees e1
WHERE salary = (SELECT MAX(salary)
                FROM employees e2
                WHERE e1.department_id = e2.department_id);
```

Best Practices for Using Subqueries

1. **Optimize Subqueries:**
    a. Ensure subqueries are optimized to avoid performance issues.
    b. Use indexes where applicable to enhance subquery performance.
2. **Limit Subquery Results:**
    a. Ensure subqueries return a limited number of rows to prevent potential performance bottlenecks.
3. **Understand Subquery Dependencies:**
    a. Be aware of dependencies between the outer query and subquery to achieve desired results.
4. **Test and Validate:**
    a. Test subqueries independently to validate their correctness before integrating them into the main query.
5. **Consider Join Alternatives:**
    a. Evaluate if JOIN operations can achieve the same result as a subquery, and choose the approach that best suits the scenario.

Mastering subquery creation opens new avenues for intricate data retrieval and manipulation in a single script that might otherwise require creation of additional views.

Creating Parameter Queries

Parameter queries empower users to interact with the database by inputting values and customizing query results. The following material examines the creation of parameterized queries, exploring how they allow for user input and enable personalized data retrieval.

# Introduction to SQL Functions and Procedures

Introduction to Parameter Queries

Parameter queries, also known as parameterized queries, provide a means for users to input values at runtime, creating a dynamic and interactive experience. This enables customized data retrieval without the need for hard-coded values in the query.

Developing Parameterized Queries

- Example: Basic Parameterized Query with WHERE Clause:

```
-- SQL SERVER
DECLARE @department_id INT;
SET @department_id = 1;

SELECT employee_id, first_name, last_name, salary
FROM employees
WHERE department_id = @department_id;
```

```
-- MySQL
SET @department_id := 1;

SELECT employee_id, first_name, last_name, salary
FROM employees
WHERE department_id = @department_id;
```

Allowing Users to Input Values

- Example: Using Parameters in a Stored Procedure:

```
-- SQL SERVER
CREATE PROCEDURE GetEmployeesByDepartment
    @department_id INT
AS
BEGIN
    SELECT employee_id, first_name, last_name, salary
    FROM employees
    WHERE department_id = @department_id;
END;
```

```
-- MySQL
DELIMITER $$

CREATE PROCEDURE GetEmployeesByDepartment(IN department_id
                                 INT)
BEGIN
    SELECT employee_id, first_name, last_name, salary
    FROM employees
    WHERE department_id = department_id;
END$$

DELIMITER ;
```

Customizing Query Results with Parameters in WHERE Clauses

- Example: Parameterized Query for Date Range:

```
-- SQL SERVER
DECLARE @start_date DATE = '2023-01-01';
DECLARE @end_date DATE = '2023-12-31';

SELECT order_id, customer_id, order_date, total_amount
FROM orders
WHERE order_date BETWEEN @start_date AND @end_date;
```

```
-- MySQL
SET @start_date := '2023-01-01';
SET @end_date := '2023-12-31';

SELECT order_id, customer_id, order_date, total_amount
FROM orders
WHERE order_date BETWEEN @start_date AND @end_date;
```

Handling NULL or Default Parameter Values

- Example: Using Default Parameter Values:

```
-- SQL SERVER
CREATE  PROCEDURE GetEmployeesBySalaryRange
```

```
    @min_salary DECIMAL = 0,
    @max_salary DECIMAL = NULL
AS
BEGIN
    SELECT employee_id, first_name, last_name, salary
    FROM employees
    WHERE salary BETWEEN @min_salary AND
    ISNULL(@max_salary,salary);
END;
```

```
-- MySQL
DELIMITER $$

CREATE PROCEDURE GetEmployeesBySalaryRange(
    IN min_salary DECIMAL(10,2),
    IN max_salary DECIMAL(10,2)
)
BEGIN
    SELECT employee_id, first_name, last_name, salary
    FROM employees
    WHERE salary BETWEEN min_salary AND
    COALESCE(max_salary, salary);
END$$

DELIMITER ;
```

Best Practices for Parameter Queries

1. **Sanitize User Input:**
   Ensure input values are validated and sanitized to prevent SQL injection attacks.
2. **Handle NULL Values:**
   Account for NULL values and provide appropriate default values or conditions.
3. **Use Appropriate Data Types:**
   Match parameter data types with the corresponding column data types for accurate comparisons.
4. **Consider Performance Implications:**
   Evaluate the performance impact of parameterized queries, especially when dealing with large datasets.
5. **Encourage Input Validation:**
   Implement mechanisms for users to input valid values, reducing the likelihood of errors.

As these examples show, parameter queries serve as bridges between users and data, enabling personalized and interactive experiences. By incorporating parameter queries into their professional skillset, DBAs can foster dynamic and user-friendly interactions with the database ecosystem.

---

## Set Operators

Set operators make possible powerful analysis of groups and sub-groups hidden within data, employing set operators such as UNION, INTERSECT, and EXCEPT. The precise list and operator names for set operators varies from one DBMS to another. You will find the list of set operators supported by Transact SQL (SQL Server) in Appendix D, and the operators supported by MySQL in Appendix E. In this section, we will learn how set operators are used for combining and comparing query results.

### Introduction to Set Operators

Set operators in SQL allow for the manipulation and combination of query results from multiple SELECT statements. They include:

- **UNION:** Combines the results of two or more queries into a single result set.

- **INTERSECT:** Returns the common rows between two result sets.

- **EXCEPT (or MINUS):** Returns the distinct rows in the first result set but not in the second.

### Using UNION to Combine Query Results

- **Example: Combining Results from Two Tables:**

```
-- COMMON SQL
SELECT employee_id, first_name, last_name
  FROM employees
UNION
SELECT customer_id, first_name, last_name
  FROM customers;
```

# Introduction to SQL Functions and Procedures

Using INTERSECT logic to Find Common Rows

- **Example: Finding Common Customers between Two Tables.** *Note that MySQL uses logically equivalent **IN** operations, **INNER JOIN**, or **WHERE EXISTS**, as MySQL does not implement the INTERSECT operator:*

```
-- SQL SERVER
SELECT customer_id, first_name, last_name
  FROM customers
INTERSECT
SELECT customer_id, first_name, last_name
  FROM preferred_customers;
```

```
-- MySQL
-- INNER JOIN solution
SELECT c.customer_id, c.first_name, c.last_name
FROM customers c
INNER JOIN preferred_customers pc
ON c.customer_id = pc.customer_id
AND c.first_name = pc.first_name
AND c.last_name = pc.last_name;
```

```
-- MySQL
-- WHERE EXISTS solution
SELECT customer_id, first_name, last_name
FROM customers c
WHERE EXISTS (
    SELECT 1
    FROM preferred_customers pc
    WHERE c.customer_id = pc.customer_id
    AND c.first_name = pc.first_name
    AND c.last_name = pc.last_name
);
```

Using EXCEPT logic to Find Differences

- **Example: Finding Employees not in Management.** *Note: MySQL uses logically equivalent **NOT IN**, or **LEFT JOIN** logic, as it does not implement the EXCEPT operator:*

```
-- SQL SERVER
SELECT employee_id, first_name, last_name
  FROM employees
EXCEPT
SELECT employee_id, first_name, last_name
  FROM management;
```

```
-- MySQL
SELECT e.employee_id, e.first_name, e.last_name
FROM employees e
LEFT JOIN management m ON e.employee_id = m.employee_id
WHERE m.employee_id IS NULL;
```

Combining Set Operators in Complex Queries

- **Example: Combining UNION and INTERSECT for Complex Conditions.** *As previously noted, MySQL uses logically equivalent* **IN**, **INNER JOIN** *or* **WHERE EXISTS** *constructs, as it does not implement the* **INTERSECT** *set operator:*

```
-- SQL SERVER
SELECT product_id, product_name
  FROM products
  WHERE product_category = 'Electronics'
UNION
SELECT product_id, product_name
  FROM products
  WHERE product_category = 'Appliances'
INTERSECT
SELECT product_id, product_name
  FROM products
  WHERE stock_quantity > 50;
```

```
-- MySQL
-- Equivalent Logic using IN operator
SELECT product_id, product_name
FROM products
WHERE (product_category = 'Electronics'
       OR product_category = 'Appliances')
AND product_id IN (
    SELECT product_id
```

```
    FROM products
    WHERE stock_quantity > 50
);
```

Best Practices for Using Set Operators

1. **Consistent Data Types:**

   - Ensure that the columns in the SELECT statements of set operations have the same data types.

2. **Column Aliases:**

   - Use column aliases to provide meaningful names for the columns in the result set.

3. **Understanding NULL Values:**

   - Be mindful of how set operators handle NULL values, as they may affect results.

4. **Order of Execution:**

   - Understand the order of execution of set operations, as it influences the final result set.

5. **Performance Considerations:**

   - Evaluate the performance impact, especially when dealing with large datasets, and consider alternative approaches if necessary.

Introduction to String Functions

String functions are important in SQL programming because they enable the manipulation and processing of textual data within the database. These functions allow for operations such as searching, replacing, concatenating, and formatting strings, which are essential for tasks like cleaning data, generating reports, and ensuring data consistency. By providing tools to handle and transform string data, string functions enhance the flexibility and power of SQL queries in managing and analyzing text-based information.

# Chapter 7

Using UPPER and LOWER to Change Case

- **Example: Converting Names to Uppercase:**

```
-- COMMON SQL
SELECT UPPER(first_name) AS uppercase_first_name,
LOWER(last_name) AS lowercase_last_name FROM employees;
```

Using CONCAT to Combine Strings

- **Example: Creating Full Names with CONCAT:**

```
-- COMMON SQL
SELECT CONCAT(first_name, ' ', last_name) AS full_name FROM
employees;
```

Combining Concatenation and String Functions in Complex Queries

- **Example: Constructing Email Addresses from First and Last Names:**

```
-- COMMON SQL
SELECT first_name,
  last_name,
  CONCAT(LOWER(SUBSTRING(first_name, 1, 1)),
  last_name,
  '@company.com') AS email_address
FROM employees;
```

- **Example: Formatting Phone Numbers with Hyphens:**

```
-- COMMON SQL
SELECT phone_number,
CONCAT(
      '(',
      SUBSTRING(phone_number, 1, 3),
      ') ',
      SUBSTRING(phone_number, 4, 3),
      '-',
      SUBSTRING(phone_number, 7, LEN(phone_number) - 6)
    ) AS formatted_phone_number
```

```
FROM customers;
```

## String Functions for Text Manipulation

String functions in SQL provide a palette of tools for manipulating and formatting text. These functions can be applied to modify the case, extract substrings, or pad strings, among other operations.

### Utilizing String Functions for Text Manipulation and Formatting

- **Example: Padding Employee IDs with Leading Zeros:**

```
-- SQL SERVER
SELECT
  employee_id,
  RIGHT('00000' + CAST(employee_id AS VARCHAR(5)), 5)
    AS padded_employee_id
FROM employees;
```

```
-- MySQL
SELECT
    employee_id,
    RIGHT(CONCAT('00000', CAST(employee_id AS CHAR(5))), 5)
      AS padded_employee_id
FROM employees;
```

## Introduction to Numeric Functions

Numeric functions are important in SQL programming because they enable the performance of mathematical operations and calculations directly within the database. These functions allow for tasks such as rounding numbers, calculating absolute values, generating random numbers, and performing complex arithmetic operations. By facilitating numerical data manipulation, numeric functions enhance the ability to analyze quantitative data, generate statistical reports, and derive insights, thus making SQL a powerful tool for data-driven decision-making. Numeric functions include functions for rounding, flooring, and other mathematical transformations.

# Chapter 7

Using ROUND for Rounding Numbers

- **Example: Rounding Salaries to the Nearest Hundred:**

```
-- COMMON SQL
SELECT employee_id, first_name, last_name, ROUND(salary, -2)
AS rounded_salary
FROM employees;
```

Using FLOOR for Rounding Down Numbers

- **Example: Flooring Discounted Prices:**

```
-- COMMON SQL
SELECT product_id, product_name, regular_price,
FLOOR(regular_price * 0.8) AS discounted_price
FROM products;
```

Combining String and Numeric Functions in Complex Queries

- **Example: Displaying Employee Names and Salaries in a Custom Format:**

```
-- COMMON SQL
SELECT
    CONCAT(
        UPPER(SUBSTRING(first_name, 1, 1)),
        LOWER(SUBSTRING(first_name, 2))
    ) AS formatted_first_name,
    CONCAT(
        UPPER(SUBSTRING(last_name, 1, 1)),
        LOWER(SUBSTRING(last_name, 2))
    ) AS formatted_last_name,
    ROUND(salary, -2) AS rounded_salary
FROM employees;
```

# Introduction to SQL Functions and Procedures

Best Practices for Using String and Numeric Functions

1. **Understand Data Types:**

   - Ensure that the data types used in string and numeric functions match the expected types.

2. **Handle NULL Values:**

   - Be aware of how string functions handle NULL values and consider appropriate handling.

3. **Performance Considerations:**

   - Evaluate the performance impact of string and numeric functions, especially when applied to large datasets.

4. **Consider Alternatives:**

   - Explore alternative methods, such as using computed columns, if string or numeric functions are applied frequently.

5. **Testing and Validation:**

   - Test functions on sample data to validate their correctness before incorporating them into production queries.

---

## Date Arithmetic and Date Functions

Date arithmetic and date functions are important in SQL programming because they enable the manipulation and calculation of dates and times, which are crucial for time-based data analysis. These functions allow for operations such as adding or subtracting intervals, extracting specific date parts (like year, month, or day), and formatting dates. This capability is essential for tasks like tracking events over time, generating time-based reports, and scheduling. By providing tools to handle date and time data efficiently, date functions enhance the accuracy and effectiveness of temporal data analysis in SQL.

# Chapter 7

## Introduction to Date Arithmetic

Date arithmetic in SQL involves performing calculations with dates, such as adding or subtracting days, months, or years. This capability allows for dynamic manipulation of date values.

## Using Date Arithmetic to Add Months or Days

- **Example: Adding Three Months to the Current Date:**

```
SELECT DATEADD(MONTH, 3, GETDATE()) AS three_months_later;
Example: Subtracting Seven Days from a Specific Date:
sqlCopy code
SELECT DATEADD(DAY, -7, '2023-01-15') AS seven_days_earlier;
```

## Introduction to Date Functions

Date functions in SQL provide a range of operations to extract and manipulate components of date values. These functions enhance the ability to perform precise calculations involving dates.

## Calculating the Number of Days Between Two Dates

- **Example: Calculating the Age of Employees in Days:**

```
SELECT employee_id, first_name, last_name, DATEDIFF(DAY,
birthdate, GETDATE()) AS age_in_days FROM employees;
```

- **Example: Finding the Difference in Days between Order and Delivery Dates:**

```
SELECT order_id, order_date, delivery_date, DATEDIFF(DAY,
order_date, delivery_date) AS delivery_duration_days FROM
orders;
```

# Introduction to SQL Functions and Procedures

Combining Date Arithmetic and Functions in Complex Queries

- **Example: Calculating Projected End Dates with Date Arithmetic:**

```
-- SQL SERVER
SELECT
  project_id,
  project_name,
  start_date,
  DATEADD(MONTH, duration_months, start_date)
  AS projected_end_date
FROM projects;
```

```
-- MySQL
SELECT
  project_id,
  project_name,
  start_date,
  DATE_ADD(start_date, INTERVAL duration_months MONTH)
  AS projected_end_date
FROM projects;
```

- **Example: Identifying Upcoming Anniversaries:**

```
-- SQL SERVER
SELECT
  employee_id,
  first_name,
  last_name,
  birthdate,
  DATEADD(YEAR, DATEDIFF(YEAR, birthdate, GETDATE()),
          birthdate)
  AS upcoming_anniversary
FROM employees;
```

```
-- MySQL
SELECT
  employee_id,
  first_name,
  last_name,
  birthdate,
```

```
TIMESTAMPADD(YEAR, TIMESTAMPDIFF(YEAR, birthdate,
            CURDATE()), birthdate)
AS upcoming_anniversary
FROM employees;
```

Best Practices for Using Date Arithmetic and Functions

1. **Consistent Date Formats:**

   - Ensure consistency in date formats to prevent unexpected results.

2. **Consider Time Components:**

   - Be mindful of time components when dealing with datetime values, and use appropriate functions or truncation if necessary.

3. **Testing Across Scenarios:**

   - Test date arithmetic and functions across various scenarios, including edge cases, to validate their accuracy.

4. **Time Zone Considerations:**

   - Consider time zone differences when dealing with date values to ensure accurate calculations.

5. **Documentation and Comments:**

   - Document the purpose of date arithmetic and function usage in queries and use comments for clarity.

In this section we explored date arithmetic and functions. We learned how to add months or days to a date, and how to calculate the number of days between two dates. Mastery of date arithmetic and date-related functions provides requisite skills for creating SQL code addressing calendaring, scheduling, and date-forecasting needs that arise frequently in database work.

---

Creating Stored Procedures

Stored procedures in SQL act as the architects of procedural database logic, offering a structured and efficient way to encapsulate sets of SQL statements. This section delves into the creation of stored procedures, explaining their use, advantages, and providing examples with SQL code. It further explores the syntax and steps for creating and executing stored procedures, serving as a comprehensive guide for practitioners seeking to harness the power of procedural logic in their SQL interactions.

## Introduction to Stored Procedures

Stored procedures are precompiled sets of one or more SQL statements stored in the database catalog. They allow for the encapsulation of logic, parameterization, and reusability of code.

## Advantages of Using Stored Procedures

1. **Modularity and Reusability:**

   - Stored procedures promote modular design, enabling the reuse of code across multiple queries or applications.

2. **Improved Performance:**

   - Precompiled execution plans in stored procedures often result in improved performance compared to ad-hoc queries.

3. **Enhanced Security:**

   - Stored procedures can control access to data and ensure that only authorized users execute specific operations.

4. **Transaction Management:**

   - Stored procedures support the management of transactions, allowing for atomic and consistent operations.

## Syntax and Steps for Creating Stored Procedures

- **Example: Creating a Simple Stored Procedure:**

```
-- SQL SERVER
CREATE PROCEDURE GetEmployeeCount AS
BEGIN
  SELECT COUNT(*) AS total_employees
  FROM employees;
```

```
END;
```

```
-- MySQL
DELIMITER $$

CREATE PROCEDURE GetEmployeeCount()
BEGIN
  SELECT COUNT(*) AS total_employees
  FROM employees;
END$$

DELIMITER ;
```

Executing Stored Procedures

- **Example: Executing the GetEmployeeCount Stored Procedure:**

```
-- SQL SERVER
EXEC GetEmployeeCount;
```

```
-- MySQL
CALL GetEmployeeCount();
```

- **Example: Executing Stored Procedure with Parameters:**

```
-- SQL SERVER
CREATE PROCEDURE GetEmployeesByDepartment @department_id INT
AS
BEGIN
  SELECT employee_id, first_name, last_name
  FROM employees
  WHERE department_id = @department_id;
END;

EXEC GetEmployeesByDepartment @department_id = 1;
```

```
-- MySQL
DELIMITER $$
```

```
CREATE PROCEDURE GetEmployeesByDepartment(IN department_id
                                    INT)
BEGIN
  SELECT employee_id, first_name, last_name
  FROM employees
  WHERE department_id = department_id;
END$$

DELIMITER ;

CALL GetEmployeesByDepartment(1);
```

Advanced Concepts in Stored Procedures

- **Example: Returning Result Sets from Stored Procedures:**

```
-- SQL SERVER
CREATE PROCEDURE GetHighSalaryEmployees AS
BEGIN
  SELECT employee_id, first_name, last_name, salary
  FROM employees
  WHERE salary > 50000;
END;
```

```
-- MySQL
DELIMITER $$

CREATE PROCEDURE GetHighSalaryEmployees()
BEGIN
  SELECT employee_id, first_name, last_name, salary
  FROM employees
  WHERE salary > 50000;
END$$

DELIMITER ;
```

- **Example: Using OUTPUT Parameters in Stored Procedures:**

```
-- SQL SERVER
CREATE PROCEDURE GetEmployeeCountByDepartment @department_id
INT, @employee_count INT OUTPUT AS
BEGIN
```

```
  SELECT @employee_count = COUNT(*)
  FROM employees
  WHERE department_id = @department_id;
END;

DECLARE @count INT;
EXEC GetEmployeeCountByDepartment @department_id = 2,
    @employee_count = @count OUTPUT;
```

```
DELIMITER $$

CREATE PROCEDURE GetEmployeeCountByDepartment(
    IN department_id INT,
    OUT employee_count INT
)
BEGIN
    SELECT COUNT(*) INTO employee_count
    FROM employees
    WHERE department_id = department_id;
END$$

DELIMITER ;

CALL GetEmployeeCountByDepartment(2, @count);
```

Best Practices for Using Stored Procedures

1. **Parameterize Inputs:**

   - Parameterize stored procedures to enhance flexibility and reusability.

2. **Error Handling:**

   - Implement error handling within stored procedures to gracefully manage exceptions.

3. **Documentation:**

   - Document the purpose, inputs, and outputs of stored procedures for clarity and future reference.

4. **Security Considerations:**

- Limit access to stored procedures based on user roles and permissions.

5. **Testing:**

- Thoroughly test stored procedures with various inputs to ensure correct functionality.

In SQL programming, stored procedures provide a structured and efficient means to encapsulate SQL statements. In this section we learned about stored procedures and their advantages. By incorporating these practices, SQL programmers can harness the power of procedural logic, enhancing modularity, reusability, and overall efficiency in their SQL interactions.

## Embedded INSERT, UPDATE, DELETE Commands

We have seen how stored procedures can serve to orchestrate data manipulation. This section focuses on embedded SQL commands within stored procedures, exploring the use of INSERT, UPDATE, and DELETE statements.

## Introduction to Embedded SQL Commands in Stored Procedures

Embedded SQL commands within stored procedures allow for the direct manipulation of data within the procedural logic, facilitating dynamic changes to the database.

## Using Embedded INSERT Commands

- **Example: Inserting a New Employee Record:**

```
-- SQL SERVER
CREATE PROCEDURE AddNewEmployee
@first_name NVARCHAR(50), @last_name NVARCHAR(50),
@salary DECIMAL(18, 2) AS
BEGIN
  INSERT INTO employees
  (first_name, last_name, salary)
  VALUES (@first_name, @last_name, @salary);
END;
```

```
-- MySQL
DELIMITER $$

CREATE PROCEDURE AddNewEmployee(
    IN first_name NVARCHAR(50),
    IN last_name NVARCHAR(50),
    IN salary DECIMAL(18, 2)
)
BEGIN
    INSERT INTO employees
    (first_name, last_name, salary)
    VALUES (first_name, last_name, salary);
END$$

DELIMITER ;
```

Using Embedded UPDATE Commands

- **Example: Updating Salary for a Specific Employee:**

```
-- SQL SERVER
CREATE PROCEDURE UpdateEmployeeSalary
@employee_id INT, @new_salary DECIMAL(18, 2) AS
BEGIN
  UPDATE employees SET salary = @new_salary
  WHERE employee_id = @employee_id;
END;
```

```
-- MySQL
DELIMITER $$

CREATE PROCEDURE UpdateEmployeeSalary(
    IN employee_id INT,
    IN new_salary DECIMAL(18, 2)
)
BEGIN
    UPDATE employees
    SET salary = new_salary
    WHERE employee_id = employee_id;
END$$
```

```
DELIMITER ;
```

Using Embedded DELETE Commands

- **Example: Deleting an Employee Record:**

```
-- SQL SERVER
CREATE PROCEDURE DeleteEmployee
@employee_id INT AS
BEGIN
  DELETE FROM employees
  WHERE employee_id = @employee_id;
END;
```

```
-- MySQL
DELIMITER $$

CREATE PROCEDURE DeleteEmployee(
    IN employee_id INT
)
BEGIN
    DELETE FROM employees
    WHERE employee_id = employee_id;
END$$

DELIMITER ;
```

Combining Embedded Commands in Complex Queries

- **Example: Transferring Employees to a New Department:**

```
-- SQL SERVER
CREATE PROCEDURE TransferEmployeesToDepartment
@from_department_id INT, @to_department_id INT AS
BEGIN
  UPDATE employees
  SET department_id = @to_department_id
  WHERE department_id = @from_department_id;
  -- Additional logic or error handling can be added
```

```
    -- as needed.
END;
```

```
-- MySQL
DELIMITER $$

CREATE PROCEDURE TransferEmployeesToDepartment(
    IN from_department_id INT,
    IN to_department_id INT
)
BEGIN
    UPDATE employees
    SET department_id = to_department_id
    WHERE department_id = from_department_id;
    -- Additional logic or error handling can be added
    -- as needed.
END$$

DELIMITER ;
```

Best Practices for Using Embedded SQL Commands

1. **Transaction Management:**

   - Implement transactions to ensure atomic and consistent execution of multiple SQL commands within a stored procedure.

2. **Error Handling:**

   - Include robust error handling to manage exceptional cases and maintain data integrity.

3. **Input Validation:**

   - Validate input parameters to prevent SQL injection and ensure data integrity.

4. **Documentation:**

   - Document the purpose and behavior of embedded SQL commands in stored procedures for future reference.

5. **Security Considerations:**

- Limit access to stored procedures based on user roles and permissions, especially those involving data modification.

---

## Using Cursors for Retrieving Multiple Rows

Many SQL queries provide large result sets, well beyond a single row. Cursors serve as navigational tools, allowing SQL programmers to traverse and process multiple rows systematically. The material which follows illuminates the use of cursors for retrieving and processing multiple rows in a result set. Through practical examples and SQL code, it provides examples for SQL programmers seeking to harness the power of row-by-row retrieval in their SQL interactions.

## Introduction to Cursors

Cursors in SQL act as pointers to result sets, enabling the traversal of rows one at a time. This capability is particularly useful when dealing with queries that yield multiple rows.

## Using Cursors for Retrieving Multiple Rows

- **Example: Retrieving and Displaying Employee Names:**

```
-- SQL SERVER
CREATE PROCEDURE RetrieveEmployeeNames AS
  BEGIN
    DECLARE @employee_id INT;
    DECLARE @first_name NVARCHAR(50);
    DECLARE @last_name NVARCHAR(50);
    DECLARE employee_cursor
    CURSOR FOR
    SELECT employee_id, first_name, last_name
    FROM employees;
    OPEN employee_cursor;
    FETCH NEXT FROM employee_cursor
    INTO @employee_id, @first_name, @last_name;
    WHILE @@FETCH_STATUS = 0 BEGIN PRINT 'Employee ID: ' +
    CAST(@employee_id AS NVARCHAR(10)) + ', Name: ' +
```

```
          @first_name + ' ' + @last_name;
        FETCH NEXT FROM employee_cursor
        INTO @employee_id, @first_name, @last_name;
      END;
    CLOSE employee_cursor;
    DEALLOCATE employee_cursor;
END;
```

```
-- MySQL
DELIMITER $$

CREATE PROCEDURE RetrieveEmployeeNames()
BEGIN
    DECLARE done INT DEFAULT 0;
    DECLARE employee_id INT;
    DECLARE first_name NVARCHAR(50);
    DECLARE last_name NVARCHAR(50);
    DECLARE employee_cursor CURSOR FOR
        SELECT employee_id, first_name, last_name
        FROM employees;
    DECLARE CONTINUE HANDLER FOR NOT FOUND SET done = 1;

    OPEN employee_cursor;

    read_loop: LOOP
        FETCH employee_cursor INTO employee_id, first_name,
            last_name;
        IF done THEN
            LEAVE read_loop;
        END IF;
        SELECT CONCAT('Employee ID: ',
                    employee_id, ',
                    Name: ',
                    first_name,
                    ' ',
                    last_name) AS employee_info;
    END LOOP;

    CLOSE employee_cursor;
END$$
```

```
DELIMITER ;
```

Syntax of Using Cursors with Embedded SQL

- **Example: Declaring and Opening a Cursor:**

```
-- SQL SERVER
DECLARE cursor_name
CURSOR FOR
SELECT column1, column2, ...
FROM table_name;
OPEN cursor_name;

-- The cursor is now open and ready for use.
-- Typically, we iterate through the returned data until
-- it is exhausted.
-- Within the iteration, you provide your logic to accomplish
-- your goals for processing/using the retrieved data.
...
```

```
-- MySQL
DELIMITER $$

DECLARE cursor_name CURSOR FOR
SELECT column1, column2, ...
FROM table_name;

-- Declare a handler to handle the end of the cursor
DECLARE CONTINUE HANDLER FOR NOT FOUND SET done = 1;

OPEN cursor_name;

-- The cursor is now open and ready for use.
-- Typically, we iterate through the returned data until
-- it is exhausted.
-- Within the iteration, you provide your logic to accomplish
-- your goals for processing/using the retrieved data.
...
```

- **Example: Fetching Rows from a Cursor:**

```
-- SQL SERVER
-- Fetch the first row from the cursor
FETCH NEXT FROM cursor_name INTO @var1, @var2, ...;

-- Initialize the done variable
SET @done = 0;

-- Start the loop
WHILE @done = 0
BEGIN
    -- Check the fetch status
    IF @@FETCH_STATUS <> 0
    BEGIN
        SET @done = 1;
        CONTINUE;
    END

    -- Process the fetched data here

    -- Fetch the next row from the cursor
    FETCH NEXT FROM cursor_name INTO @var1, @var2;
END
```

```
-- MySQL
-- Fetching data from the cursor typically involves a loop
structure, which should be handled properly in MySQL
read_loop: LOOP
    FETCH cursor_name INTO var1, var2, ...;
    IF done THEN
        LEAVE read_loop;
    END IF;
    -- Process the fetched data here
END LOOP;
```

- **Example: Closing and Deallocating a Cursor:**

```
-- SQL Server
CLOSE cursor_name;
DEALLOCATE cursor_name;
```

```
-- MySQL
CLOSE cursor_name;
-- MySQL does not require explicit deallocation of the cursor.
```

Advanced Concepts with Cursors

- **Example: Updating Records Using a Cursor:**

```
-- SQL SERVER
CREATE PROCEDURE UpdateEmployeeSalaries AS
BEGIN
  DECLARE @employee_id INT;
  DECLARE @new_salary DECIMAL(18, 2);
  DECLARE salary_update_cursor CURSOR FOR
  SELECT employee_id, salary
  FROM employees
  WHERE department_id = 1;
  OPEN salary_update_cursor;
  FETCH NEXT FROM salary_update_cursor INTO
  @employee_id, @new_salary;
  WHILE @@FETCH_STATUS = 0
    BEGIN
      UPDATE employees
      SET salary = @new_salary * 1.1
      WHERE employee_id = @employee_id;
      FETCH NEXT FROM salary_update_cursor
      INTO @employee_id, @new_salary;
    END;
  CLOSE salary_update_cursor;
  DEALLOCATE salary_update_cursor;
END;
```

```
-- MySQL
DELIMITER $$

CREATE PROCEDURE UpdateEmployeeSalaries()
BEGIN
    DECLARE done INT DEFAULT 0;
    DECLARE employee_id INT;
```

```
    DECLARE new_salary DECIMAL(18, 2);

    -- Declare the cursor
    DECLARE salary_update_cursor CURSOR FOR
    SELECT employee_id, salary
    FROM employees
    WHERE department_id = 1;

    -- Declare a handler to set the done variable when
    -- there are no more rows
    DECLARE CONTINUE HANDLER FOR NOT FOUND SET done = 1;

    -- Open the cursor
    OPEN salary_update_cursor;

    -- Fetch the first row
    FETCH salary_update_cursor INTO employee_id, new_salary;

    -- Loop until there are no more rows
    read_loop: LOOP
        IF done THEN
            LEAVE read_loop;
        END IF;

        -- Update the salary
        UPDATE employees
        SET salary = new_salary * 1.1
        WHERE employee_id = employee_id;

        -- Fetch the next row
        FETCH salary_update_cursor INTO employee_id,
            new_salary;
    END LOOP;

    -- Close the cursor
    CLOSE salary_update_cursor;

END$$

DELIMITER ;
```

Best Practices for Using Cursors

1. **Minimize Cursor Use:**

   - Use cursors judiciously, as they may impact performance compared to set-based operations.

2. **Fetch in Batches:**

   - Fetch rows in manageable batches to reduce the impact on system resources.

3. **Proper Cursor Management:**

   - Close and deallocate cursors promptly to release associated resources.

4. **Optimize Queries:**

   - Optimize queries within cursors to ensure efficient data retrieval.

5. **Documentation:**

   - Document the purpose and behavior of cursors within stored procedures for future reference.

In SQL, cursors act as magnifying glasses, allowing SQL programmers to focus on and process individual rows within a result set. In this section, we learned about using cursors for retrieving and processing multiple rows, providing practical examples with SQL code. By incorporating these techniques, SQL programmers can confidently navigate and manipulate result sets with precision in their SQL interactions.

Error Handling in Procedures

Error handling is a crucial aspect of procedural logic. This section examines the incorporation of error handling in SQL code procedures, focusing on handling errors in procedures containing embedded SQL commands. Practical examples and explanations illustrate how error handling mechanisms can safeguard data integrity, providing a comprehensive guide for SQL programmers seeking to fortify their SQL procedures against potential pitfalls.

# Chapter 7

Introduction to Error Handling in SQL Procedures

Error handling in SQL procedures involves the implementation of mechanisms to gracefully manage unexpected situations, ensuring that procedures can respond to errors without compromising data integrity.

Handling Errors in Procedures with Embedded SQL Commands

- **Example: Handling Insert Errors in a Procedure:**

```
-- SQL SERVER
CREATE PROCEDURE InsertEmployee
@employee_id INT, @first_name NVARCHAR(50),
@last_name NVARCHAR(50) AS
BEGIN
  BEGIN TRY
    INSERT INTO employees (employee_id, first_name, last_name)
    VALUES (@employee_id, @first_name, @last_name);
  END TRY
  BEGIN CATCH
    -- Log or handle the error appropriately
    PRINT 'Error occurred while inserting employee. Details: '
    + ERROR_MESSAGE();
  END CATCH
END;
```

```
-- MySQL
DELIMITER $$

CREATE PROCEDURE InsertEmployee (
    IN employee_id INT,
    IN first_name VARCHAR(50),
    IN last_name VARCHAR(50)
)
BEGIN
    DECLARE EXIT HANDLER FOR SQLEXCEPTION
    BEGIN
        -- Log or handle the error appropriately
        SELECT 'Error occurred while inserting employee.';
```

```
    END;

    -- Attempt to insert the employee record
    INSERT INTO employees (employee_id, first_name, last_name)
    VALUES (employee_id, first_name, last_name);
END$$

DELIMITER ;
```

Implementation of Error Handling Mechanisms for Data Integrity

- **Example: Updating Records with Error Handling:**

```
-- SQL SERVER
CREATE PROCEDURE UpdateEmployeeSalary
@employee_id INT, @new_salary DECIMAL(18, 2) AS
BEGIN
  DECLARE @previous_salary DECIMAL(18, 2);
  BEGIN TRY -- Capture the previous salary
    SELECT @previous_salary = salary FROM employees
    WHERE employee_id = @employee_id; -- Update the salary
    UPDATE employees
    SET salary = @new_salary
    WHERE employee_id = @employee_id;
  END TRY
  BEGIN CATCH -- Rollback the transaction if an error occurs
    IF @@TRANCOUNT > 0 ROLLBACK;
    -- Log or handle the error appropriately
    PRINT 'Error occurred while updating employee salary.
          Details: ' + ERROR_MESSAGE();
  END CATCH
END;
```

```
-- MySQL
DELIMITER $$

CREATE PROCEDURE UpdateEmployeeSalary (
    IN employee_id INT,
    IN new_salary DECIMAL(18, 2)
)
BEGIN
```

```
DECLARE previous_salary DECIMAL(18, 2);
DECLARE EXIT HANDLER FOR SQLEXCEPTION
BEGIN
    -- Rollback the transaction in case of an error
    ROLLBACK;
    -- Log or handle the error appropriately
    SELECT 'Error occurred while updating employee
            salary.' AS ErrorMessage;
END;

-- Start a new transaction
START TRANSACTION;

-- Capture the previous salary
SELECT salary INTO previous_salary FROM employees
WHERE employee_id = employee_id;

-- Update the salary
UPDATE employees
SET salary = new_salary
WHERE employee_id = employee_id;

-- Commit the transaction
COMMIT;
END$$

DELIMITER ;
```

Best Practices for Error Handling in SQL Procedures

1. **Specific Error Handling:**

   - Handle specific errors with detailed messages for better diagnostics.

2. **Transaction Management:**

   - Implement transaction management to ensure atomic operations and data consistency.

3. **Logging:**

   - Log errors to a dedicated error log or table for future analysis.

4. **Graceful Degradation:**

   - Plan for graceful degradation in case of errors to prevent cascading failures.

5. **Testing Scenarios:**

   - Test error handling mechanisms with various scenarios to validate their effectiveness.

SQL error handling guards and protects data integrity in the face of unforeseen circumstances. By incorporating these practices, SQL programmers can fortify their SQL procedures, ensuring robust responses to errors and maintaining the integrity of their database operations.

---

## Revisiting Triggers – A Deeper Dive

You will recall from our introduction of triggers for updating data, in Chapter 5, that triggers are powerful tools for SQL automation, responding to specific events and executing predefined actions. This section further explores the creation and utilization of triggers and their role in automating actions on data changes. Practical examples and discussions illustrate how triggers can be harnessed to respond to database events, providing SQL programmers powerful automation capabilities of their SQL databases.

## Triggers in SQL Databases

Triggers in SQL are special types of stored procedures that are automatically executed in response to specific events on tables or views.

## Use of Triggers and Their Role in Automation

Triggers serve the following key purposes:

1. **Automating Actions:**

   - Triggers automate actions in response to INSERT, UPDATE, DELETE, or other events.

2. **Ensuring Data Integrity:**

   - Triggers help enforce data integrity rules by performing checks or modifications.

3. **Logging and Auditing:**

   - Triggers can be used for logging or auditing changes to maintain a history of data modifications.

Creating Triggers to Respond to Specific Database Events

- **Example: Creating a Trigger for Audit Logging:**

```sql
-- SQL SERVER
CREATE TRIGGER AuditLogTrigger
ON employees AFTER INSERT, UPDATE, DELETE AS
BEGIN -- Perform audit logging actions
  INSERT INTO audit_log
  (action, table_name, record_id, timestamp)
  SELECT CASE
    WHEN EXISTS (SELECT * FROM inserted) AND
      EXISTS (SELECT * FROM deleted)
    THEN 'UPDATE'
    WHEN EXISTS (SELECT * FROM inserted)
    THEN 'INSERT'
    WHEN EXISTS (SELECT * FROM deleted)
    THEN 'DELETE'
  END,
  'employees',
  COALESCE
    (
      (SELECT TOP 1 employee_id
       FROM inserted),
      (SELECT TOP 1 employee_id
       FROM deleted)
    ),
  GETDATE();
END;
```

```sql
-- MySQL
DELIMITER $$
```

```
CREATE TRIGGER AuditLogTrigger AFTER INSERT, UPDATE, DELETE
ON employees
FOR EACH ROW
BEGIN
    DECLARE action VARCHAR(10);

    -- Determine the action (INSERT, UPDATE, DELETE)
    IF NEW IS NOT NULL AND OLD IS NOT NULL THEN
        SET action = 'UPDATE';
    ELSEIF NEW IS NOT NULL THEN
        SET action = 'INSERT';
    ELSE
        SET action = 'DELETE';
    END IF;

    -- Perform audit logging actions
    INSERT INTO audit_log (action, table_name, record_id,
                timestamp)
    SELECT action, 'employees',
            COALESCE(NEW.employee_id, OLD.employee_id), NOW();
END$$

DELIMITER ;
```

Advanced Concepts in Trigger Creation

- **Example: Enforcing Referential Integrity with a Trigger:**

```
-- SQL SERVER
CREATE TRIGGER EnforceReferentialIntegrity
ON orders INSTEAD OF INSERT AS
BEGIN
  -- Check if the referenced customer exists
  IF NOT EXISTS
    (
      SELECT 1 FROM inserted i
      LEFT JOIN customers c
      ON i.customer_id = c.customer_id
      WHERE c.customer_id IS NULL
    )
    BEGIN -- Perform the insert if the customer exists
```

```
      INSERT INTO orders
      (order_id, customer_id, order_date, total_amount)
      SELECT order_id, customer_id, order_date, total_amount
      FROM inserted;
    END
  ELSE
    BEGIN
    -- Raise an error or handle the situation where
    -- the customer doesn't exist
    RAISEERROR ('Referenced customer does not exist.', 16, 1);
  END
END;
```

```
-- MySQL
DELIMITER $$

CREATE TRIGGER EnforceReferentialIntegrity BEFORE INSERT
ON orders
FOR EACH ROW
BEGIN
    DECLARE customer_exists INT;

    -- Check if the referenced customer exists
    SELECT COUNT(*)
    INTO customer_exists
    FROM customers c
    WHERE c.customer_id = NEW.customer_id;

    -- Perform the insert if the customer exists
    IF customer_exists > 0 THEN
        -- Perform the insert
        INSERT INTO orders
          (order_id, customer_id, order_date, total_amount
        VALUES
          (NEW.order_id, NEW.customer_id, NEW.order_date,
          NEW.total_amount);
    ELSE
        -- Raise an error or handle the situation where the
        -- customer doesn't exist
        SIGNAL SQLSTATE '45000' SET MESSAGE_TEXT =
          'Referenced customer does not exist.';
    END IF;
```

```
END$$

DELIMITER ;
```

Best Practices for Creating and Using Triggers

1. **Keep Triggers Concise:**

   • Triggers should perform their actions efficiently without unnecessary complexity.

2. **Avoid Recursive Triggers:**

   • Be cautious about recursive triggers, which can lead to unintended behavior.

3. **Logging and Error Handling:**

   • Include logging and error handling mechanisms within triggers for diagnostic purposes.

4. **Testing Scenarios:**

   • Thoroughly test triggers with various scenarios to ensure they behave as expected.

5. **Documentation:**

   • Document the purpose and behavior of triggers for future reference and maintenance.

SQL triggers act as automated guardians, responding to specific events and executing predefined actions. This section presented details of creating and using triggers in SQL databases, providing practical examples and explanations. By incorporating these techniques, SQL programmers can harness the automation capabilities of triggers, streamlining data management and ensuring the integrity of their database operations.

# Appendix A – Commonly Used SQL Server Functions

AVG(): Calculates the average value of a numeric column in a set of rows.

CHARINDEX(): Returns the starting position of a substring within a string.

COALESCE(): Returns the first non-null expression from a list of expressions.

COALESCE(): Returns the first non-null expression in a list.

CONCAT(): Concatenates two or more strings into a single string.

COUNT(): Returns the number of rows that match a specified condition.

DATEADD(): Adds a specified time interval to a date.

DATEDIFF(): Calculates the difference between two dates in terms of a specified date part (such as days, months, years, etc.).

DATEDIFF(): Returns the difference between two dates in a specified time interval.

DATEPART(): Returns a specific part of a date, such as day, month, year, etc.

FORMAT(): Formats a value with a specified format.

GETDATE(): Retrieves the current date and time from the system.

IIF(): Returns one value if a specified condition is true, and another value if it's false.

ISNULL(): Returns a replacement value if an expression is null.

LEFT(): Returns a specified number of characters from the beginning of a string.

LEN(): Returns the length (number of characters) of a string.

LOWER(): Converts a string to lowercase.

MAX(): Returns the maximum value in a column.

MIN(): Returns the minimum value in a column.

MONTH(): Extracts the month from a date.

NULLIF(): Compares two expressions and returns null if they are equal.

RANK(): Assigns a unique rank to each distinct row within a result set.

RIGHT(): Returns a specified number of characters from the end of a string.

ROUND(): Rounds a numeric value to a specified number of decimal places.

ROW_NUMBER(): Returns a unique number for each row within a result set.

STUFF(): Replaces a specified portion of a string with another string.

SUBSTRING(): Extracts a substring from a string.

SUM(): Calculates the sum of values in a numeric column.

UPPER(): Converts a string to uppercase.

YEAR(): Extracts the year from a date.

ABS(): Returns the absolute value of a number.

COALESCE(): Returns the first non-null value in a list of expressions.

CONCAT(): Concatenates two or more strings together.

CONCAT_WS(): Concatenates multiple strings with a specified delimiter.

COUNT(): Returns the number of rows in a result set or the number of occurrences of a specified expression.

DATE_ADD(): Adds a specified time interval to a date.

DATE_FORMAT(): Formats a date or datetime value according to a specified format string.

DATE_SUB(): Subtracts a specified time interval from a date.

DATEDIFF(): Calculates the difference between two dates.

FIND_IN_SET(): Searches for a value in a comma-separated list.

GROUP_CONCAT(): Concatenates values from multiple rows into a single string with a specified delimiter.

IF(): Returns one value if a condition is true and another value if the condition is false.

IFNULL(): Returns a specified value if a expression is null; otherwise, it returns the expression.

LCASE() or LOWER(): Converts a string to lowercase.

LEFT(): Returns a specified number of characters from the left of a string.

LENGTH(): Returns the length (number of characters) of a string.

MAX(): Returns the maximum value in a set of values.

MIN(): Returns the minimum value in a set of values.

NOW(): Returns the current date and time.

NULLIF(): Returns null if two expressions are equal; otherwise, it returns the first expression.

RAND(): Generates a random floating-point value between 0 and 1.

ROUND(): Rounds a numeric value to a specified number of decimal places.

STR_TO_DATE(): Converts a string to a date using a specified format.

SUBSTRING(): Returns a portion of a string, starting from a specified position.

SUM(): Calculates the sum of a set of values.

TIMESTAMPADD(): Adds a specified time interval to a datetime value.

TIMESTAMPDIFF(): Calculates the difference between two datetime values in a specified unit.

TRIM(): Removes leading and trailing spaces or specified characters from a string.

UCASE() or UPPER(): Converts a string to uppercase.

# Appendix C – Summary of mathematical, Boolean, and logical operators in SQL

| Precedence | Operator Type | Operators | Associativity |
|---|---|---|---|
| 1 | Parentheses | () | N/A |
| 2 | Exponentiation | ^ | Right |
| 3 | Unary Operators | + (Positive), - (Negative), NOT | Right |
| 4 | Multiplication/Division | *, /, % | Left |
| 5 | Addition/Subtraction | +, - | Left |
| 6 | Comparison | =, <, >, <=, >=, <>, !=, <=>, BETWEEN, IN, LIKE, IS NULL, IS NOT NULL | N/A |
| 7 | Logical NOT | NOT | Right |
| 8 | Logical AND | AND | Left |
| 9 | Logical OR | OR | Left |

Note:

- Operators of higher precedence are evaluated before operators of lower precedence.
- Operators with the same precedence are evaluated based on their associativity (Left or Right).
- Some operators, like the BETWEEN, IN, LIKE, IS NULL, and IS NOT NULL operators, do not strictly follow left-to-right associativity but rather depend on the specific context of their usage.

# Appendix C

This table provides a general overview of operator precedence in SQL, but keep in mind that different database systems might have slight variations in operator precedence. Always refer to the documentation of your specific database management system for the most accurate information

# Appendix D – Summary of Set Operators Supported in TRANSACT SQL (SQL Server)

Transact-SQL (T-SQL), which is an extension of SQL used in Microsoft SQL Server, supports various set operators for combining and manipulating query results. Here's a list of set operators implemented in Transact-SQL:

APPLY: A combination of CROSS APPLY and OUTER APPLY, which can be used to invoke a table-valued function.

CROSS APPLY: Applies a table-valued function to each row of the left table expression, returning the combined result.

CROSS JOIN: Combines all rows from both tables, creating a Cartesian product.

EXCEPT: Returns the distinct rows from the left result set that are not present in the right result set.

FULL (OUTER) JOIN: Returns all rows from both tables, with NULL values in columns where no match is found.

INNER JOIN: Returns only matching rows from both tables.

INTERSECT: Returns the common rows between the result sets of two or more SELECT statements.

JOIN: Combines rows from two or more tables based on a specified condition.

LEFT (OUTER) JOIN: Returns all rows from the left table and the matching rows from the right table.

OUTER APPLY: Similar to CROSS APPLY, but includes unmatched rows from the left table expression.

RIGHT (OUTER) JOIN: Returns all rows from the right table and the matching rows from the left table.

UNION ALL: Similar to UNION, but includes all rows, even if they are duplicates.

UNION: Combines the result sets of two or more SELECT statements, removing duplicates.

These set operators provide powerful tools for manipulating and combining data in Transact-SQL queries. Remember to consult the official documentation for the specific version of SQL Server you are using, as there might be variations or additional features available in different versions.

# Appendix E – Summary of Set Operators Supported in MySQL

MySQL supports various set operators that allow you to perform operations on sets of data, typically within the context of queries involving multiple tables or subqueries. Here's a list of set operators implemented in MySQL:

ALL: Used with comparison operators to compare a value to all values returned by a subquery. Equivalent to using a combination of AND and comparison operators.

ANY / SOME: Used with comparison operators to compare a value to a set of values returned by a subquery. Equivalent to using IN.

CROSS JOIN: Returns the Cartesian product of two or more tables, resulting in a combination of all rows from each table.

EXCEPT / MINUS: MySQL does not have a direct EXCEPT or MINUS operator. You can achieve the same effect using various techniques, such as NOT IN or LEFT JOIN with NULL check.

EXISTS / NOT EXISTS: Checks for the existence (or non-existence) of rows in a subquery and returns a Boolean value.

EXISTS: Checks for the existence of rows in a subquery and returns a Boolean value.

FULL OUTER JOIN: MySQL does not have a direct FULL OUTER JOIN operator. You can achieve a similar result using a combination of LEFT JOIN and RIGHT JOIN with UNION or UNION ALL.

IN: Tests whether a value is present in a set of values returned by a subquery or specified explicitly.

INTERSECT: MySQL does not have a direct INTERSECT operator like some other databases. You can achieve intersection using INNER JOIN or EXISTS subqueries.

LIMIT: While not a traditional set operator, LIMIT is used to restrict the number of rows returned by a query.

NOT IN: Opposite of the IN operator; tests whether a value is not present in a set of values.

UNION ALL: Similar to UNION, but includes all rows from the combined result sets, including duplicates.

UNION: Combines the result sets of two or more SELECT queries into a single result set, removing duplicate rows by default.

It's important to note that MySQL's set operator support is not as extensive as some other database systems like PostgreSQL. Some set operations might need to be achieved through creative use of joins, subqueries, and conditional logic. Always refer to the MySQL documentation for the most accurate and up-to-date information on set operators and their usage

# Appendix F – MySQL Data Types

As of the date of this writing, MySQL supports the following data types for storing different kinds of data. Keep in mind that software can evolve, so it's a good practice to consult the official MySQL documentation for the most up-to-date information.

1. Numeric Types:

   - INT

   - TINYINT

   - SMALLINT

   - MEDIUMINT

   - BIGINT

   - FLOAT

   - DOUBLE

   - DECIMAL

2. Date and Time Types:

   - DATE

   - TIME

   - DATETIME

   - TIMESTAMP

   - YEAR

3. String Types:

   - CHAR

   - VARCHAR

   - BINARY

   - VARBINARY

   - TINYTEXT

   - TEXT

   - MEDIUMTEXT

   - LONGTEXT

   - ENUM

- SET

4. Binary Data Types:

  - BLOB

  - MEDIUMBLOB

  - LONGBLOB

  - TINYBLOB

5. Spatial Data Types:

  - GEOMETRY

  - POINT

  - LINESTRING

  - POLYGON

  - GEOMETRYCOLLECTION

  - MULTIPOINT

  - MULTILINESTRING

  - MULTIPOLYGON

6. JSON Data Type:

  - JSON

7. Boolean Type:

  - BOOLEAN or BOOL (synonym for TINYINT)

8. Miscellaneous Types:

  - AUTO_INCREMENT (for generating unique identifiers)

  - SERIAL (a synonym for BIGINT UNSIGNED NOT NULL AUTO_INCREMENT UNIQUE)

Remember that some data types might have variations or synonyms, and new types might be introduced in newer versions of MySQL. Always consult the official MySQL documentation or resources for the most accurate and up-to-date information on data types and their usage.

# Appendix G – SQL Server Data Types

As of this writing, Microsoft SQL Server supports the following data types for storing different types of data. Keep in mind that software evolves, so it's recommended to consult the official SQL Server documentation for the most up-to-date information. Here's a list of common data types supported by SQL Server:

1. **Exact Numeric Types:**

   - INT

   - BIGINT

   - SMALLINT

   - TINYINT

   - DECIMAL

   - NUMERIC

   - MONEY

   - SMALLMONEY

2. **Approximate Numeric Types:**

   - FLOAT

   - REAL

3. **Date and Time Types:**

   - DATE

   - TIME

   - DATETIME

   - DATETIME2

   - SMALLDATETIME

   - TIMESTAMP

   - OFFSETDATETIME (starting from SQL Server 2016)

   - DATETIMEOFFSET

4. **Character String Types:**

   - CHAR

   - VARCHAR

- TEXT

- NCHAR

- NVARCHAR

- NTEXT

5. **Binary Data Types:**

- BINARY

- VARBINARY

- IMAGE

6. **Large Object Types:**

- VARCHAR(MAX)

- NVARCHAR(MAX)

- TEXT

- NTEXT

- VARBINARY(MAX)

- IMAGE

7. **Bit Data Type:**

- BIT

8. **Uniqueidentifier Type:**

- UNIQUEIDENTIFIER

9. **Rowversion Type:**

- TIMESTAMP

10. **Hierarchyid Type:**

- HIERARCHYID

11. **Geospatial Data Types:**

- GEOMETRY

- GEOGRAPHY

12. **JSON Data Type:**

- JSON

13. **Table Types:**

- TABLE

14. **Cursor Types:**

- CURSOR

15. **User-Defined Data Types (UDTs):**

- These are custom data types created by users.

16. **XML Type:**

- XML

17. **User-Defined Table Types:**

- These are used to define table structures for passing as parameters to stored procedures and functions.

Remember that SQL Server might have introduced new data types or variations in more recent versions. Always refer to the official SQL Server documentation or relevant resources for the most accurate and current information on data types and their usage.

# Appendix H – System Catalog Commands: SQL Server vs. MySQL

Frequently used system catalog commands, SQL Server vs. MySQL:

| SQL Server Command | Description | MySQL Equivalent Command | Description |
|---|---|---|---|
| **sp_help** | Displays information about a database object. | **DESCRIBE or SHOW CREATE TABLE** | Provides information about a table structure. |
| **sp_columns** | Lists the columns in a table. | **DESCRIBE** | Shows the columns of a table. |
| **sp_tables** | Lists tables and their types in the current database. | **SHOW TABLES** | Displays a list of tables in the current database. |
| **sp_indexes** | Lists the indexes for a given table. | **SHOW INDEX FROM <table_name>** | Lists indexes of a table. |
| **sp_pkeys** | Lists the primary key columns for a given table. | **SHOW KEYS FROM <table_name> WHERE Key_name = 'PRIMARY'** | Displays primary key columns of a table. |
| **sp_fkeys** | Lists the foreign key columns for a given table. | - | MySQL automatically includes foreign key information in **SHOW CREATE TABLE**. |
| **sp_helpindex** | Displays information about indexes on a table. | **SHOW INDEX FROM <table_name>** | Shows indexes of a table. |

| SQL Server Command | Description | MySQL Equivalent Command | Description |
|---|---|---|---|
| **sp_depends** | Displays the objects that depend on a specified object. | - | MySQL does not have a direct equivalent. |
| **sys.tables** | Retrieves information about tables in the database. | **INFORMATION_SCHEMA.TABLES** | Provides metadata about tables in the database. |
| **sys.columns** | Retrieves information about columns of a table. | **INFORMATION_SCHEMA.COLUMNS** | Provides metadata about columns in a table. |
| **sys.indexes** | Retrieves information about indexes on tables. | **SHOW INDEX FROM <table_name>** | Displays information about indexes on tables. |
| **sys.objects** | Retrieves information about all objects in the database. | **SHOW FULL TABLES** | Lists all tables in the database. |
| **sys.schemas** | Retrieves information about schemas in the database. | **SHOW CREATE TABLE <table_name>** | Shows the schema of a table. |

# Appendix H

These commands provide various ways to explore the database schema, including information about tables, columns, indexes, keys, and dependencies.

# Index

# Index

# Index

www.ingramcontent.com/pod-product-compliance
Lightning Source LLC
Chambersburg PA
CBHW042031220326
41598CB00073BA/7448